MathFlare

Name: ____________________________

Class: ___________

Teacher: ____________________________

Introduction

As parents and educators, we recognize the pivotal role mathematics plays in shaping a child's academic journey and future success. Yet, the path to mathematical proficiency can often seem daunting, fraught with challenges and complexities. That's where the transformative power of MathFlare Workbooks shine through, illuminating the way forward with clarity, precision, and purpose.

Introducing MathFlare Workbooks – a beacon of guidance, a testament to excellence, and a catalyst for achievement. Crafted with meticulous care and expertise, MathFlare Workbooks stand as paragons of educational excellence, designed to nurture young minds, ignite a passion for learning, and develop a deep-rooted understanding of mathematical concepts.

Picture this: your child eagerly delves into the pages of Mathflare Workbook, greeted by a step-by-step guide illuminated with vivid examples that demystify complex mathematical concepts. With each turn of the page, they embark on a journey of discovery, encountering thoughtfully curated practice questions that reinforce learning and hone problem-solving skills. And when they unveil the answers to those very questions, a sense of accomplishment blossoms within them – a tangible reward for their hard work and dedication.

But MathFlare Workbooks are more than just tools for learning; they are pathways to comprehension, fostering a deep-seated understanding of mathematical concepts through a sequential, logical flow. From fundamental principles to advanced problem-solving strategies, every chapter builds upon the last, ensuring a robust foundation upon which future knowledge can be constructed.

As parents, we yearn for nothing more than to see our children thrive, to witness the spark of inspiration ignited within them as they conquer academic challenges with confidence and poise. MathFlare Workbooks serve as partners in this noble endeavor, offering not just practice questions, but the keys to unlocking a world of opportunity.

And for teachers, MathFlare Workbooks stand as invaluable allies in the quest to cultivate mathematical proficiency in the classroom. With answers readily available, instructors can focus on guiding and nurturing their students, confident in the knowledge that MathFlare Workbooks provide a solid framework upon which to build.

In the pages of MathFlare Workbooks, we find not just the promise of academic excellence, but the seeds of a brighter tomorrow. So let us embrace the power of mathematics, let us champion the journey of learning, and let us pave the way for a generation of young minds poised to shape the world. With MathFlare Workbooks as our guide, the possibilities are infinite, and the future, bright.

Table of Contents

Chapter. 01
Ratio, Proportion and Percentage

Proportional Relationship	1
Percentage	4
Percent Word Problems	11
Ratio and Proportion Word Problems	18
Convert Ratio, Fractions, Percent and Decimals	28

Chapter. 02   37
Algebra

Order of Operations (PEMDAS)	33
Evaluate Expressions	38
Solving Inequalities	48
Find Numbers	58
Solving Equations (One Step)	73
Equations (Two Step)	82

Chapter. 03
Cartesian Plane

Cartesian Coordinates	98
Cartesian Coordinates (Four Quadrants)	103

Chapter. 04
Geometry

Area and Perimeter	118
Pythagorean Theorem	138
Volume and Surface Area	143

Chapter. 05
Statistics

Mean, Median, Mode and Range	158

Answers

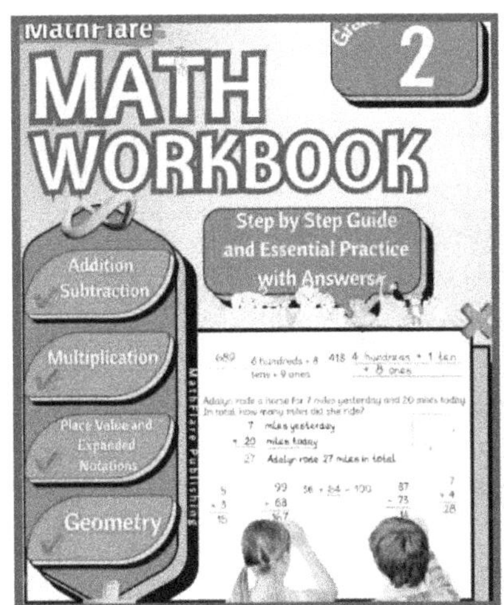
MathFlare
MATH WORKBOOK
Grade 2
Step by Step Guide and Essential Practice with Answers
Addition Subtraction
Multiplication
Place Value and Expanded Notations
Geometry
MathFlare Publishing

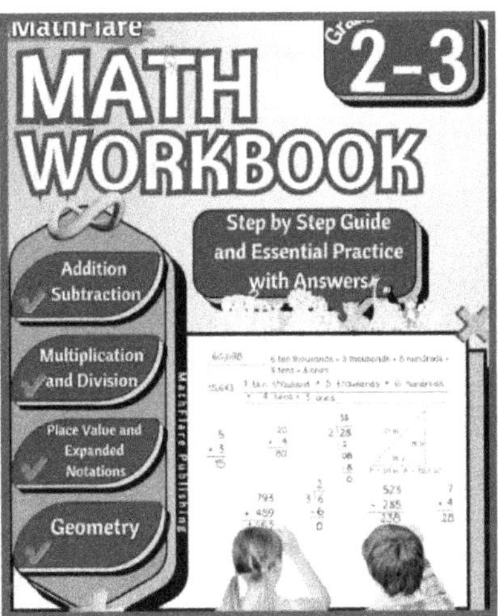
MathFlare
MATH WORKBOOK
Grade 2-3
Step by Step Guide and Essential Practice with Answers
Addition Subtraction
Multiplication and Division
Place Value and Expanded Notations
Geometry
MathFlare Publishing

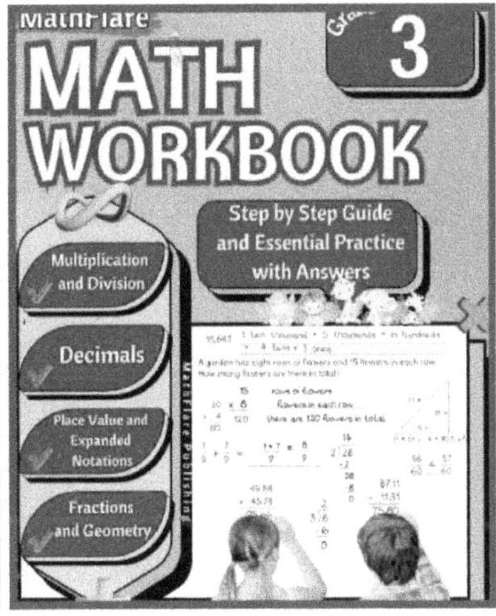
MathFlare
MATH WORKBOOK
Grade 3
Step by Step Guide and Essential Practice with Answers
Multiplication and Division
Decimals
Place Value and Expanded Notations
Fractions and Geometry
MathFlare Publishing

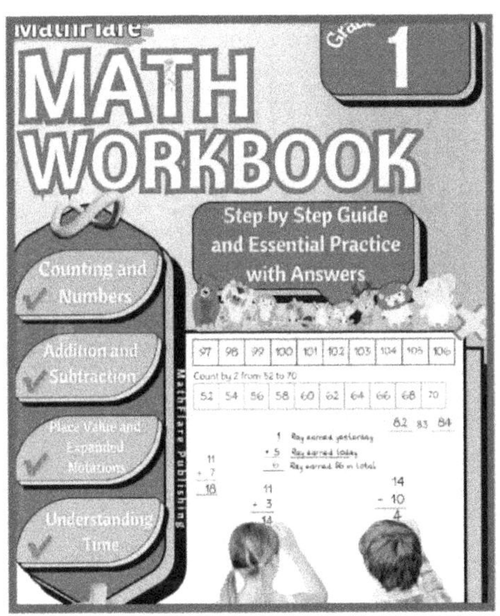
MathFlare
MATH WORKBOOK
Grade 1
Step by Step Guide and Essential Practice with Answers
Counting and Numbers
Addition and Subtraction
Place Value and Expanded Notations
Understanding Time
MathFlare Publishing

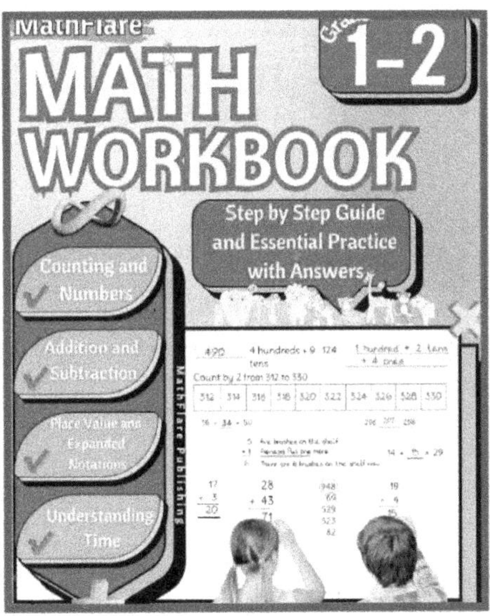
MathFlare
MATH WORKBOOK
Grade 1-2
Step by Step Guide and Essential Practice with Answers
Counting and Numbers
Addition and Subtraction
Place Value and Expanded Notations
Understanding Time
MathFlare Publishing

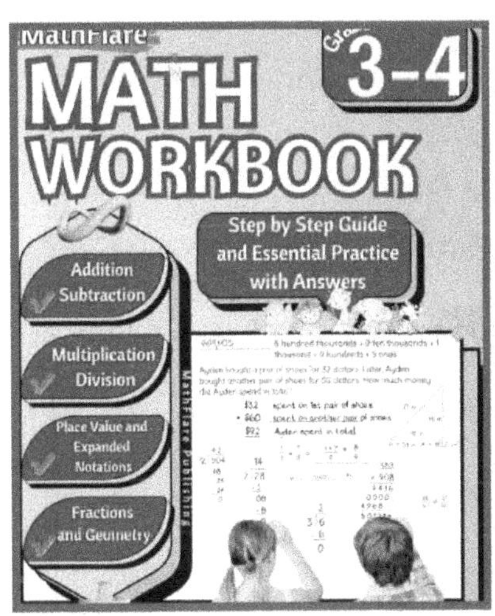
MathFlare
MATH WORKBOOK
Grade 3-4
Step by Step Guide and Essential Practice with Answers
Addition Subtraction
Multiplication Division
Place Value and Expanded Notations
Fractions and Geometry
MathFlare Publishing

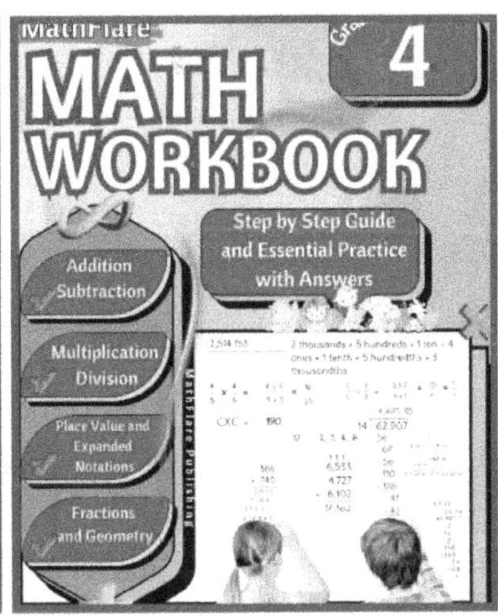
MathFlare
MATH WORKBOOK
Grade 4
Step by Step Guide and Essential Practice with Answers
Addition Subtraction
Multiplication Division
Place Value and Expanded Notations
Fractions and Geometry
MathFlare Publishing

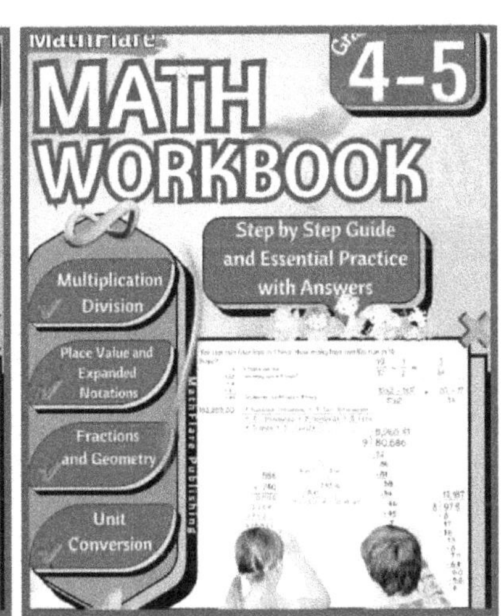
MathFlare
MATH WORKBOOK
Grade 4-5
Step by Step Guide and Essential Practice with Answers
Multiplication Division
Place Value and Expanded Notations
Fractions and Geometry
Unit Conversion
MathFlare Publishing

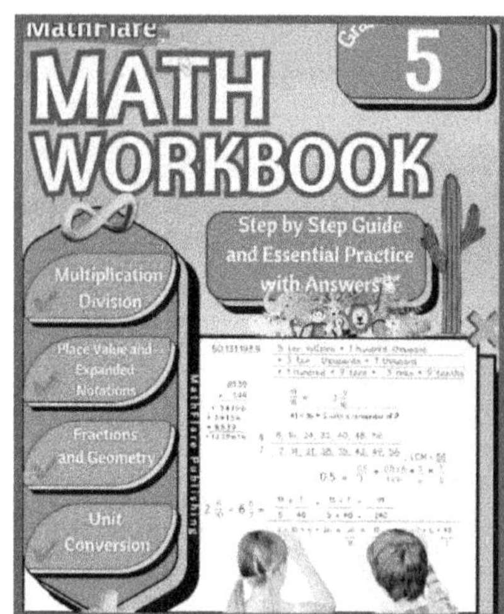
MathFlare
Grade 5
MATH WORKBOOK
Step by Step Guide and Essential Practice with Answers
Multiplication Division
Place Value and Expanded Notations
Fractions and Geometry
Unit Conversion
MathFlare Publishing

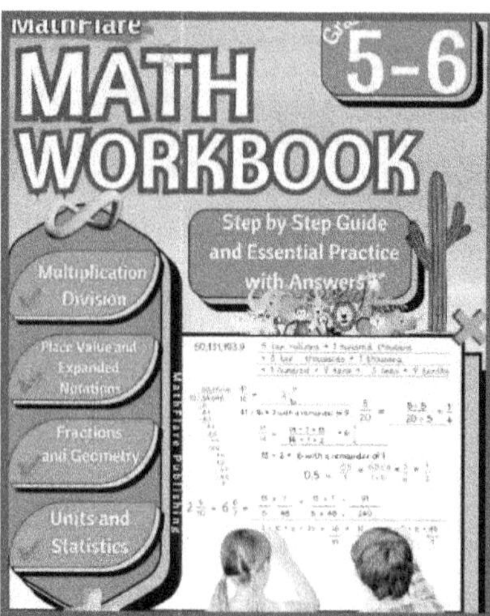
MathFlare
Grade 5-6
MATH WORKBOOK
Step by Step Guide and Essential Practice with Answers
Multiplication Division
Place Value and Expanded Notations
Fractions and Geometry
Units and Statistics
MathFlare Publishing

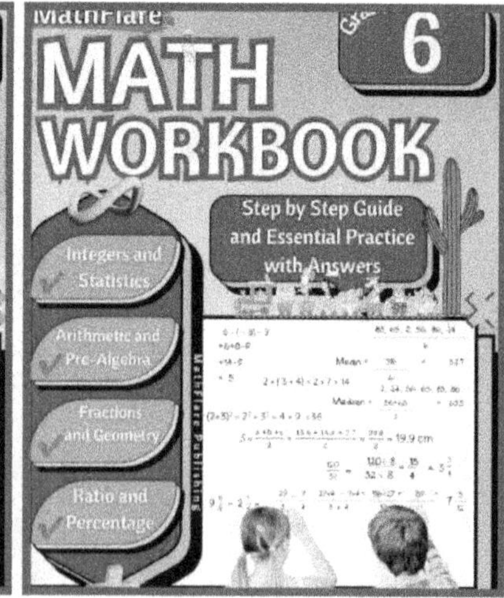
MathFlare
Grade 6
MATH WORKBOOK
Step by Step Guide and Essential Practice with Answers
Integers and Statistics
Arithmetic and Pre-Algebra
Fractions and Geometry
Ratio and Percentage
MathFlare Publishing

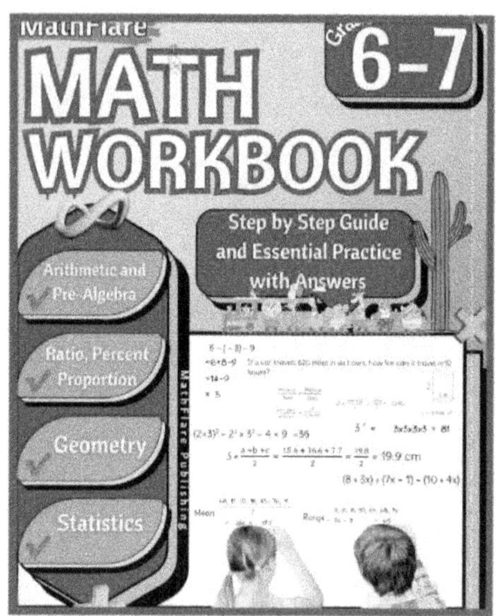
MathFlare
Grade 6-7
MATH WORKBOOK
Step by Step Guide and Essential Practice with Answers
Arithmetic and Pre-Algebra
Ratio, Percent Proportion
Geometry
Statistics
MathFlare Publishing

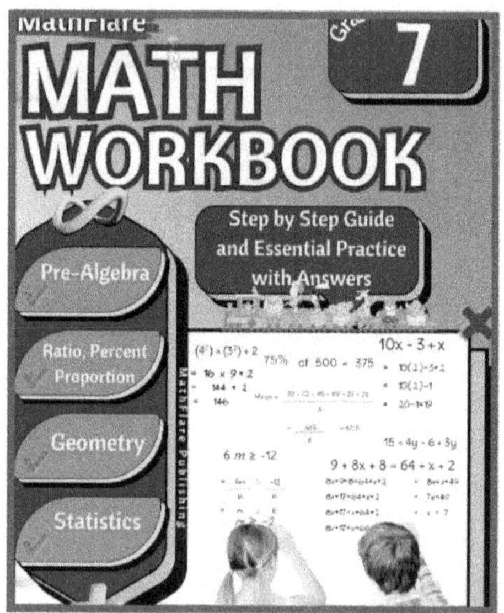
MathFlare
Grade 7
MATH WORKBOOK
Step by Step Guide and Essential Practice with Answers
Pre-Algebra
Ratio, Percent Proportion
Geometry
Statistics
MathFlare Publishing

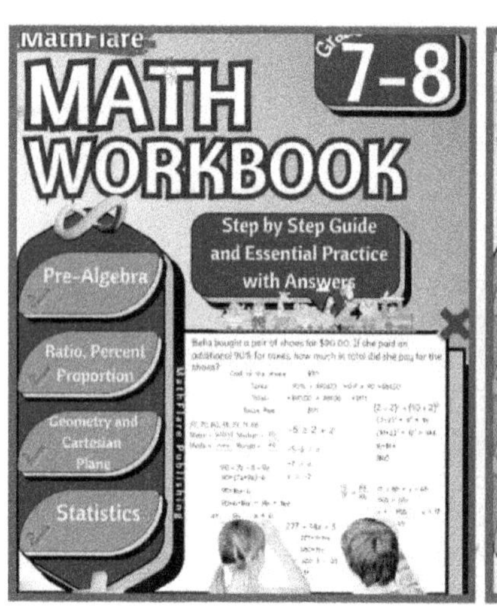
MathFlare
Grade 7-8
MATH WORKBOOK
Step by Step Guide and Essential Practice with Answers
Pre-Algebra
Ratio, Percent Proportion
Geometry and Cartesian Plane
Statistics
MathFlare Publishing

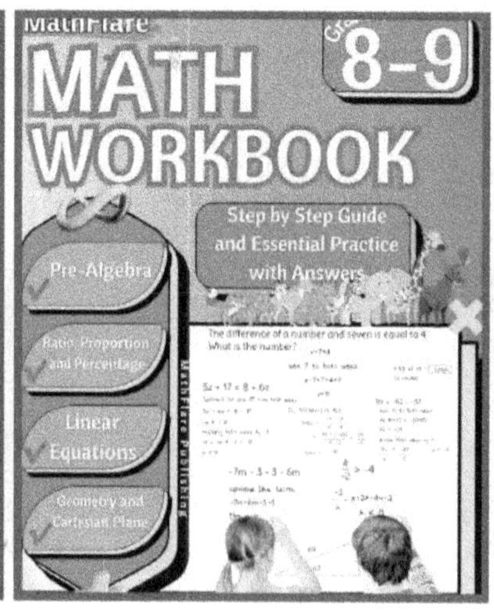
MathFlare
Grade 8-9
MATH WORKBOOK
Step by Step Guide and Essential Practice with Answers
Pre-Algebra
Ratio, Proportion and Percentage
Linear Equations
Geometry and Cartesian Plane
MathFlare Publishing

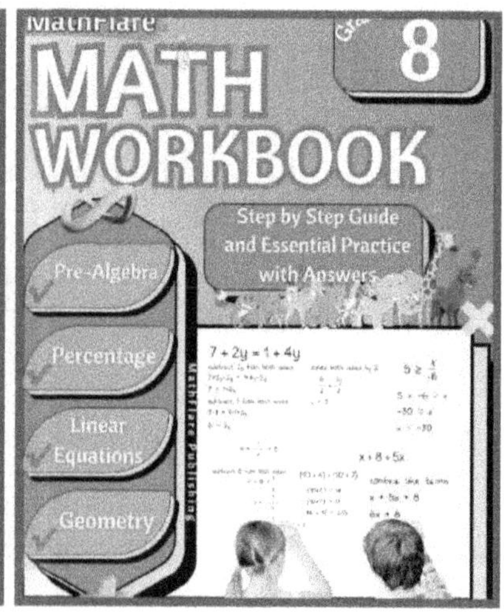
MathFlare
Grade 8
MATH WORKBOOK
Step by Step Guide and Essential Practice with Answers
Pre-Algebra
Percentage
Linear Equations
Geometry
MathFlare Publishing

Chapter. 01

Ratio and Proportion and Percentage

A proportional relationship between two quantities exists when they have a constant ratio or when one is a multiple of the other. In other words, if we increase one quantity, the other quantity will increase or decrease by the same factor. For example, if we double one quantity, the other quantity will also double.

Let's solve a problem:

$$\frac{}{9} = \frac{8}{18}$$

Step 1: Cross Multiply: Cross multiply by multiplying the numerator of one fraction by the denominator of the other, and vice versa:

$$x \times 18 = 9 \times 8$$

Step 2: Solve for the Unknown: Perform the multiplication on both sides of the equation:

$$18x = 72$$

Step 3: Divide Both Sides by the Coefficient of the Unknown: To isolate x, divide both sides of the equation by the coefficient of x, which is 18:

$$\frac{18x}{18} = \frac{72}{18}$$

$$x = 4$$

Step 4: Verify Check your solution by substituting x = 4 back into the original equation:

$$\frac{4}{9} = \frac{8}{18}$$

Since both sides are equal, the solution x = 4 is correct.

Ratio and Proportion Word Problems

We can use the concept of proportionality in solving many word problems, for example:

If a car travels 620 miles in six hours, how far can it travel in 12 hours?

Since the car travels a certain distance in a certain amount of time, we can assume that the distance traveled is directly proportional to the time taken.

Let d be the distance the car can travel in 12 hours.

We can set up a proportion:

$$\frac{\text{Distance1}}{\text{Time1}} = \frac{\text{Distance2}}{\text{Time2}}$$

Substituting the given values:

$$\frac{620 \text{ miles}}{6 \text{ hours}} = \frac{d}{12 \text{ hours}}$$

Now, let's solve for d.

$$d = \frac{620 \times 12}{6} = \frac{7440}{6} = 1240$$

So, the car can travel 1240 miles in 12 hours.

Percentage

Percentage is a way of expressing a number as a fraction of 100. It is commonly used to represent proportions, rates, and comparisons. The symbol "%" is used to denote percentages.

To calculate a percentage, we multiply the given number by the appropriate fraction or decimal equivalent.

How to calculate a percentage:

Convert Percentage to Decimal: If the percentage is given as a percentage value (e.g., 25%), convert it to its decimal equivalent by dividing by 100.

$$\text{For example, 25\% as a decimal is } \frac{25}{100} = 0.25$$

Multiply: Multiply the decimal equivalent of the percentage by the given number. This gives us the portion of the number that represents the percentage.

$$100 \times 0.25 = 25\%$$

Result: The result is the calculated percentage value.

For example, to calculate 25% of 80:

Convert 25% to a decimal: 25% = 0.25.

Multiply 0.25 by 80: $0.25 \times 80 = 20$. The result is 20.

Percent Word Problems

Percent word problems involve situations where percentages are used to calculate quantities or amounts. These problems often require converting percentages to decimals and then applying them to the given values.

For example:

Bella bought a pair of shoes for $90.00. If she paid an additional 90% for taxes, how much in total did she pay for the shoes?

- Bella bought a pair of shoes for $90.00.

- She paid an additional 90% for taxes.

Calculate 90% of $90:

Tax= 90% × 90

Tax= 0.90 × 90

Tax= $81

Add the tax amount to the original price:

Total cost= $90 + $81

Total cost= $171

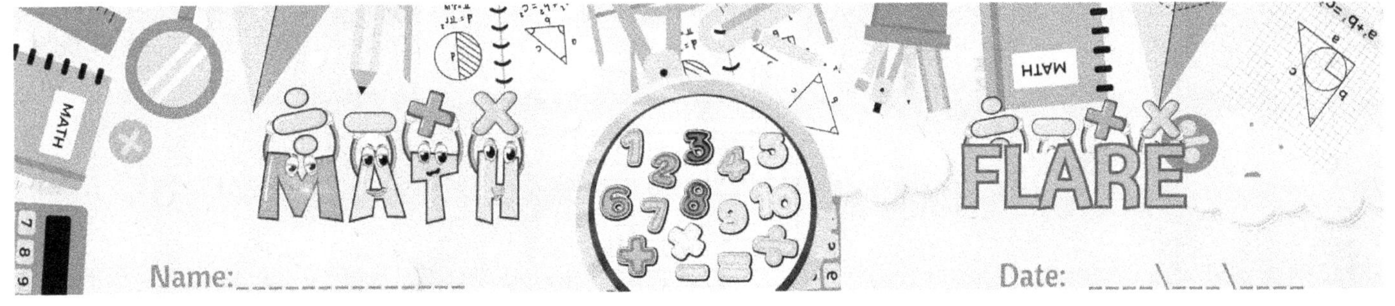

Proportional Relationship

1) $\dfrac{13}{17} = \dfrac{65}{85}$ 13 × 85 = x × 65
    1105 = 65x
    x = $\dfrac{1105}{65}$ x = 17

2) $\dfrac{1}{4} = \dfrac{6}{}$

3) $\dfrac{9}{13} = \dfrac{}{130}$

4) $\dfrac{1}{18} = \dfrac{2}{}$

5) $\dfrac{}{6} = \dfrac{28}{42}$

6) $\dfrac{}{11} = \dfrac{36}{66}$

7) $\dfrac{}{8} = \dfrac{10}{80}$

8) $\dfrac{7}{14} = \dfrac{}{28}$

9) $\dfrac{2}{12} = \dfrac{10}{}$

10) $\dfrac{3}{5} = \dfrac{15}{}$

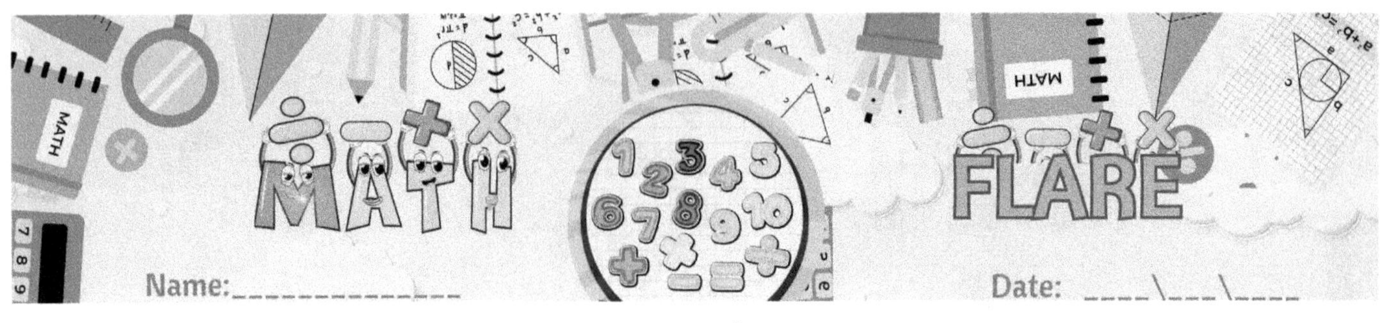

11) $\dfrac{\ }{14} = \dfrac{60}{140}$

12) $\dfrac{1}{4} = \dfrac{7}{\ }$

13) $\dfrac{4}{19} = \dfrac{12}{\ }$

14) $\dfrac{4}{9} = \dfrac{\ }{54}$

15) $\dfrac{3}{10} = \dfrac{15}{\ }$

16) $\dfrac{4}{\ } = \dfrac{20}{35}$

17) $\dfrac{12}{\ } = \dfrac{48}{64}$

18) $\dfrac{10}{\ } = \dfrac{30}{33}$

19) $\dfrac{4}{18} = \dfrac{\ }{144}$

20) $\dfrac{12}{\ } = \dfrac{60}{85}$

21) $\dfrac{2}{3} = \dfrac{\ }{6}$

22) $\dfrac{19}{20} = \dfrac{190}{\ }$

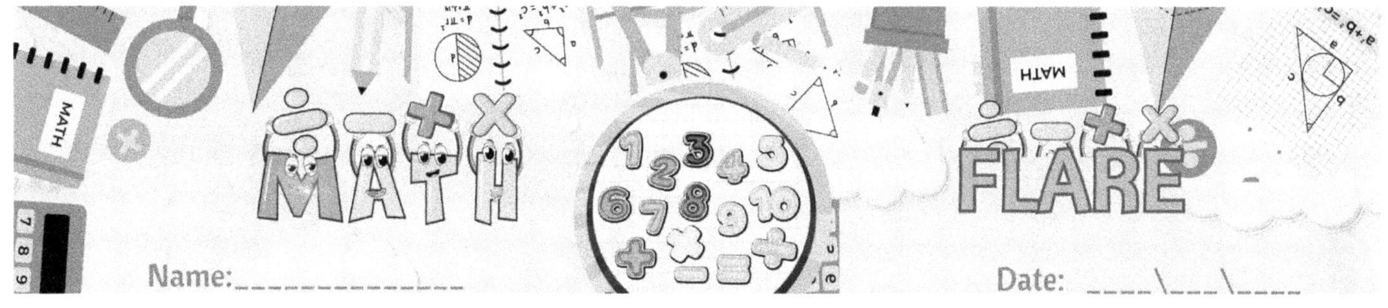

23) $\dfrac{2}{15} = \dfrac{}{150}$

24) $\dfrac{6}{13} = \dfrac{}{130}$

25) $\dfrac{4}{8} = \dfrac{}{48}$

26) $\dfrac{2}{} = \dfrac{18}{54}$

27) $\dfrac{1}{} = \dfrac{8}{16}$

28) $\dfrac{17}{19} = \dfrac{136}{}$

29) $\dfrac{2}{} = \dfrac{4}{16}$

30) $\dfrac{}{11} = \dfrac{100}{110}$

31) $\dfrac{6}{} = \dfrac{24}{28}$

32) $\dfrac{8}{20} = \dfrac{24}{}$

33) $\dfrac{10}{} = \dfrac{40}{72}$

34) $\dfrac{1}{10} = \dfrac{}{30}$

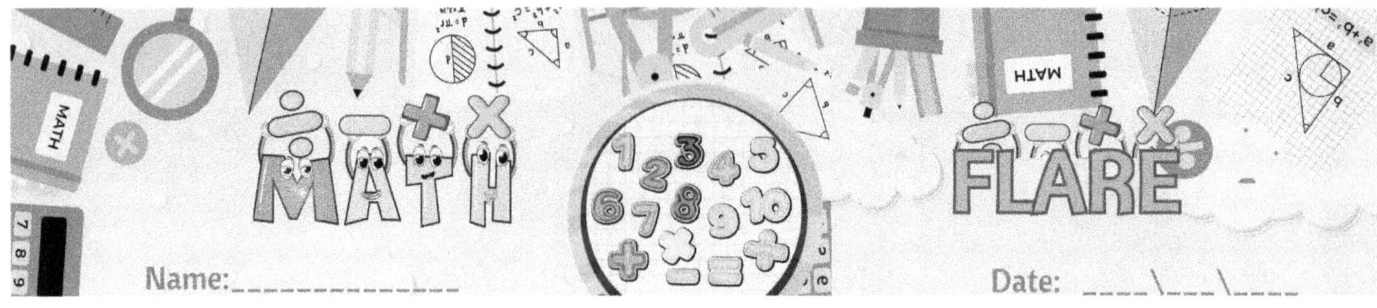

Percentage

Find the percentage of given numbers.

1) | 10% | of 70 = 7

2) | | of 300 = 150

3) | | of 200 = 200

4) | | of 600 = 420

5) | | of 800 = 560

6) | | of 200 = 8

7) 2% of | | = 6

8) | | of 200 = 70

9) 3% of 600 = | |

10) | | of 600 = 1200

11) | | of 40 = 10

12) 6% of 300 = | |

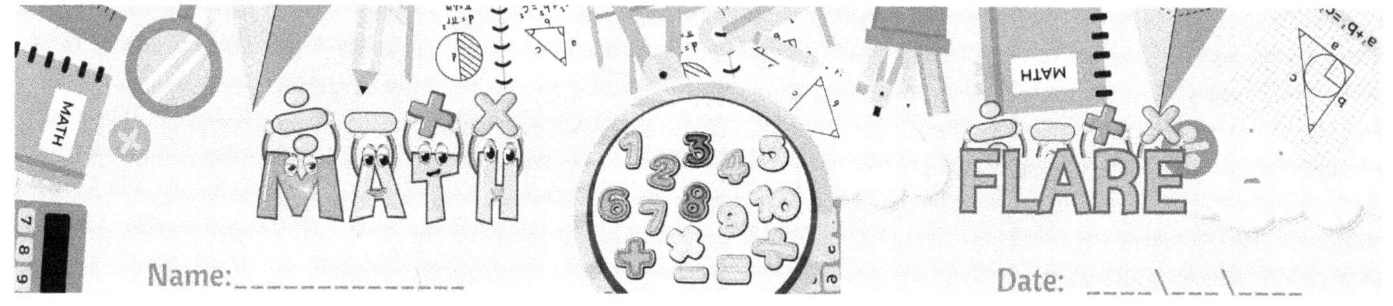

13) 30% of ☐ = 9

14) 15% of 200 = ☐

15) 60% of 400 = ☐

16) 10% of ☐ = 80

17) 40% of 100 = ☐

18) 50% of 600 = ☐

19) 8% of 900 = ☐

20) ☐ of 50 = 50

21) 1% of 20 = ☐

22) 90% of 800 = ☐

23) ☐ of 100 = 75

24) ☐ of 20 = 1.8

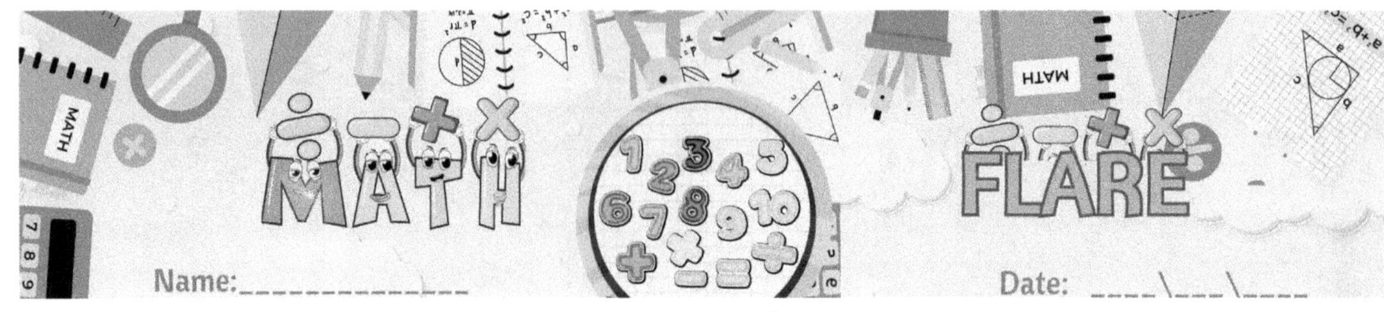

25) 7% of ☐ = 14

26) ☐ of 600 = 120

27) ☐ of 200 = 160

28) ☐ of 800 = 40

29) ☐ of 30 = 90

30) ☐ of 900 = 180

31) 200% of 700 = ☐

32) ☐ of 900 = 2700

33) 50% of 80 = ☐

34) ☐ of 500 = 200

35) ☐ of 100 = 6

36) ☐ of 50 = 0.5

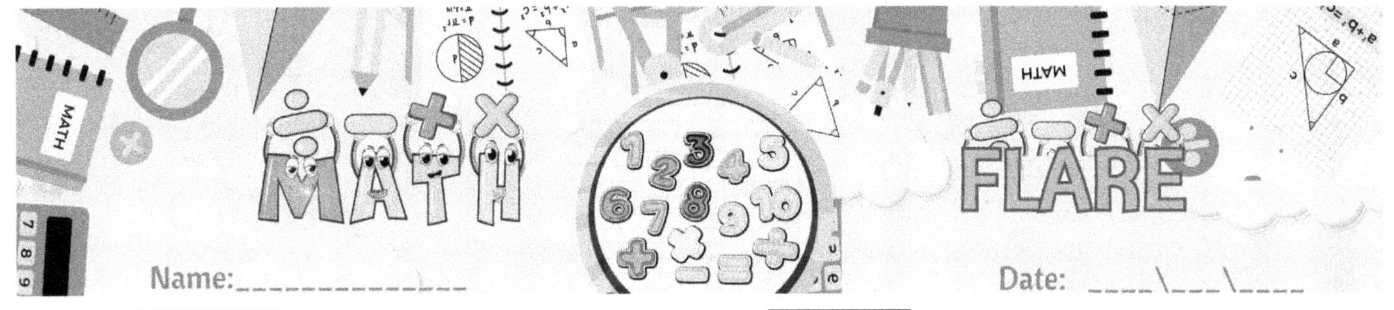

1) [ ] of 98 = 0.588

2) [ ] of 8 = 0.016

3) 3.4% of [ ] = 11.186

4) 38.8% of [ ] = 2.716

5) [ ] of 6 = 0.03

6) 2.2% of 8 = [ ]

7) 12.6% of [ ] = 116.802

8) 0.3% of 569 = [ ]

9) [ ] of 884 = 7.956

10) 2.4% of 5 = [ ]

11) 8.8% of [ ] = 7.392

12) [ ] of 8 = 0.184

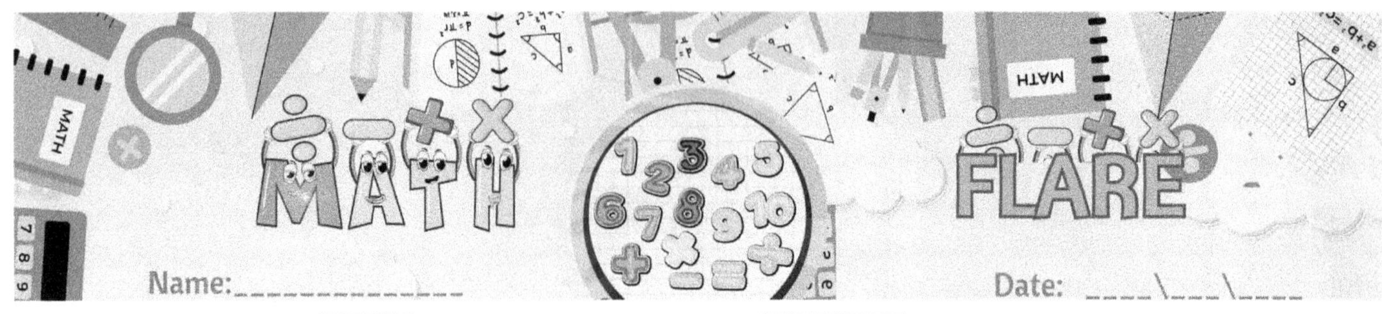

13) 26.1% of ☐ = 1.305

14) ☐ of 4 = 0.3

15) 0.4% of 478 = ☐

16) 44.2% of 733 = ☐

17) 9.6% of 16 = ☐

18) 48.0% of 789 = ☐

19) 36.2% of ☐ = 2.534

20) 5.7% of ☐ = 0.285

21) ☐ of 5 = 2.49

22) 2.5% of 45 = ☐

23) 0.2% of 63 = ☐

24) 3.0% of ☐ = 6.51

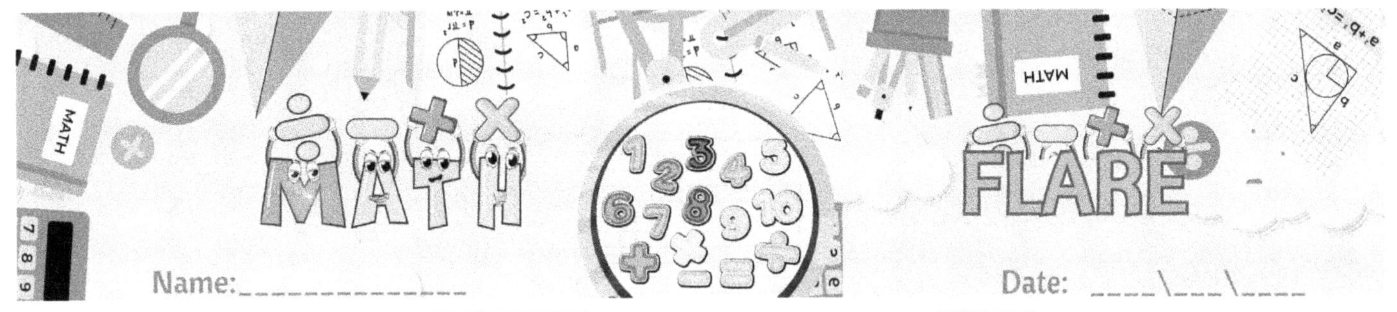

25) 6.2% of 73 = [＿＿＿]

26) 8.4% of [＿＿] = 6.804

27) [＿＿] of 4 = 0.028

28) 40.2% of [＿＿] = 2.814

29) [＿＿] of 497 = 36.778

30) [＿＿] of 50 = 19.7

31) [＿＿] of 6 = 0.012

32) 23.7% of [＿＿] = 178.461

33) 3.5% of 527 = [＿＿＿]

34) [＿＿] of 6 = 0.036

35) 0.2% of [＿＿] = 0.006

36) 3.4% of 2 = [＿＿＿]

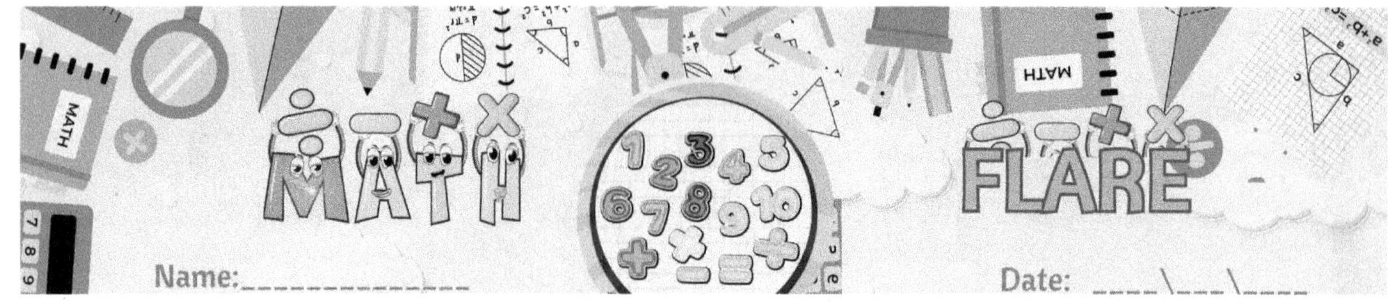

37) [ ] of 52 = 20.176

38) [ ] of 1 = 0.005

39) 2.2% of 6 = [ ]

40) 12.6% of [ ] = 9.324

41) 0.3% of 98 = [ ]

42) [ ] of 293 = 2.637

43) 2.4% of [ ] = 0.048

44) 8.8% of [ ] = 22.616

45) 2.3% of [ ] = 3.726

46) 26.1% of 877 = [ ]

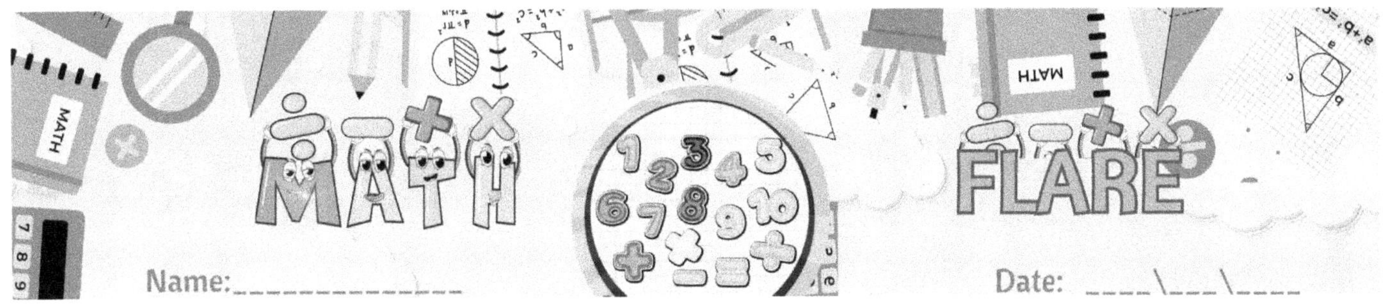

Word Problems: Percent

1) Bella bought a shoes for $90.00. If she paid an additional 90% for sales tax, how much in total did she pay for the shoes?

Cost of the shoes: $90

Taxes: 90% × $90.00   = 0.9 × 90 = $81.00

Total: = $90.00 + $81.00   = $171

Bella Paid $171

2) Avery bought needles for $50.00. If she paid an additional 44% for sales tax, how much in total did she pay for the needles?

3) A store has 20 deodorants. If 85% of them are sold at the end of the day, how many deodorants are sold?

4) Ariana bought some compasses for $50.00. If she paid an additional 8% for sales tax, how much in total did she pay for the compasses?

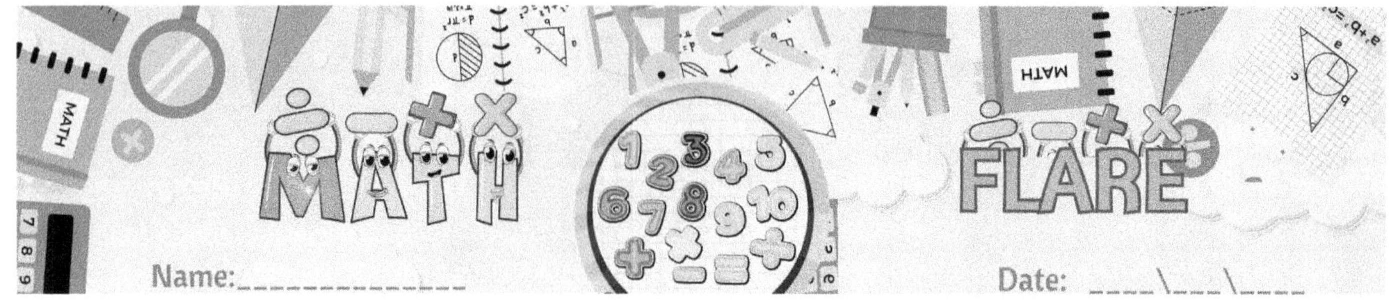

5) Natalie bought a camera for $25.00. If she paid an additional 8% for sales tax, how much in total did she pay for the camera?

6) Savannah had a collection of 60 baseball cards. She gave away 85% of them. How many did she have left?

7) A car dealership sold 20 cars last month. If the sales increased by 90% this month, how many cars did they sell this month?

8) Carson buys bananas for $100.00 to sell them in market. If he wants to earn 1% profit. What must be the selling price of bananas?

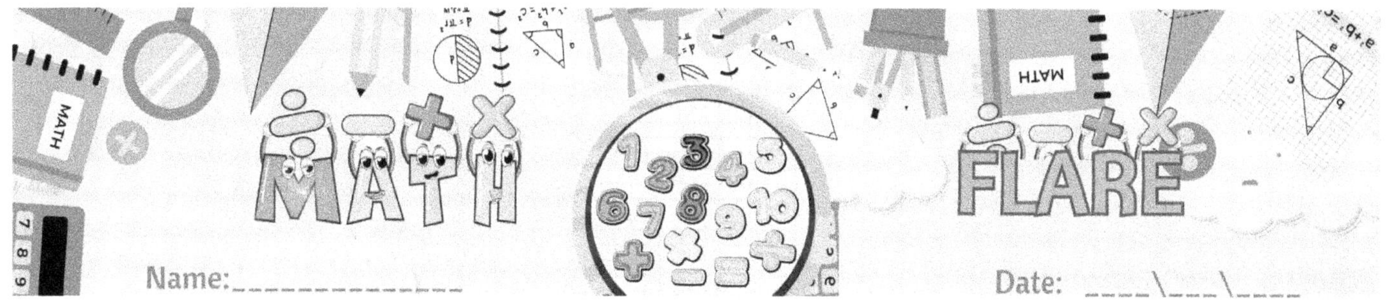

9) Kennedy bought a bag for $50.00. If she paid an additional 8% for sales tax, how much in total did she pay for the bag?

10) A school has a total of 100 teachers. If 73% of them are men, how many male teachers are there?

11) A store offers a 5% discount on all items. If Genesis buys bagels originally priced at $80.00, how much money did she save?

12) If the number 50 is increased by 2%, what is the value of the new number?

13) Nicholas's monthly sales of erasers was $25.00. If he earned 8% of profit, what was his profit?

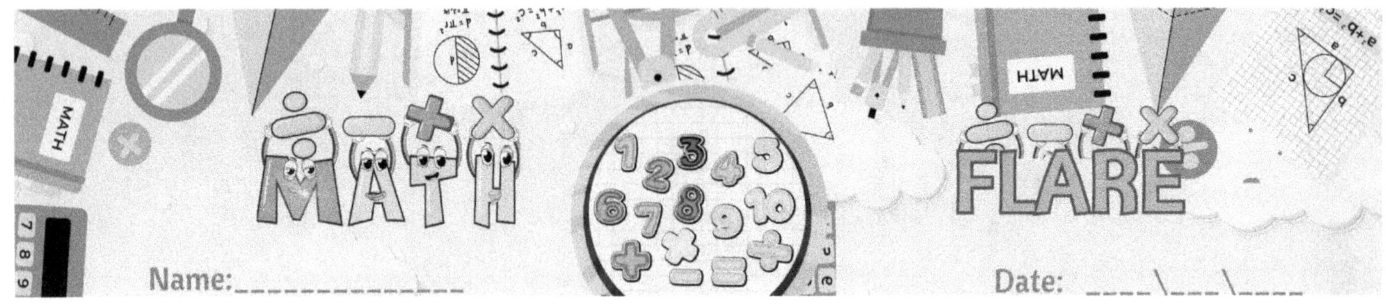

14) A school has 60 students. If 85% of them play baseball, how many students play baseball?

15) A store is having a sale where everything is 71% off. The chairs originally priced at $100.00 is now on sale. How much is the new price of chairs now?

16) A school has 25 students. If 8% of them play tennis, how many students play tennis?

17) A classroom has 40 students, of which 85% are girls. How many boys are in the classroom?

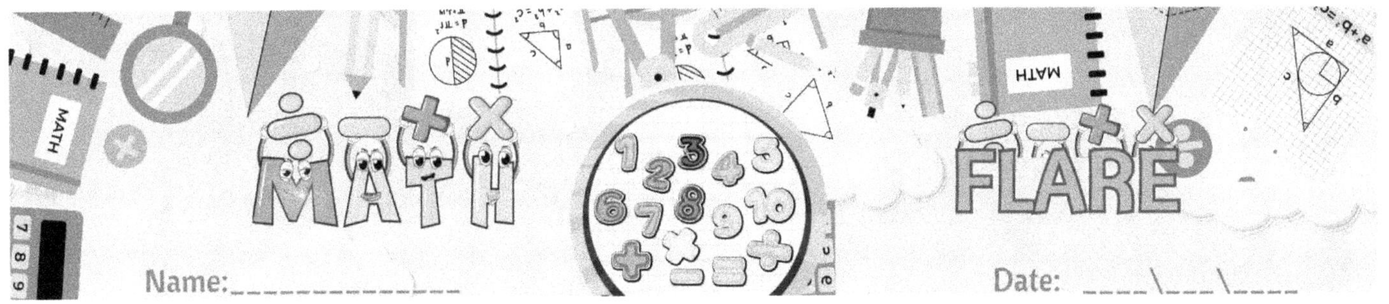

18) In a class of 50 students, 4% of them are in the Math Club. How many students are in the Math Club?

19) A teacher gave a math test with 50 questions. If a student got 2% questions correct, how many questions were correct?

20) In a survey of 60 people, 5% said they prefer cats over dogs. How many people prefer cats?

21) In a class of 80 students, 85% are girls. How many are girls?

22) Alice bought a book for $50.00. If she paid an additional 78% for sales tax, how much in total did she pay for the book?

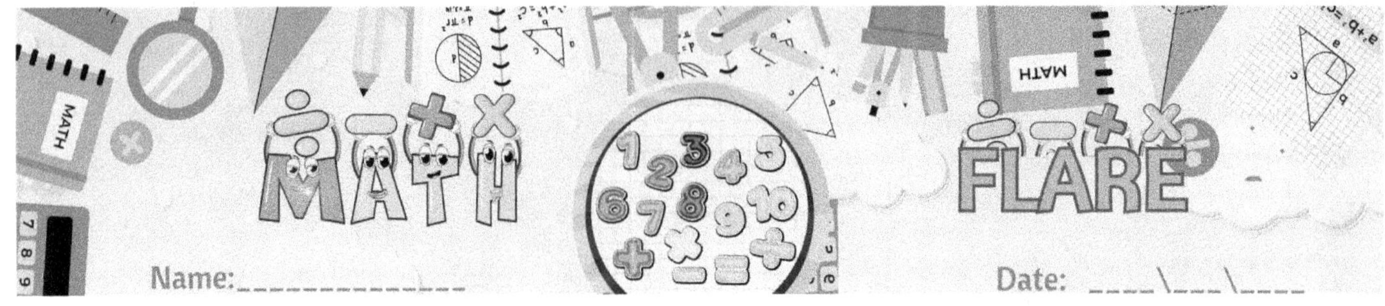

23) A school has a total of 20 teachers. If 90% of them are men, how many female teachers are there?

24) In a class of 80 students, 5% are boys. How many are boys?

25) Luna bought a pizza for $40.00. If she paid an additional 85% for sales tax, how much in total did she pay for the pizza?

26) A person wants to make a 4% tip on a $75.00 meal. How much should the tip be?

27) In a basket of 50 thermometers, 4% are red thermometers. How many are red thermometers?

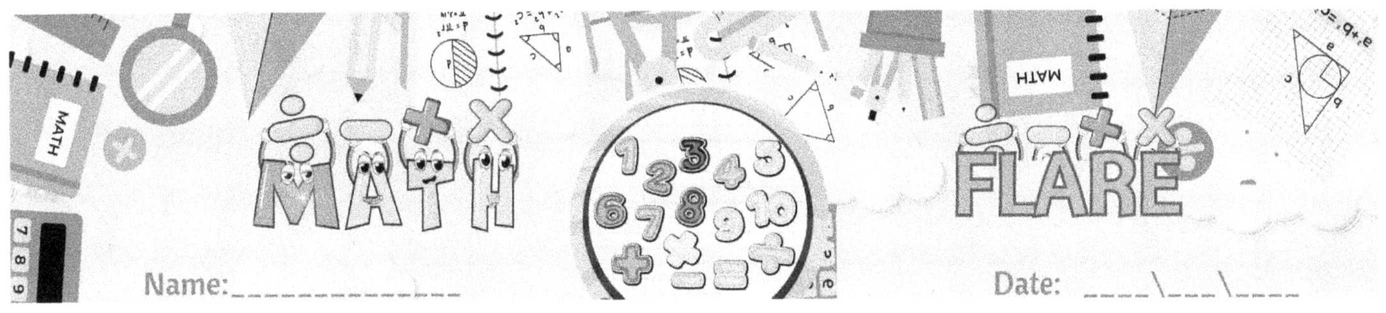

28) A restaurant makes a pizza that is 100 inches in diameter. If they want to increase the size of the pizza by 8%, what will be the new diameter?

29) A store increases the prices of all items by 6%. If the balls originally costs $50.00, what is the sale price?

30) A school has 50 students. If 8% of them play football, how many students play football?

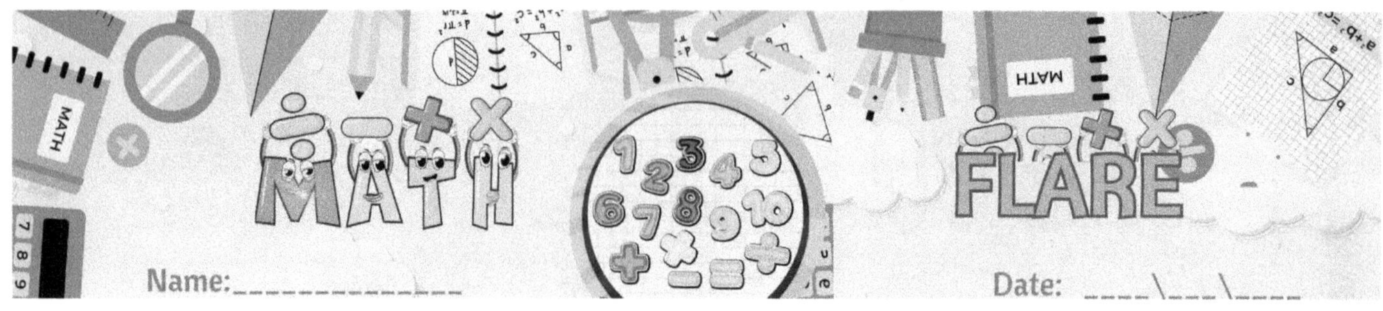

Ratio and Proportion Word Problems

1) If nine workers can build a house in 18 hours, how many workers are needed to build the house in seven hours?

$$9 \times 18 = 162$$

$$\text{Number of workers} \times 7 = 162$$

$$= \frac{162}{7}$$

$$\approx 23.14$$

$$\text{Number of workers} = 24$$

2) A company has a ratio of four managers for every 30 employees. If the company has 112 employees, how many managers are there?

3) If five workers can build a wall in 13 hours, how many workers are needed to build the wall in seven hours?

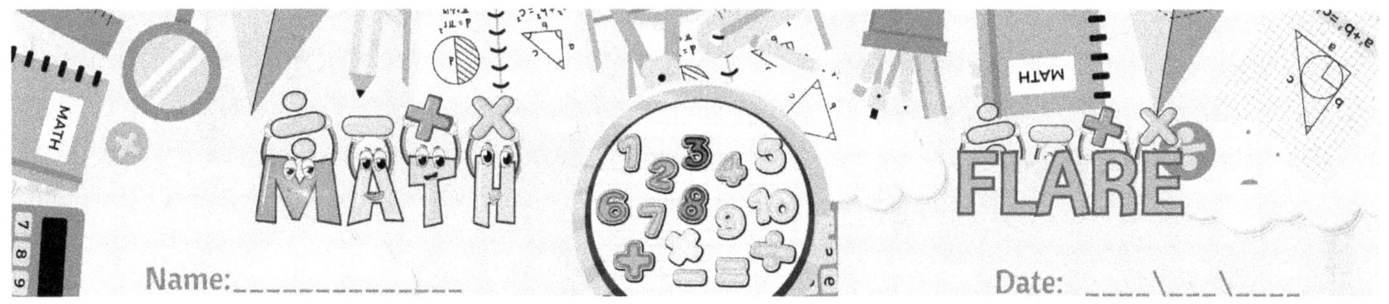

Name:_________________   Date: ____________

4) Carter drives 139 miles in five hours. How far can he travel in 13 hours?

5) If it takes six students 13 hours to complete a science project, how many students are needed to finish the project in four hours?

6) A room has an area of 184 square meters and a length of 16 meters. What is the width of the room?

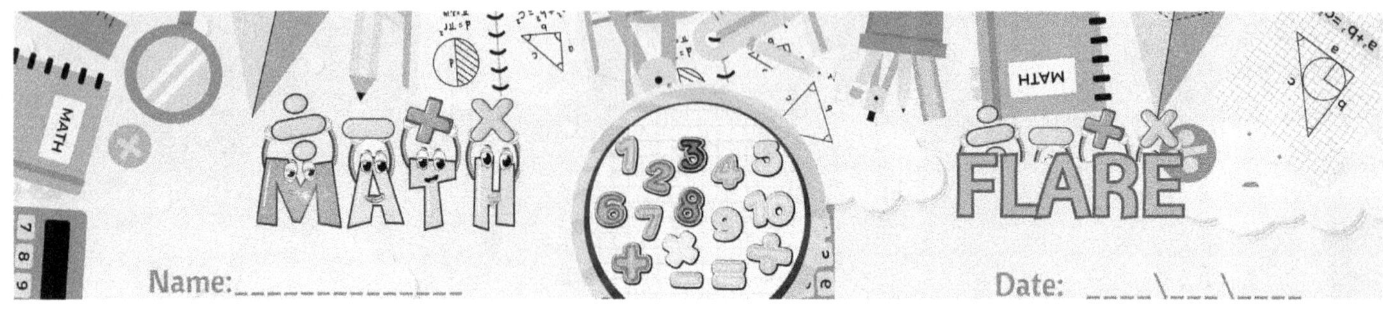

7) A class has a ratio of two girls to every 10 boys. If there are 21 boys, how many girls are there?

8) In a classroom, the ratio of boys to girls is two:nine. If there are 16 girls, how many boys are there?

9) If a recipe calls for two cups of water for every five cups of rice, how much water is needed for nine cups of rice?

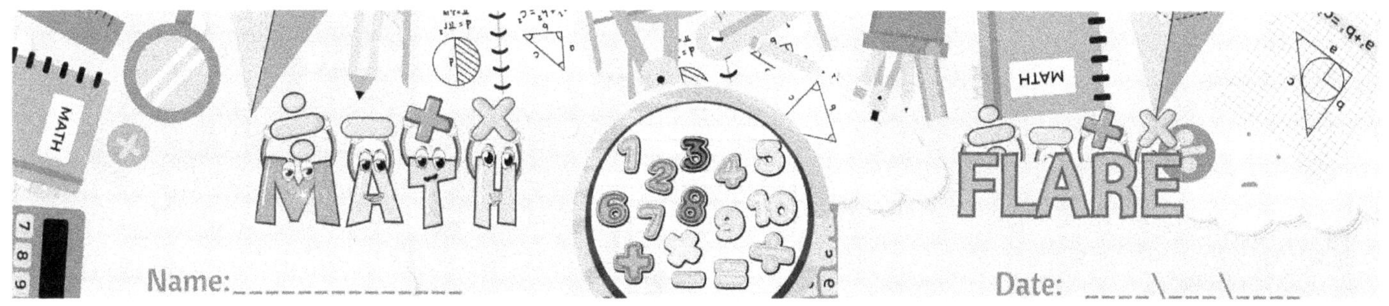

10) If a recipe calls for six eggs for every 10 cups of flour, how many eggs are needed for 10 cups of flour?

11) If four painters can paint a house in 18 days, how many painters are needed to paint the same house in five days?

12) A train travels 227 miles in five hours. How far can it travel in 12 hours?

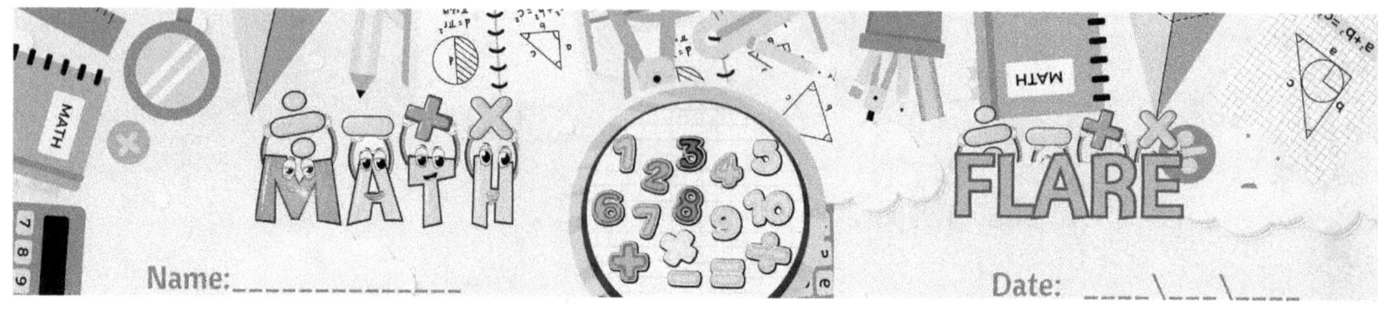

13) A bus travels at a speed of 69 miles per hour. How long will it take to travel 156 miles?

14) Luna sells five surgical masks for every eight balls. If there are 88 surgical masks, how many balls are there?

15) If a recipe calls for five cups of sugar for every 10 cups of flour, how many cups of sugar are needed for 18 cups of flour?

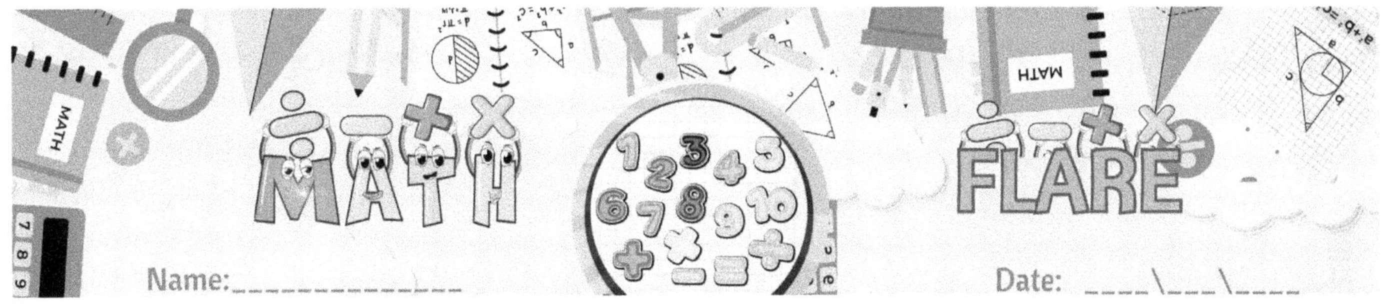

16) A recipe calls for five cups of sugar for every seven cups of flour. If you have 15 cups of flour, how much sugar is needed?

17) A school has a teacher-student ratio of 1:38. If there are 927 students, how many teachers are needed?

18) If a map scale is 1 inch to four miles, how far apart are two cities that are nine inches apart on the map?

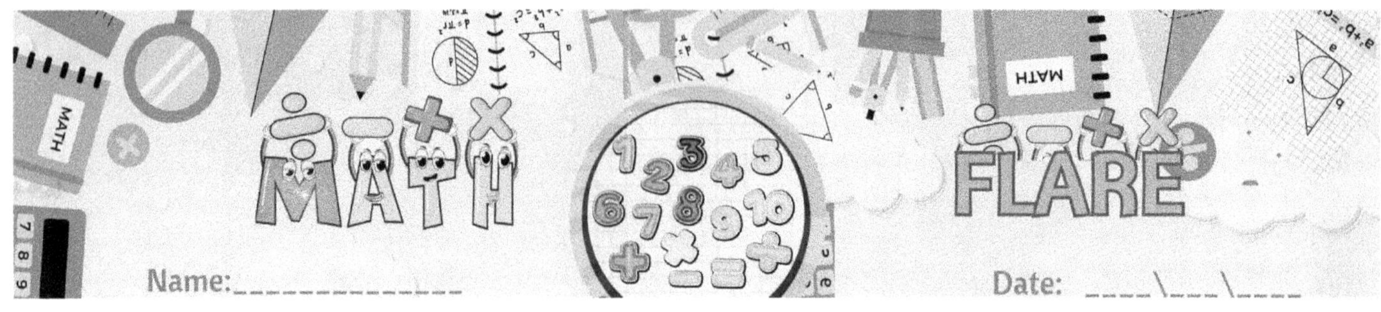

19) A farmer has a ratio of four sheep to every eight cows in his pasture. If there are 47 cows in the pasture, how many sheep are there?

20) If a car travels 192 miles using 12 gallons of gas, how far can it travel using 17 gallons of gas?

21) If six workers can complete a job in 13 days, how many workers are needed to complete the job in eight days?

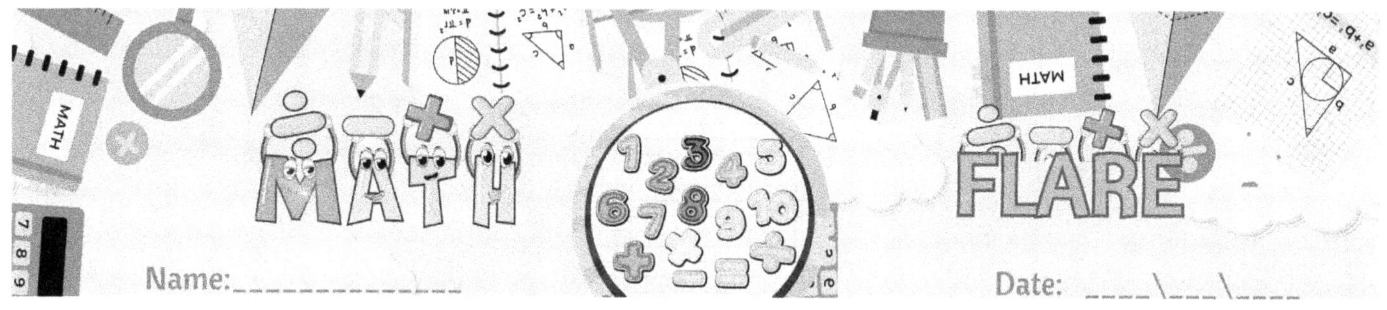

22) A rectangular pool has an area of 370 square meters and a width of 11 meters. What is the length of the pool?

23) A school has a ratio of four female teachers to every eight male teachers. If there are 21 male teachers, how many female teachers are there?

24) A car can travel 42 miles per gallon of gas. How many gallons of gas are needed to travel 149 miles?

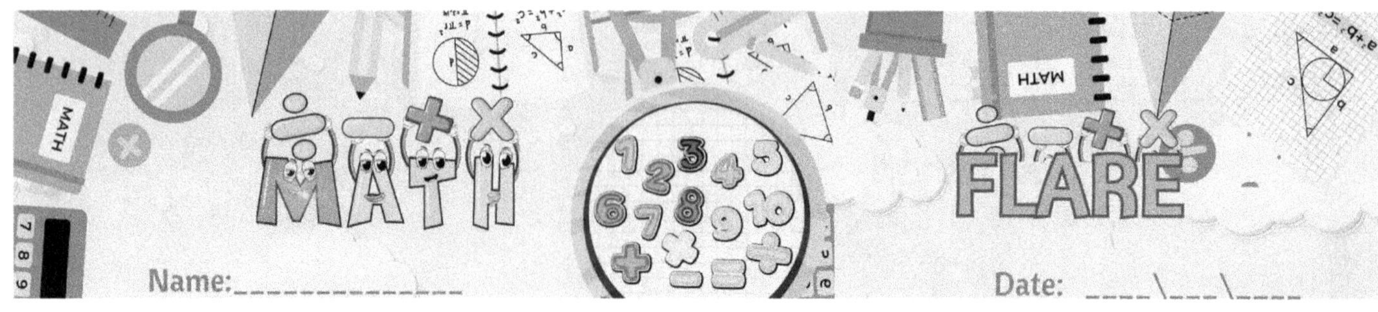

25) A road is 151 miles long and it takes a car three hour to travel the entire length. What is the speed of the car in miles per hour?

26) If a team of two construction workers can build a road in 18 days, how many workers are required to complete the road in seven days?

27) A school has a ratio of four teachers for every 22 students. If the school has 116 students, how many teachers are there?

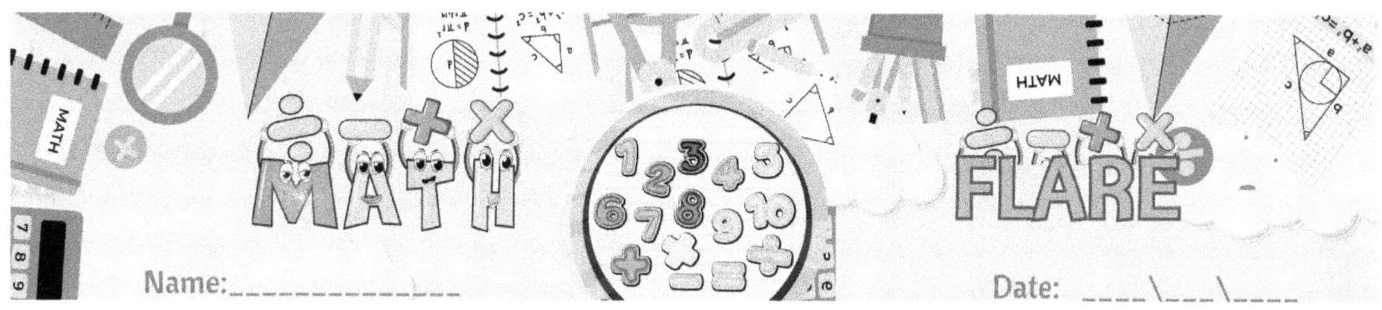

28) A bike travels at a speed of 17 miles per hour. How long will it take to travel 63 miles?

29) If a car travels 266 miles in six hours, how far can it travel in 11 hours?

30) In a bag of candies, the ratio of chocolate candies to fruit candies is one:nine. If there are 13 fruit candies, how many chocolate candies are there?

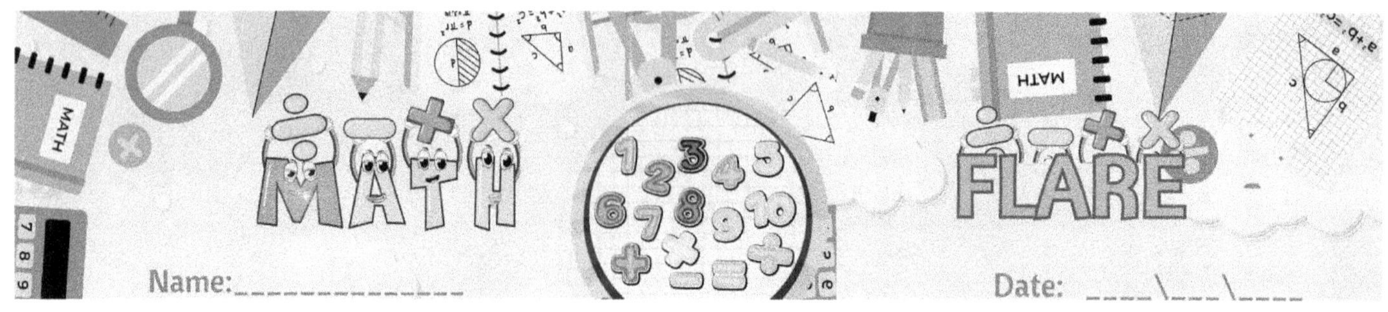

Ratio Conversions

1)

	Ratio	Fraction	Percent	Decimal
a.	12:19	12/19	63.2%	0.632
b.	1:2	1/2	50%	0.5
c.				0.6
d.		1/4		
e.	3:14			
f.			55.6%	
g.		2/5		
h.				0.688
i.				1
j.			40%	
k.	8:11			
l.	6:16			
m.				0.667
n.			36.8%	
o.				0.75

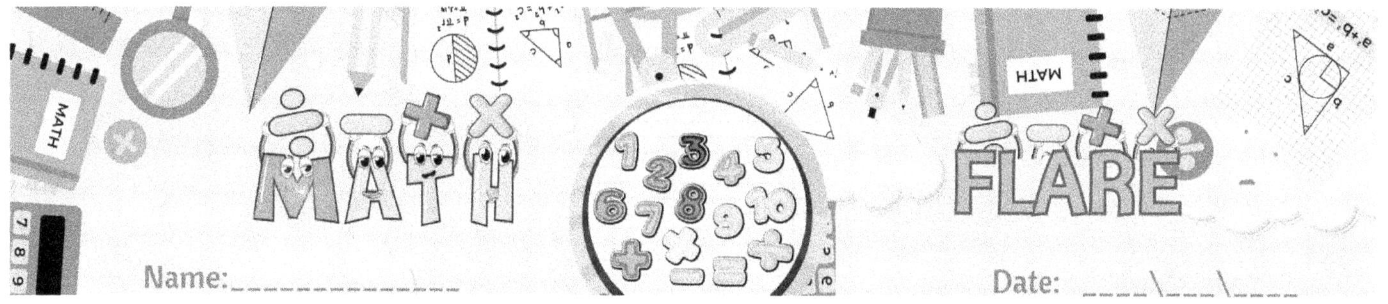

2)

	Ratio	Fraction	Percent	Decimal
a.			100%	
b.				0.4
c.		1/4		
d.	16:19			
e.				0.1
f.		6/18		
g.				0.182
h.		5/18		
i.		14/16		
j.				0.833
k.	7:13			
l.	4:5			
m.		4/6		
n.			55%	
o.			40%	

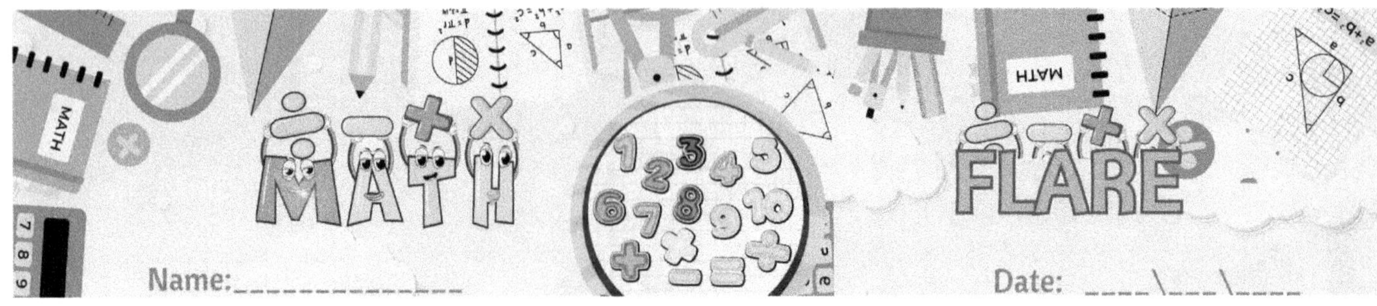

3)

	Ratio	Fraction	Percent	Decimal
a.			100%	
b.			21.4%	
c.				0.7
d.	9:18			
e.				0.5
f.			76.5%	
g.		9/16		
h.	1:4			
i.				0.5
j.			12.5%	
k.				0.059
l.				0.5
m.				0.75
n.				0.412
o.	1:7			

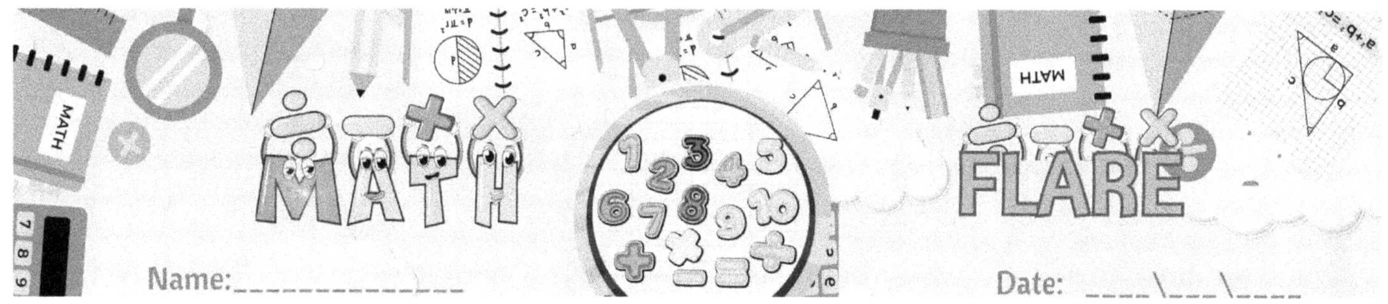

4)

	Ratio	Fraction	Percent	Decimal
a.				0.526
b.				1
c.				0.25
d.	7:17			
e.		9/15		
f.				0.077
g.			75%	
h.			18.2%	
i.			22.2%	
j.				0.824
k.			65%	
l.			58.3%	
m.		1/3		
n.			46.2%	
o.			29.4%	

5)

	Ratio	Fraction	Percent	Decimal
a.			22.2%	
b.			100%	
c.			35%	
d.			80%	
e.			80%	
f.	11:15			
g.				0.857
h.				0.75
i.	4:20			
j.			25%	
k.		1/10		
l.		4/11		
m.				0.6
n.	10:18			
o.			50%	

Chapter. 02

Pre-Algebra

Order of Operations (PEMDAS)

The order of operations, often remembered by the acronym PEMDAS, stands for:

- **Parentheses**: Perform operations inside parentheses first.
- **Exponents**: Evaluate exponents (powers and roots) next.
- **Multiplication and Division**: Perform multiplication and division from left to right.
- **Addition and Subtraction**: Perform addition and subtraction from left to right.

The order of operations helps to clarify which operations should be performed first in a mathematical expression to ensure consistent and accurate results.

- **Parentheses**: Evaluate expressions within parentheses first. If there are nested parentheses, start with the innermost ones and work your way out.

  1. Example: $2 \times (3 + 4) = 2 \times 7 = 14$

- **Exponents**: Evaluate expressions with exponents (powers and roots) next.

  1. Example: $2^3 + 4 = 8 + 4 = 12$

- **Multiplication and Division**: Perform multiplication and division from left to right.

  1. Example: $2 \times 3 + 4 = 6 + 4 = 10$

  2. Example: $6 \div 2 \times 3 = 3 \times 3 = 9$

- **Addition and Subtraction**: Perform addition and subtraction from left to right.

  1. Example: $2 + 3 \times 4 = 2 + 12 = 14$

  2. Example: $10 - 4 \div 2 = 10 - 2 = 8$

Evaluate Expressions

Evaluating expressions involves substituting given values for variables in an expression and then performing the indicated operations to find the result.

For example: Let's evaluate $4x - 10$, when $x = 3$:

Step 1: Substitute the given value for the variable:

Replace every occurrence of x in the expression $4x - 10$ with the given value, which is 3:

$$= 4(3) - 10$$

Step 2: Perform the operations:

Perform the indicated operations according to the order of operations (PEMDAS - Parentheses, Exponents, Multiplication and Division, Addition and Subtraction):

$$= 4 \times 3 - 10$$

Step 3: Simplify:

Calculate the result:

$$12 - 10 = 2$$

Solving Equations (One Step)

Solving one-step equations involves performing a single operation to isolate the variable and find its value.

Let's solve an equation step by step: $16 + x = 31$

1. **Identify the Goal:**

   The goal is to isolate the variable x on one side of the equation.

2. **Simplify the Equation**: Combine like terms on both sides of the equation, if necessary.

   The equation is already simplified.

3. **Undo Addition or Subtraction**: If there's addition or subtraction involving the variable, undo it by performing the opposite operation on both sides of the equation.

   Since x is being added to 16, we'll undo this operation by subtracting 16 from both sides of the equation:

   $$16 + x - 16 = 31 - 16$$

4. **Isolate the Variable**: Ensure that the variable is alone on one side of the equation.

   $$X = 15$$

5. **Check Your Solution**: Substitute the value of x back into the original equation to verify that it satisfies the equation.

   $$16 + 15 = 31$$

   $$31 = 31$$

   The equation is balanced, so the solution.

Equations (Two Sides)

A two-sided equation is an equation where both sides have expressions with variables and constants. The goal when solving a two-sided equation is to find the value of the variable that makes both sides equal.

For example: Let's solve an equation:

$$9 + 8x + 8 = 64 + x + 2$$

- **Combine Like Terms:** Simplify each side of the equation by combining like terms (terms with the same variable or constants).

$$9 + 8x + 8 = 64 + x + 2$$

$$17 + 8x = 66 + x$$

- **Isolate the Variable:** Use inverse operations to isolate the variable on one side of the equation.

subtract x from both sides:

$$17 + 8x - x = 66 + x - x$$

$$17 + 7x = 66$$

subtracting 17 from both sides:

$$17 - 17 + 7x = 66 - 17$$

$$7x = 49$$

divide both sides by 7:

$$\frac{7x}{7} = \frac{49}{7} = x = 7$$

- **Check Solution:** Once you find the solution, substitute it back into the original equation to ensure it makes the equation true.

Substitute $x = 7$ back into the original equation:

$$9 + 8(7) + 8 = 64 + 7 + 2$$

$$9 + 56 + 8 = 64 + 7 + 2$$

$$73 = 73$$

Find Numbers (Verbal Algebra)

Verbal algebra involves translating word problems or verbal statements into algebraic expressions or equations.

For example: The product of the two numbers is 91. One number is six less than the other. What are the numbers?

We're given a verbal description of a problem, and we need to represent it using algebraic symbols and equations.

Let's break down the given problem into algebraic expressions:

- Given that the product of the two numbers is 91, we can write the equation: $xy = 91$
- Also, given that one number is six less than the other, we can write another equation: $x = y - 6$

Now, we can use algebraic techniques to solve the system of equations to find the values of x and y, which represent the two numbers.

$$x(x - 6) = 91$$

1. Solve the equation:

   - Expand the equation:

     $$x^2 - 6x = 91$$

   - Rearrange the equation into standard quadratic form:

     $$x^2 - 6x - 91 = 0$$

   - Factor the quadratic equation:

     $$(x - 13)(x + 7) = 0$$

2. Find the solutions for x:

- From the factored form, we have two possible values for x:

$$x = 13 \text{ or } x = -7$$

3. **Check the validity of the solutions:**

   - Since one number is six less than the other, we discard the negative solution.

   - Therefore, the solution is $x = 13$.

4. **Find the other number:**

   - Substitute $x = 13$ into the expression for the other number:

   Other number $= x - 6 = 13 - 6 = 7$

So, the two numbers are 13 and 7.

Solving Inequalities

Inequalities are mathematical expressions that compare the relative sizes of two values. They are used to express relationships where one quantity is:

- "<" (less than),
- ">" (greater than),
- "<=" (less than or equal to),
- ">=" (greater than or equal to),
- and "≠" (not equal to) another quantity.

For example:

$$y + -10 \leq -8$$

To isolate y, we need to get rid of the constant term -10. Since -10 is being subtracted from y, we can undo this operation by adding 10 to both sides of the inequality:

$$y - 10 + 10 \leq -8 + 10$$

$$y \leq 2$$

To check the solution:

$$2 - 10 \leq -8$$

$$-8 = -8$$

The inequality is true when $y = 2$

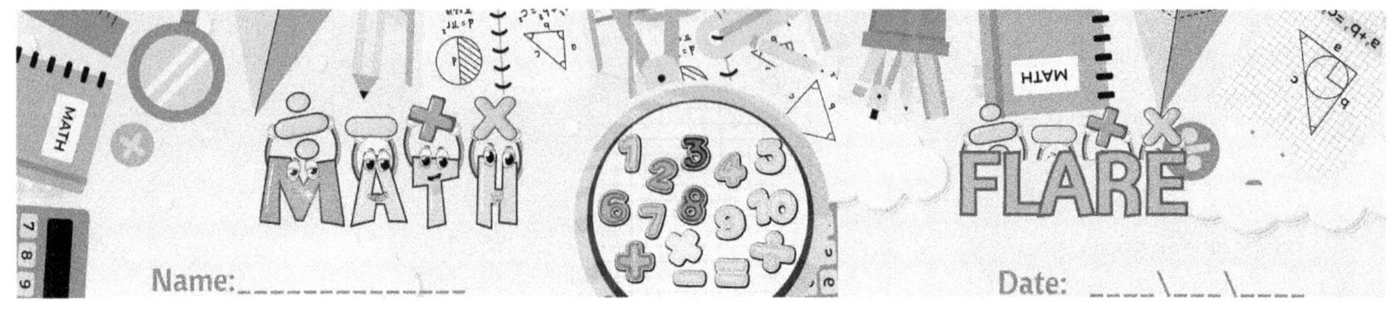

Order of Operations (PEMDAS)

Evaluate Expressions.

1) $(2 + 2)^2 + (10 + 2)^2 =$

$= (2+2)^2 = 4^2 = 16$

$= (10+2)^2 = 12^2 = 144$

$= 16+144$

$= \$160$

2) $5 + 3^2 =$

3) $10 + 9 - 4 + 3 =$

4) $[5 - (6 + 1)] \div 3 =$

5) $[9 - (10 + 8)] - 1 =$

6) $5 \times (1 + 1) =$

7) $4 + 6 - 9 + 8 =$

8) $(6 \times 7) - (1 + 4) =$

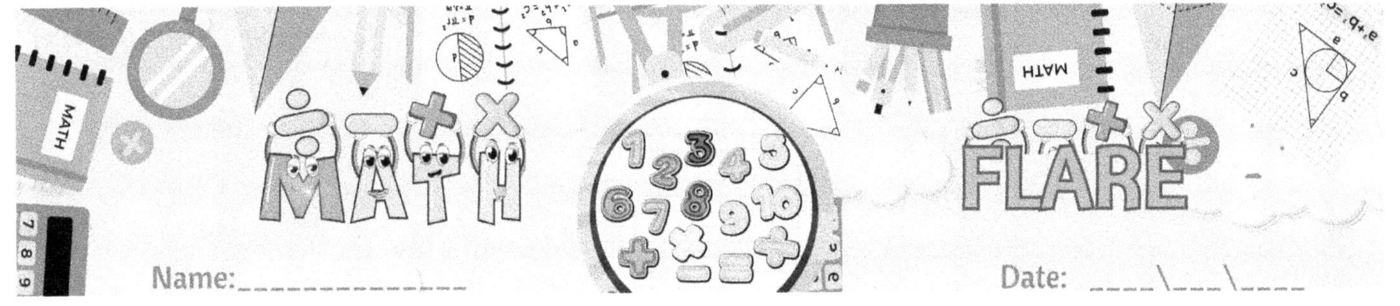

9) $10 + 1 - 4 + 9 =$

10) $1 + 6 - 1 + 5 =$

11) $9 + 9^2 + 2 + 5^2 =$

12) $4(8 + 6) =$

13) $(5 + 4)^2 =$

14) $8 + 7 + 2 =$

15) $8 + 7 + 7 =$

16) $3 \times 5 \times 8 =$

17) $[8 - (7 + 1)] - 5 =$

18) $10 + 6^2 =$

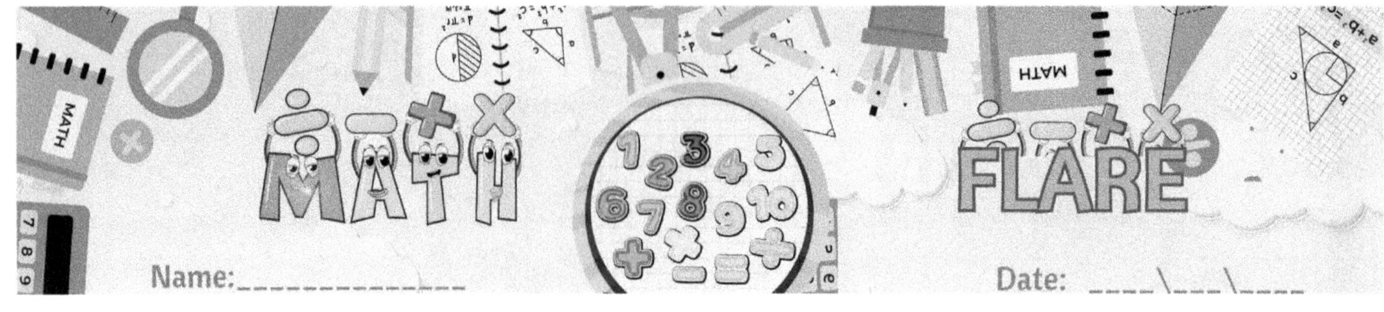

19) $10 + 5^2 + 5 + 3^2 =$

20) $(1 + 8) \div 10 =$

21) $7 + (8 + (5 - 9))^2 =$

22) $2 + (3 - (7 + 8)) =$

23) $6 + 10^2 + 5 + 4^2 =$

24) $8 + 1 + 9 + 7 =$

25) $(3 \times 5) - (2 + 4) =$

26) $3 \times 9 + 4 =$

27) $5 \times (5 + 10) =$

28) $7 + (6 - (9 - 4)) =$

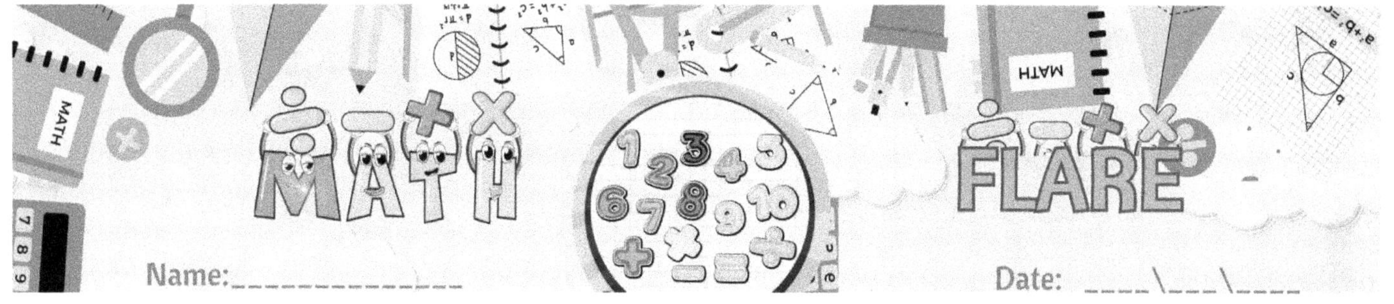

29) $4 + (5 - (6 - 9)) =$

30) $10 + 4 + 3 + 8 =$

31) $(5 + 10) \div 9 =$

32) $1 + 2^2 + 8 + 7^2 =$

33) $1 + 2^2 =$

34) $6 + 1 + 8 + 2 =$

35) $9 \times 9 \times 5 =$

36) $7 \times 9 + 5 =$

37) $(1 + 5)^2 + (3 + 7)^2 =$

38) $2(9 + 3) =$

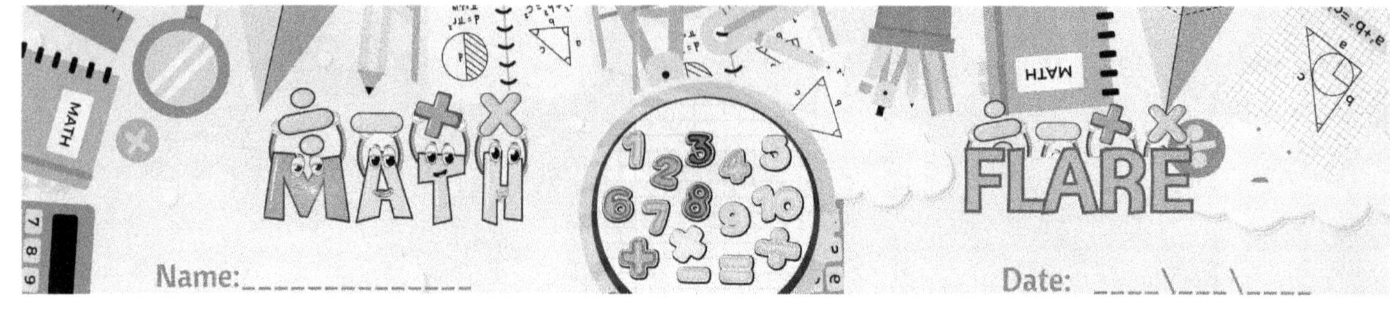

39) $(7 + 1)^2 + (8 + 10)^2 =$

40) $2 + 6 - 4 + 5 =$

41) $(10 + 3) \div 5 =$

42) $[3 - (7 + 7)] - 8 =$

43) $4 + 8 - 1 + 5 =$

44) $2 \times (3 + 5) =$

45) $6 + 2 + 2 =$

46) $1 + 10^2 =$

47) $(3 \times 4) - (3 + 4) =$

48) $(8^2) \times (3^2) + 10 =$

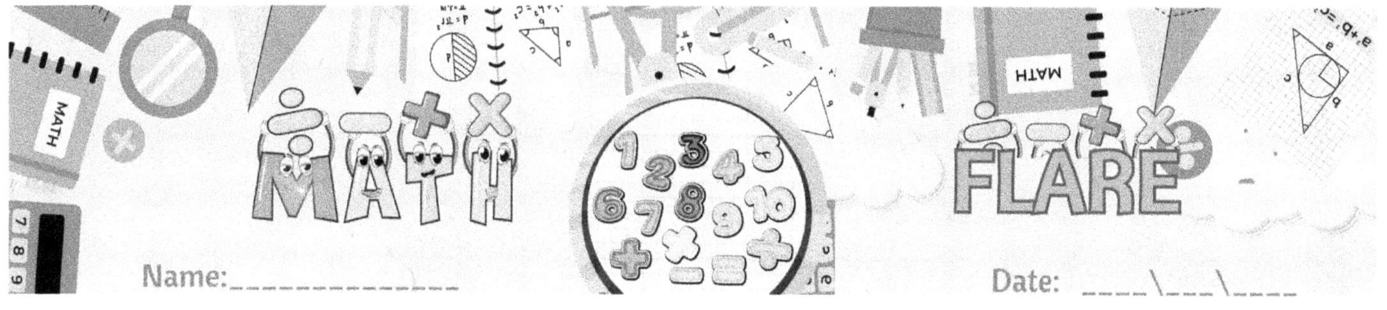

Name:_______________   Date: ______________

Evaluate Expressions

Solve for the variable.

1) $90 = 7z - 6 + 9z$

$$90 = (7z + 9z) - 6$$
$$90 = 16z - 6$$
$$90 + 6 = 16z \quad = \quad 96 = 16z$$
$$z = \frac{96}{16} \qquad z = 6$$

2) $3z - 7 + 2z = 28$

3) $9 - z = 5$

4) $8x^2 + x^2 = 441$

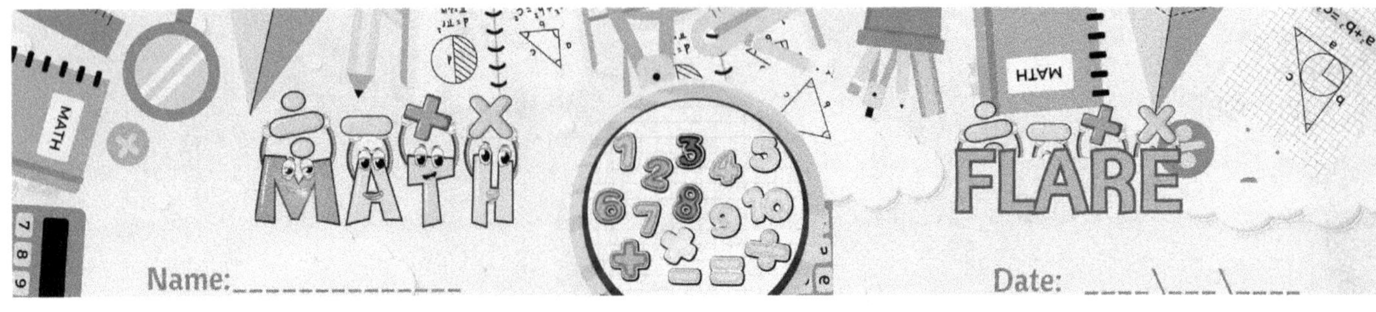

5) $30 = y(1 + y)$

6) $9 + y = 11$

7) $y^2 + y - 3 = 39$

8) $x^2 + x - 9 = 3$

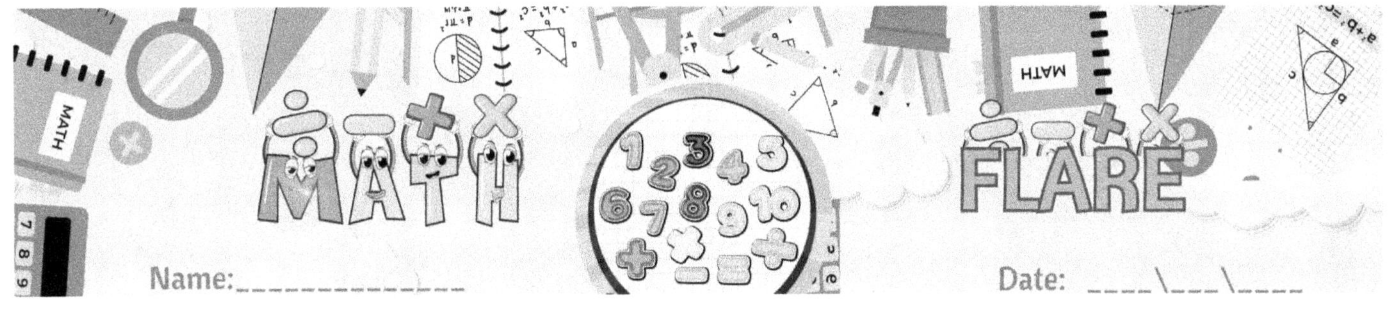

9) $z^2 + z - 5 = 1$

10) $20 = 2 + (7y + 4) - 6 + (3y)$

11) $1 \div (z + 8) = 0.059$

12) $8 \div x + 4 = 12$

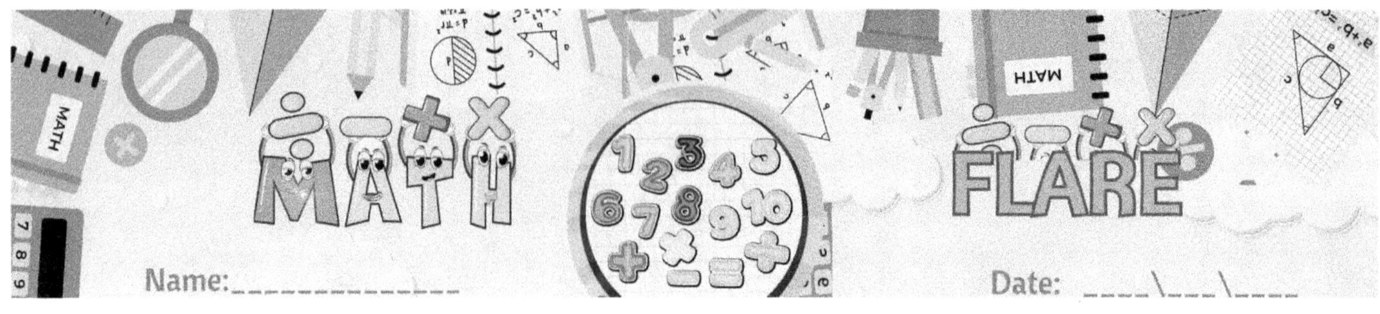

13) $z - 5 = 1$

14) $-4 = 4(2 - z)$

15) $\dfrac{y}{4} = 1$

16) $21 = 2x + x$

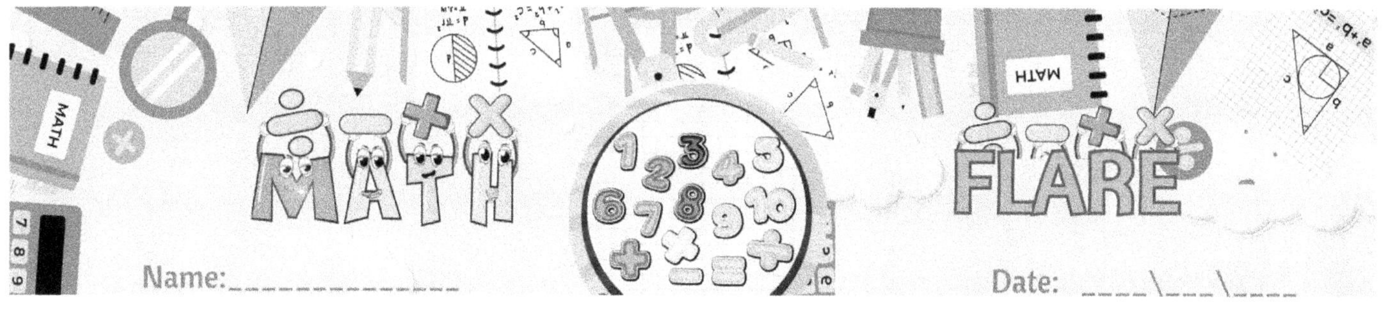

17) $324 = (9z)^2$

18) $0 = 6(6 - x)$

19) $37 = 6^2 + z^2$

20) $8 = 4 + \dfrac{4 + z}{z} - 1$

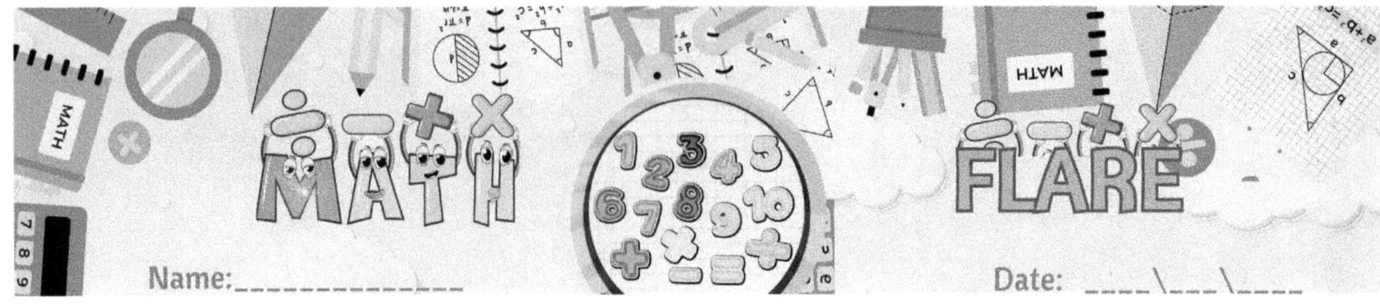

21) $0.625 = (y + 1) \div 8$

22) $z \div 4 = 2.25$

23) $-4.25 = 1 + \dfrac{8 + z}{4z} - 6$

24) $-1 = 3(2y - 5) + 1(7 + y)$

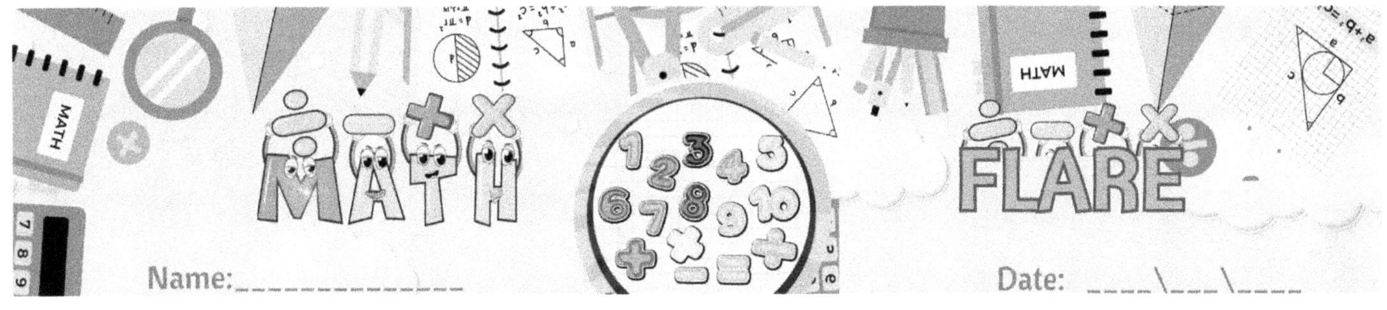

25) $2(6x - 8) + 9(7 + x) = 173$

26) $90 = 9x + 4x + 5x$

27) $6(5 - z) = 12$

28) $48 = 3(4x)$

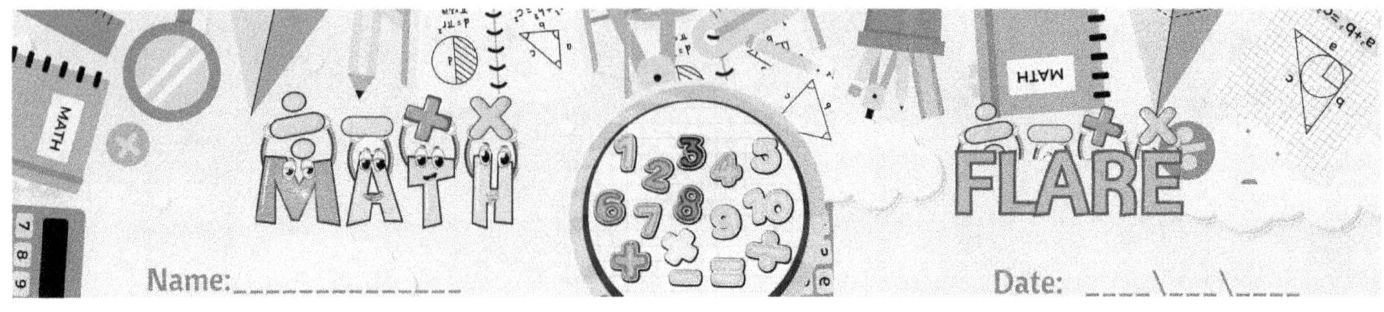

29) $21 = 8y + 5 + (2y - 4)$

30) $10 = 9 + \dfrac{y}{1}$

31) $41 = 9y + 5$

32) $2 = \dfrac{6}{z}$

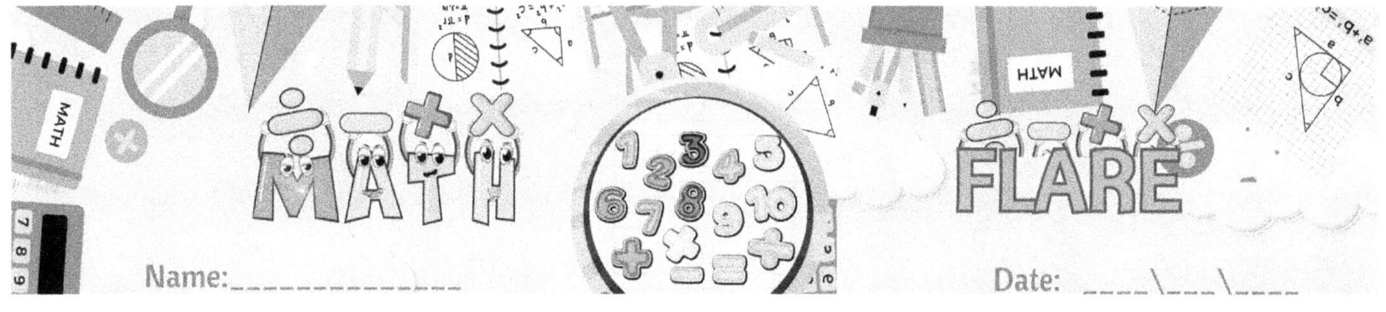

33) $15 = 4z - z$

34) $12 = 2x^2 + x^2$

35) $3 = 9 - x$

36) $(x + 9) \div 4 = 4.25$

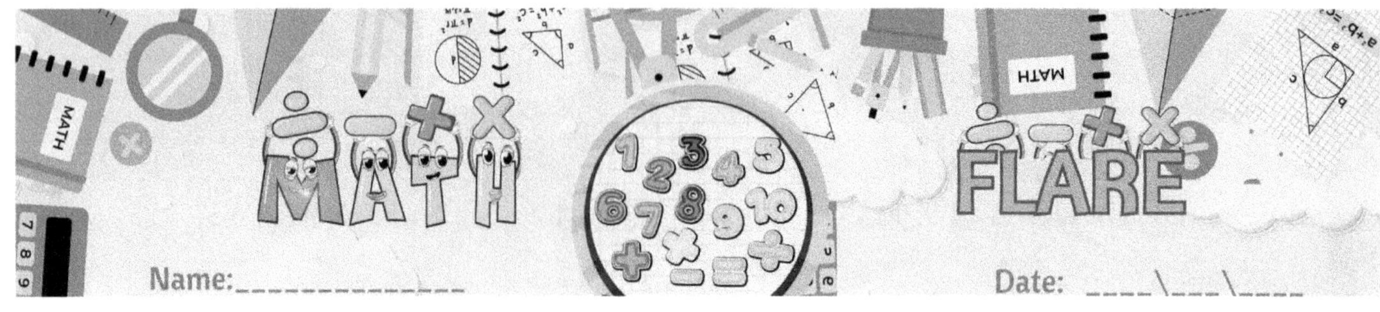

37) $104 = 1(3y - 3) + 8(1 + y)$

38) $35 = (z^2 + 4) - 3(3 + z)$

39) $28 = 4(7x)$

40) $4 + \dfrac{1}{x} + 9^2 = 86$

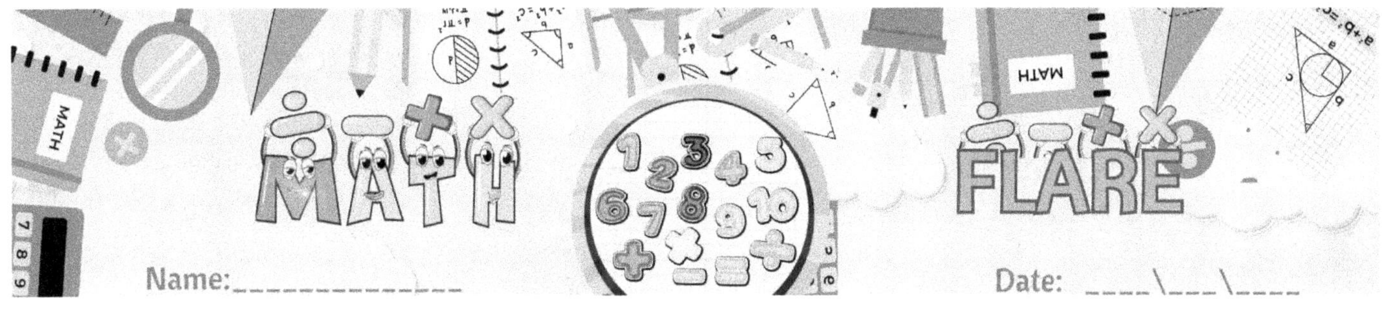

Solving Inequalities

1)

$-5 \geq 2 + z$

$-5-2 \geq z$

$-7 \geq z$

$z \leq -7$

$z \leq -7$

2)

$\dfrac{z}{-2} \geq -1$

3)

$x - -4 < -3$

4)

$-15\,k < -12$

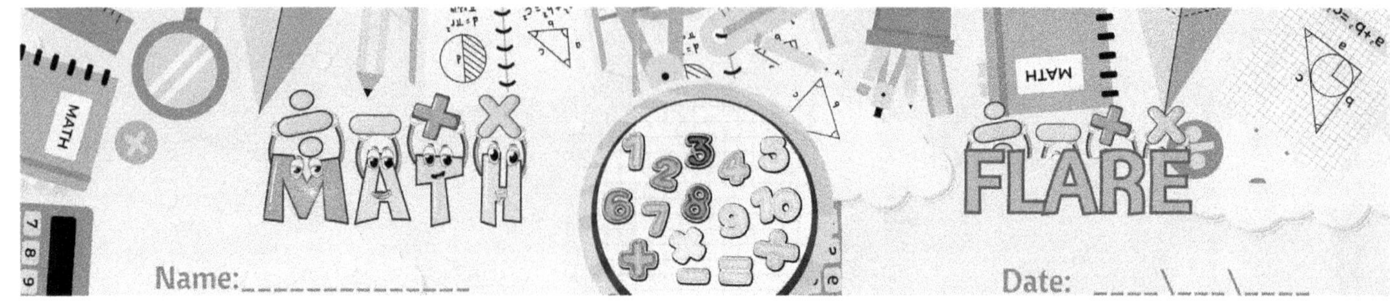

5)
$$m - 3 > 6$$

6)
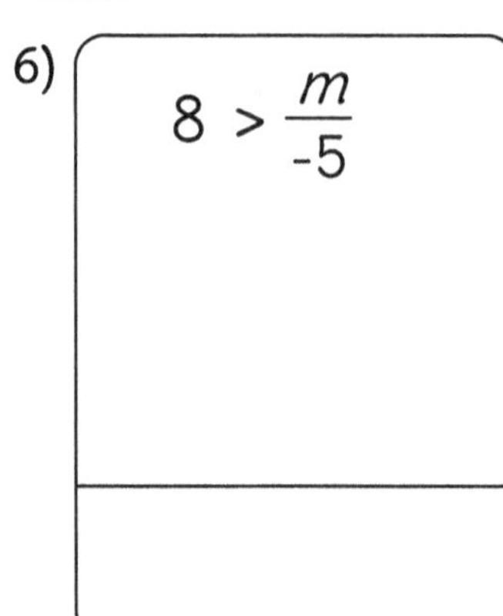
$$8 > \frac{m}{-5}$$

7)
$$-2\ k < 12$$

8)
$$y + -7 > -7$$

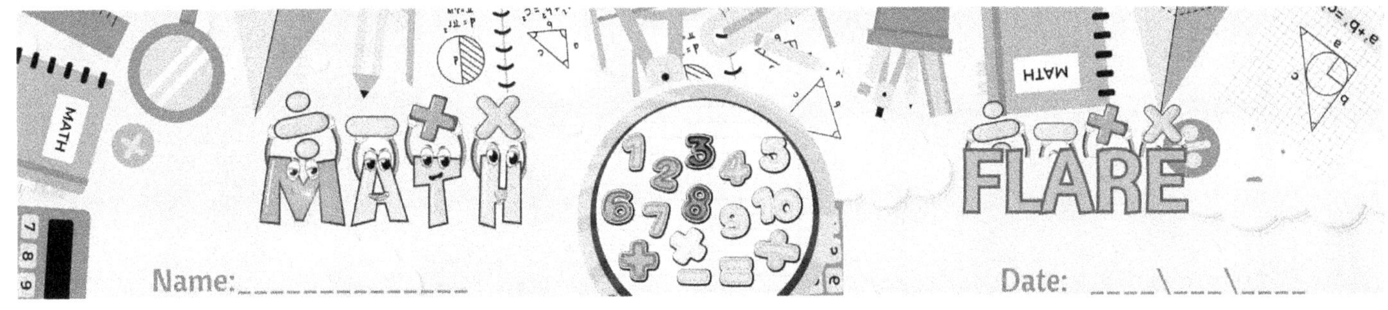

9)

$$6 - m \geq 8$$

10)

$$-6x > -8$$

11)

$$-3 \leq -6 + x$$

12)

$$-6 \leq \frac{k}{8}$$

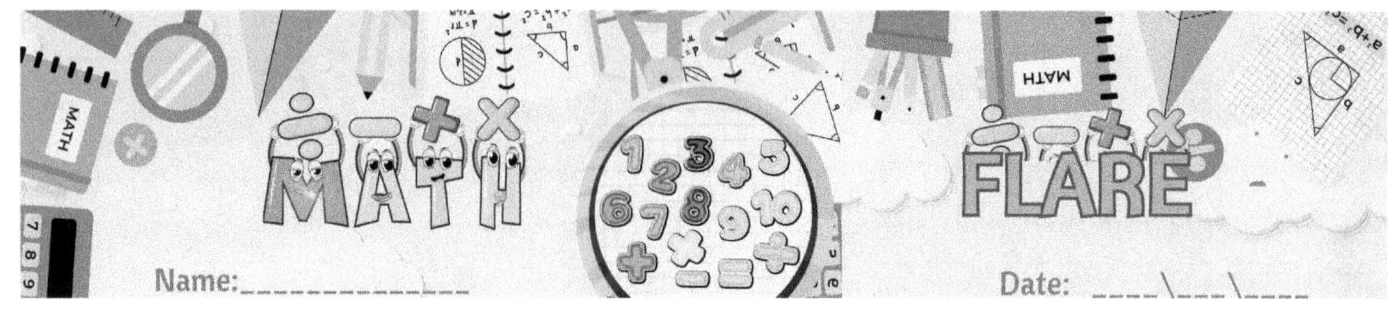

Name:_________________   Date: _____________

13)

$$7 > y - -8$$

14)

$$3 + m < -8$$

15)

$$12 \leq 10\,z$$

16)

$$\frac{m}{-7} < -1$$

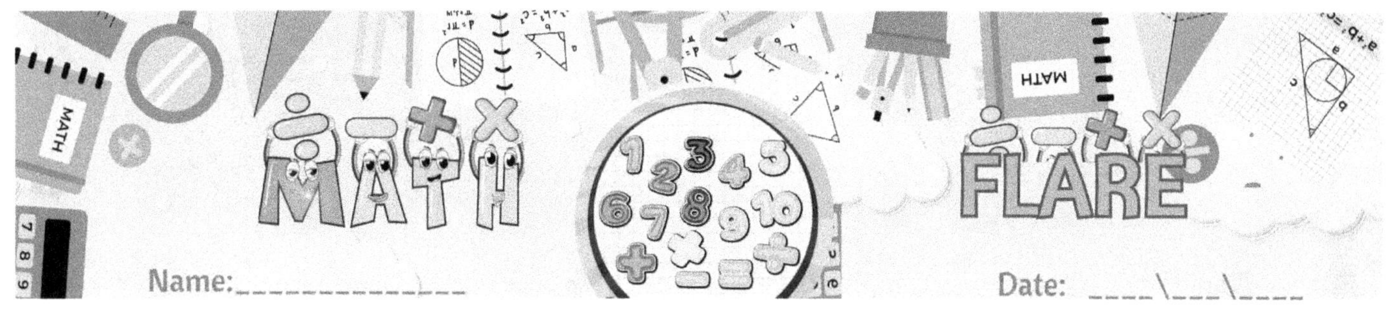

17)
$$-1\,x \le 3$$

18) 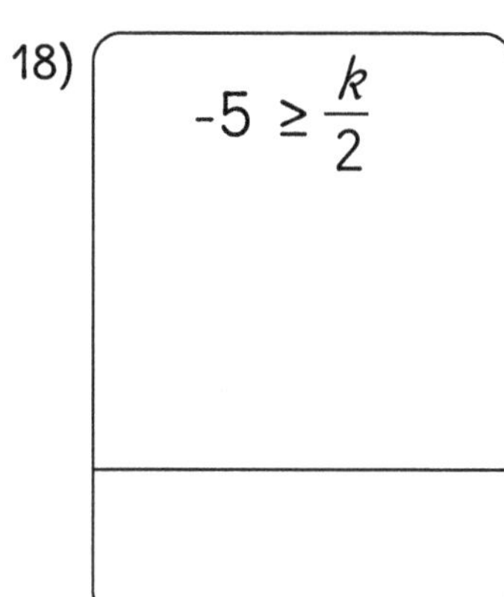
$$-5 \ge \frac{k}{2}$$

19)
$$2 + x < -5$$

20)
$$x - 2 \le 5$$

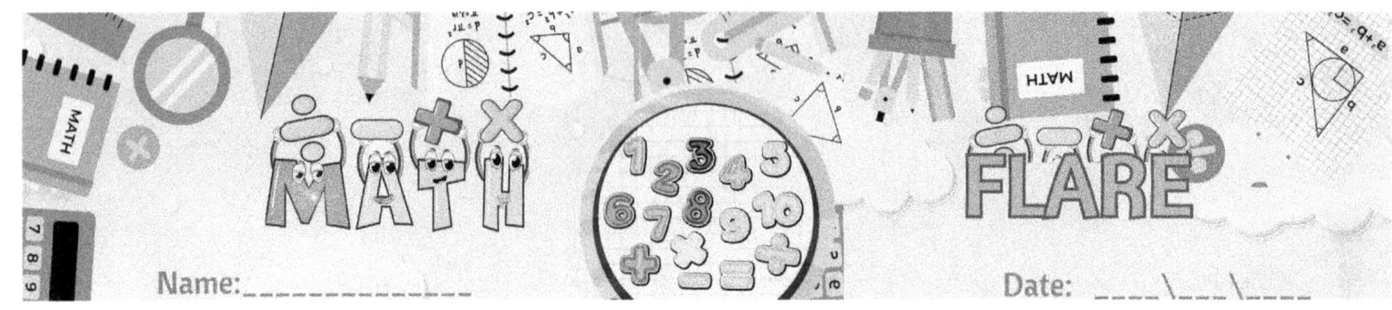

21)

$$9 > m + -10$$

22)

$$-7 < k - -9$$

23)

$$3 \leq \frac{k}{-4}$$

24)

$$-2x \geq 4$$

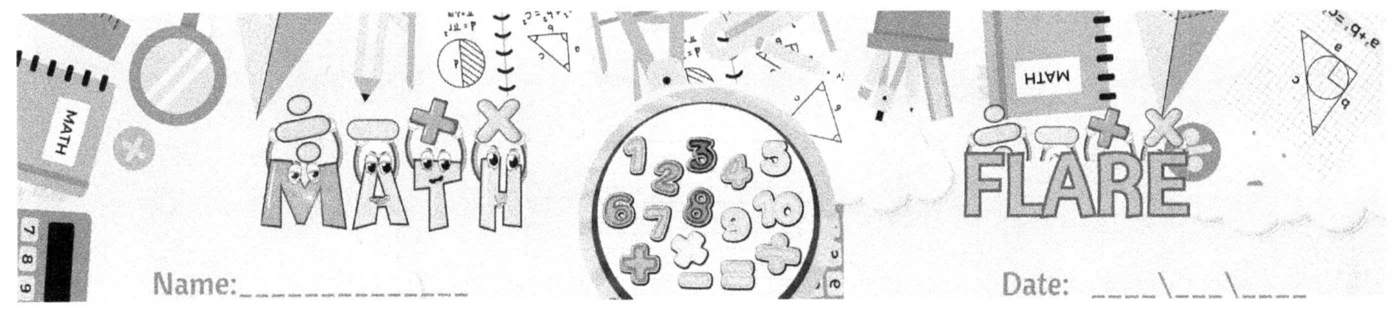

25)

$$-2 + k > -7$$

26)

$$-16 < 8\,m$$

27)

$$8 < k - 4$$

28)

$$\frac{k}{-9} > -1$$

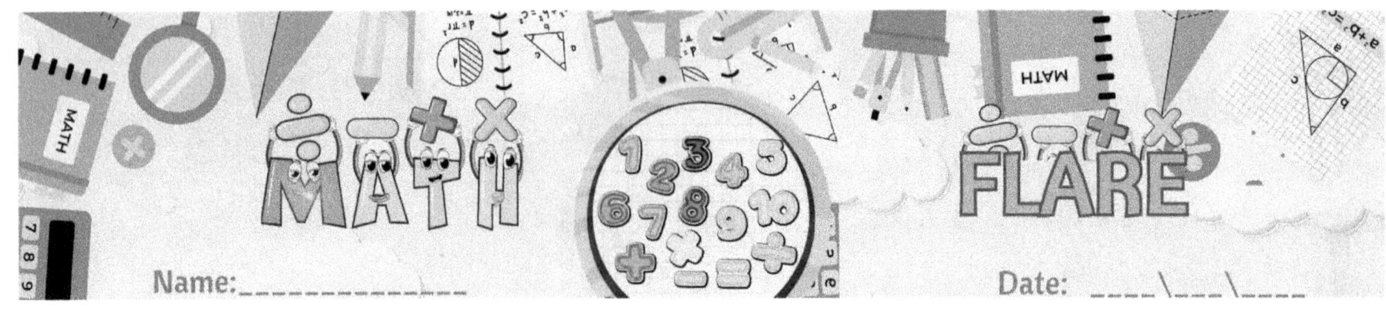

29)

$$-9 + m \leq -5$$

30)

$$\frac{y}{2} \leq 4$$

31)

$$y - 4 \leq 8$$

32)

$$-16 < -4\,m$$

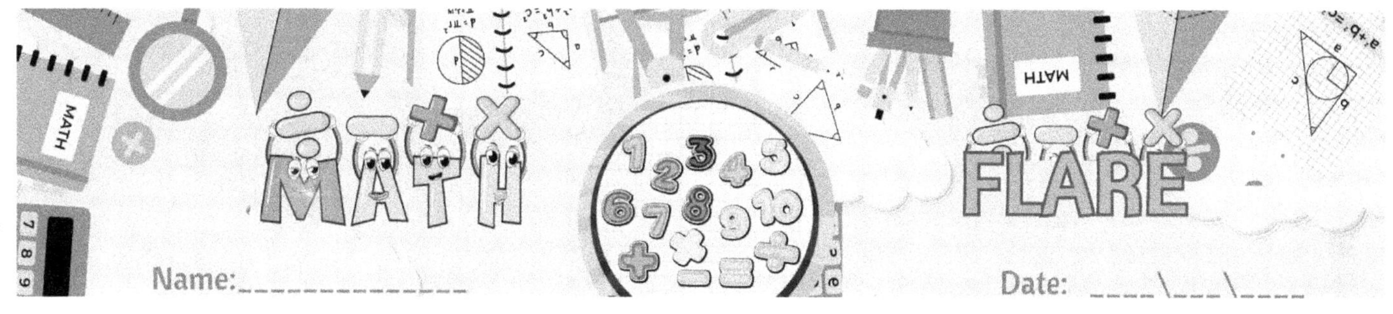

33)

$$-9 \geq \frac{m}{-3}$$

34)

$$z - {-4} \geq -1$$

35)

$$4x > 6$$

36)

$$-6 > m + {-3}$$

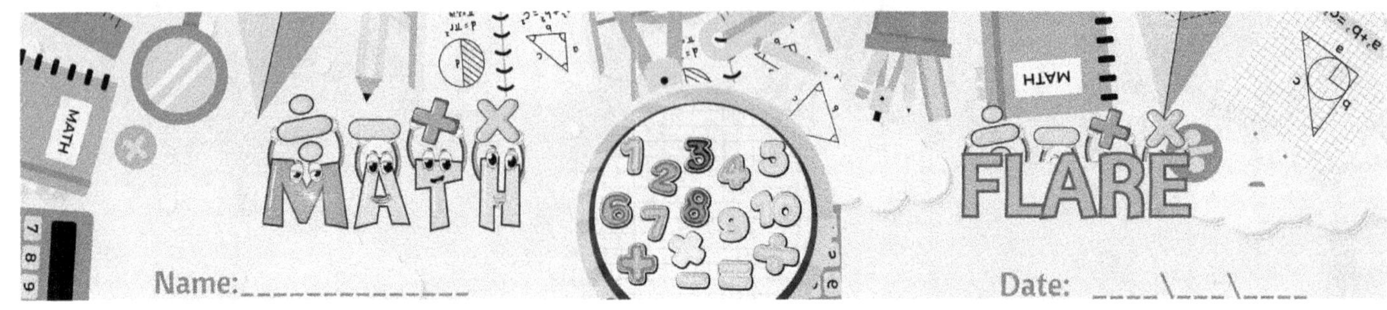

37)
$$\frac{z}{5} < 7$$

38)
$$-8 \le 12\,z$$

39)
$$5 > x - 1$$

40)
$$x + -3 \ge -4$$

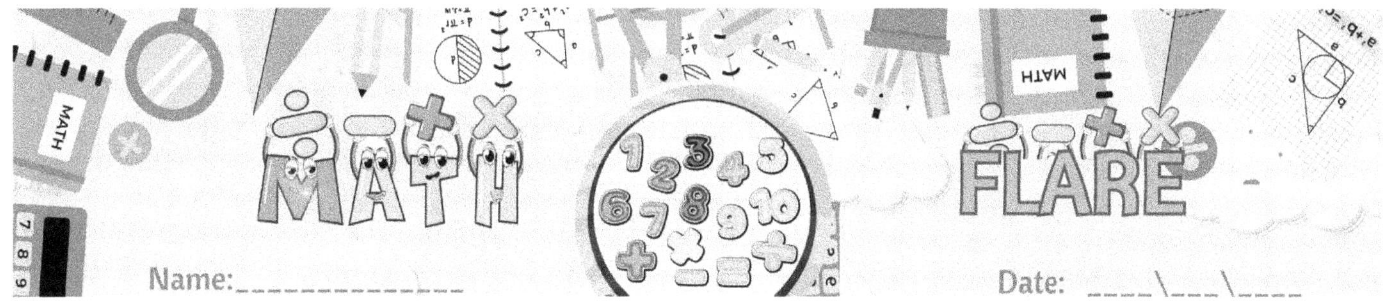

Find Numbers

Think Algebraically and find the numbers.

1) The quotient of a number and seven increased by 2 is 3. What is the number?

2) If the product of five and a number is increased by 4, the result is 54. Find the number?

3) Eight more than ten times a number is 98. What is the number?

4) The sum of the largest and six times the smallest of three consecutive numbers is equal to 16. Find the numbers.

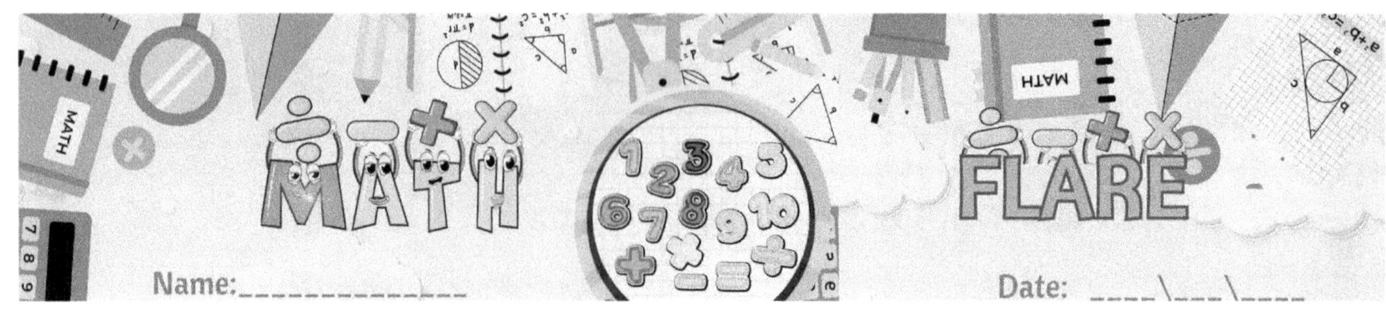

5) The sum of four consecutive numbers is 26. What are the numbers?

6) Two more than a number is 10. What is the number?

7) The sum of three numbers is 55. The largest number is ten times the smallest, and the smallest is seven less than the middle number. Find the numbers.

8) Eight less than a number is 8. Find the number.

9) One less than seven times a number is 48. Find the number.

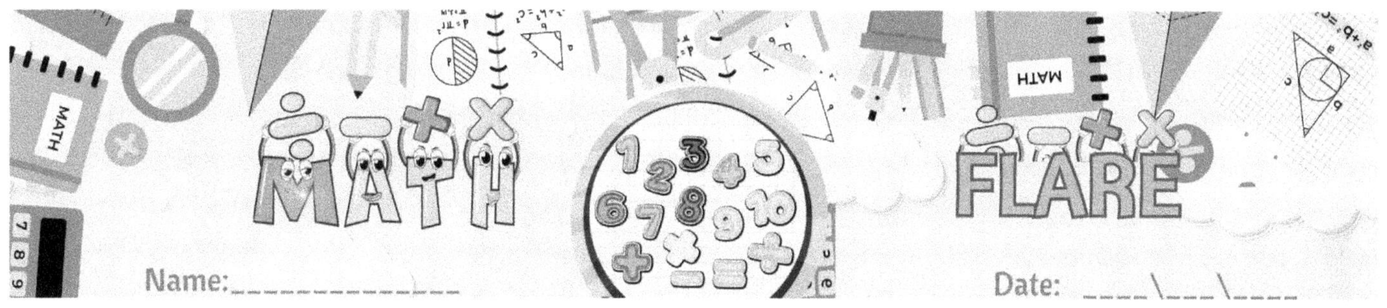

10)   The quotient of a number and ten increased by 6 is 12. What is the number?

11)   The sum of two numbers is 35. The larger number is four times the smaller number. What are the numbers?

12)   Three-fourths of a number increased by 4 is 10. What is the number?

13)   Four more than three times a number is equal to the number increased by 26. What is the number?

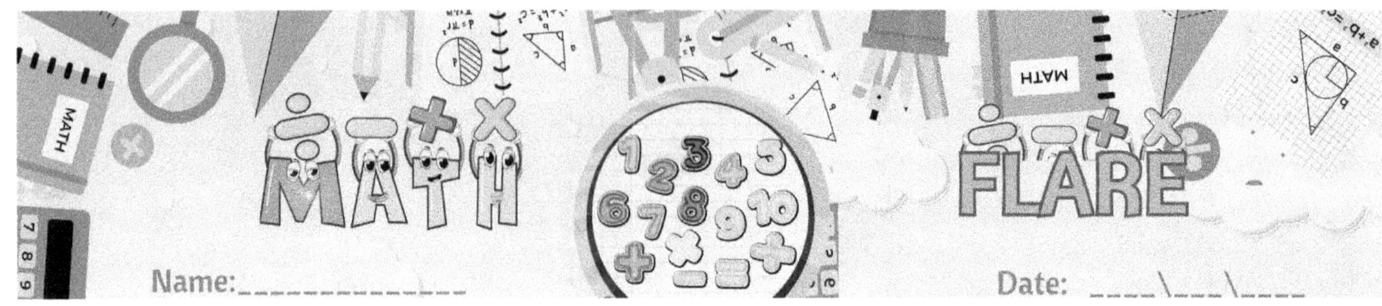

14) The sum of two numbers is 19. The difference of the same two numbers is three. Find the numbers.

15) The difference of a number and three is equal to 7. What is the number?

16) Four more than a number is 8. What is the number?

17) Find two consecutive even integers such that six times the smaller decreased by the larger is 18.

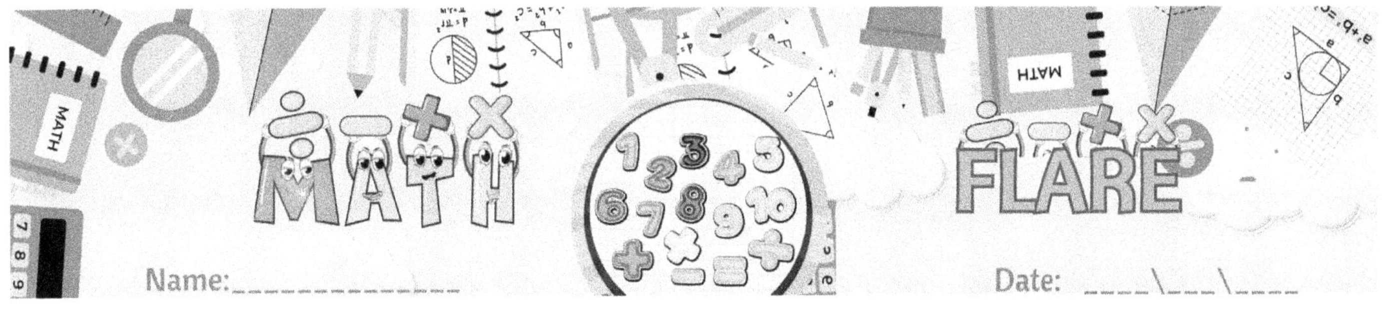

18) One number is 10 more than another number. The sum of twice the larger number and four times the smaller is 68. What are the numbers?

19) The sum of four consecutive numbers is 30. What are the numbers?

20) The product of four and some number is equal to the sum of that number and 18. What is the number?

21) The sum of two consecutive odd numbers is 20. Find the numbers.

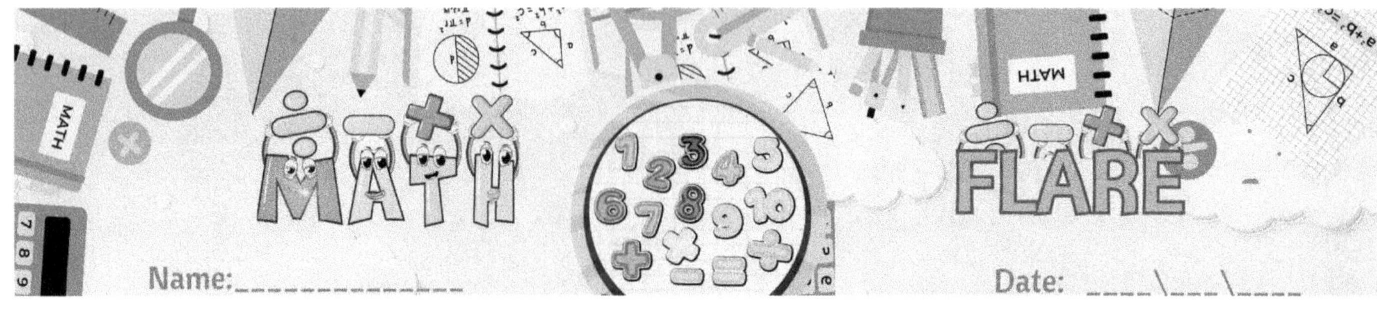

22) One number is four times another. Their sum is 20. Find the numbers.

23) The sum of two numbers is 9. One number is seven less than the other. Find the numbers.

24) The sum of three consecutive even numbers is 24. What are the numbers?

25) One less than eight times a number is 15. Find the number.

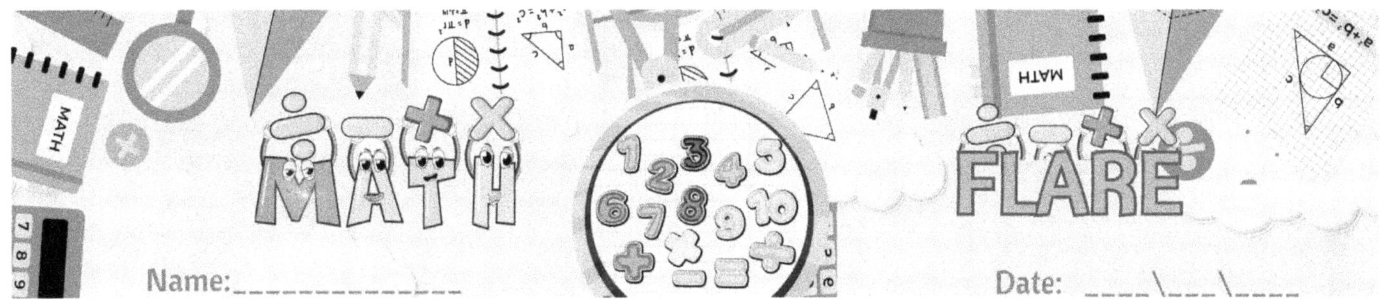

Name:_________________   Date: _______________

26)   Nine more than three times a number is equal to the number increased by 29. What is the number?

27)   One number is 10 more than another number. The sum of seven times the larger number and eight times the smaller is 145. What are the numbers?

28)   Two-fifths of a number increased by 5 is 11. What is the number?

29)   Three times a number is 3. What is the number?

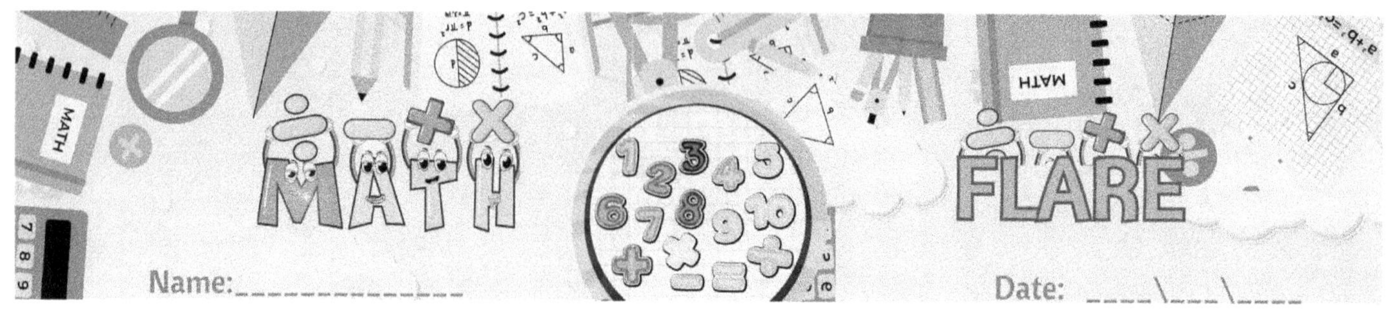

30) The sum of a number and nine is 17. Find the number.

31) A number diminished by 7 is 6. Find the number.

32) When a number is divided by seven, the result is 5. What is the number?

33) One number is five more than another number. The sum of the larger number and twice the smaller number is 17. Find the numbers?

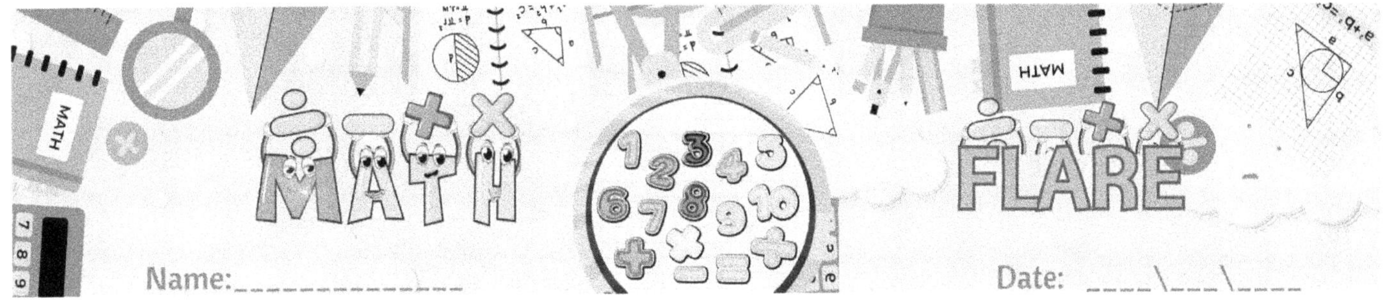

Name:_________________________   Date: ______________

34)   One of two numbers is two-fifths of the other number. The sum of the numbers is 0. Find the numbers.

35)   Eight times the sum of a number and six times the number is 392. Find the number.

36)   A number increased by four is 10. Find the number.

37)   The sum of the largest and nine times the smallest of three consecutive numbers is equal to 72. Find the numbers.

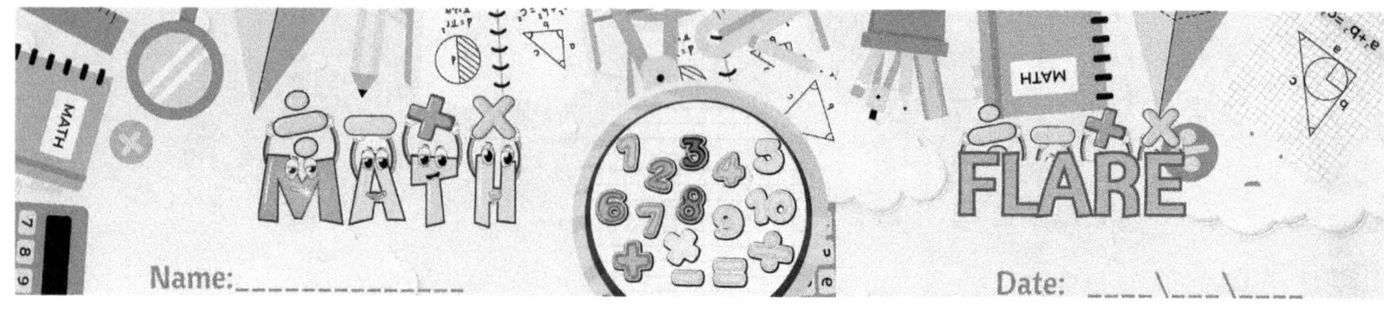

38) The sum of a number and seven is 11. Find the number.

39) Nine times a number decreased by 27 is 0. Find the number.

40) If the product of five and a number is increased by 3, the result is 43. Find the number?

41) One-fourth of a number is 2. Find the number.

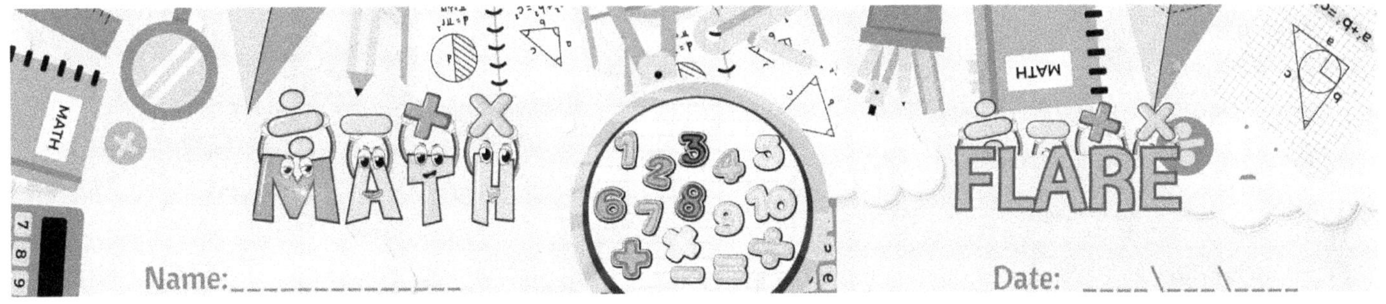

42) One of two numbers is three-fourths of the other number. The sum of the numbers is 7. Find the numbers.

43) One-third of a number diminished by 3 is -1. Find the number.

44) Two more than a number is 8. What is the number?

45) One of two numbers is one-half of the other number. The sum of the numbers is 3. Find the numbers.

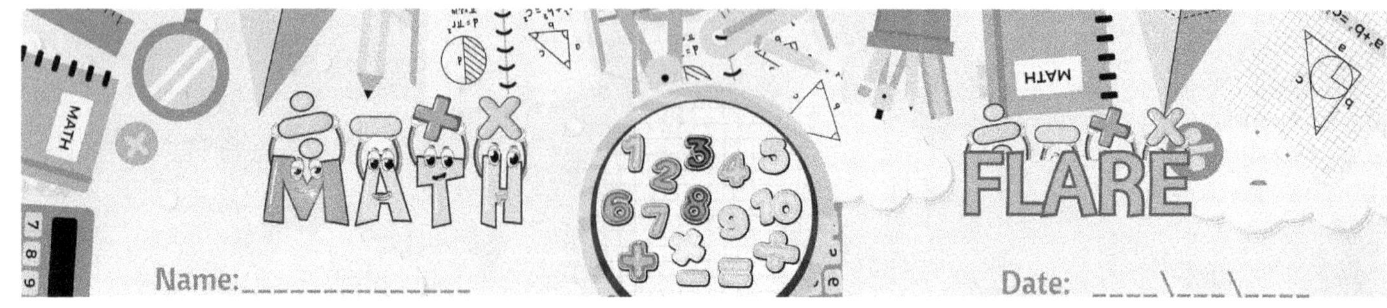

46) Find two consecutive even integers such that five times the smaller decreased by the larger is 22.

47) Four less than a number is 9. Find the number.

48) The product of two and some number is equal to the sum of that number and 4. What is the number?

49) The sum of the largest and five times the smallest of three consecutive numbers is equal to 20. Find the numbers.

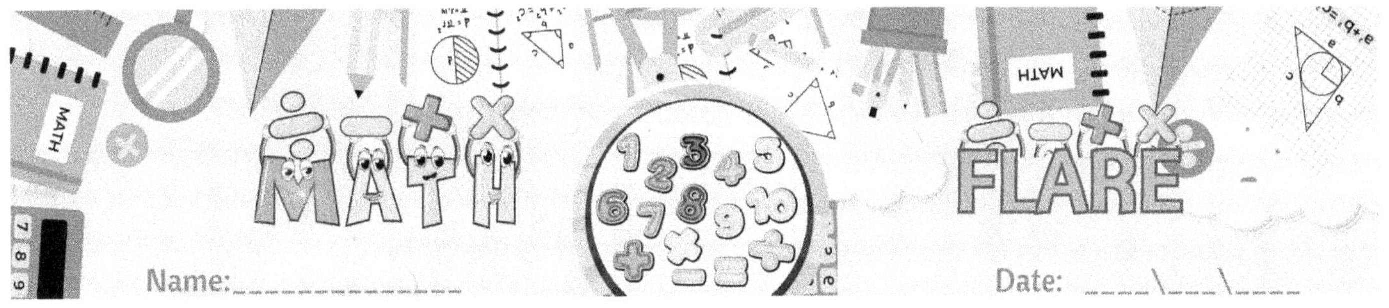

50) The sum of four consecutive numbers is 38. What are the numbers?

51) One-half of a number is 1. Find the number.

52) The sum of two consecutive odd numbers is 16. Find the numbers.

53) One more than four times a number is 49. What is the number?

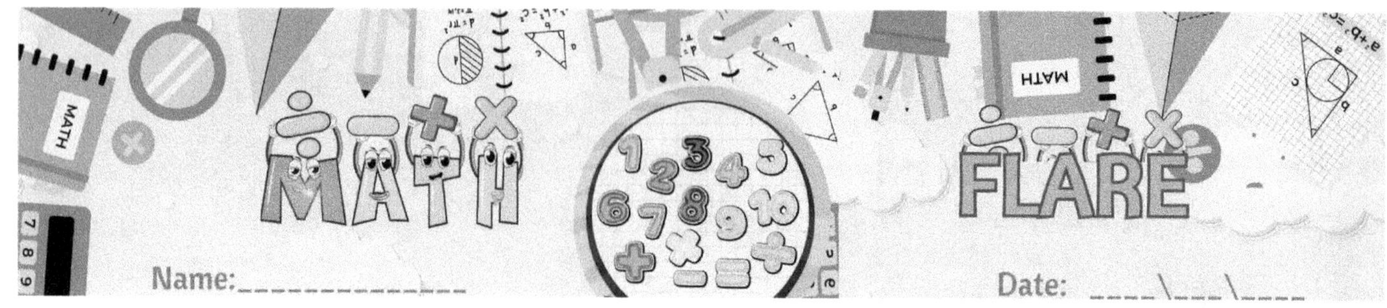

54) Ten more than the second of three consecutive even integers is the same as the difference between the third and four times the first. Find the numbers.

55) One less than seven times a number is 41. Find the number.

56) The sum of three consecutive even numbers is 24. What are the numbers?

57) The sum of two consecutive odd numbers is 4. Find the numbers.

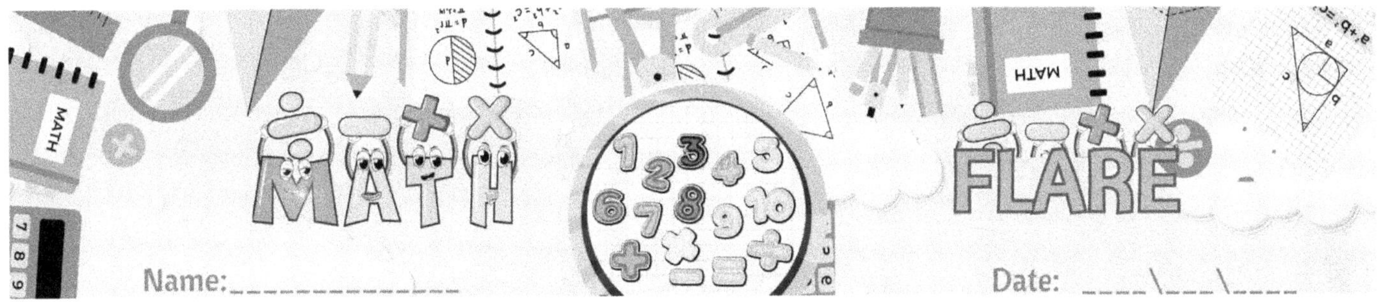

58)   The sum of three numbers is 27. The largest number is eight times the smallest, and the smallest is seven less than the middle number. Find the numbers.

59)   Find two consecutive odd integers such that twice the larger decreased by the smaller is 7.

60)   Six more than twice a number is equal to the number increased by 9. What is the number?

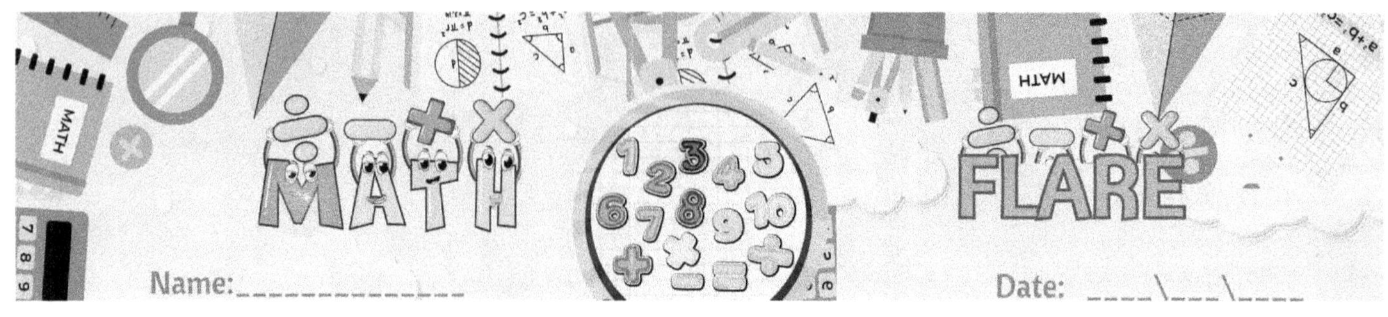

Solving Equations: (One Step)

1) $277 = 14x - 3$

$277 + 3 = 14x$

$280 = 14x$

$X = \dfrac{280}{14}$ $X = 20$

2) $x + 3 = 20$

3) $17k - 2 = 168$

4) $6 = 406 - 20y$

5) $20 = 180 \div k$

6) $y \div 16 = 18$

7) $211 = 11 + 20k$

8) $m + 5 = 14$

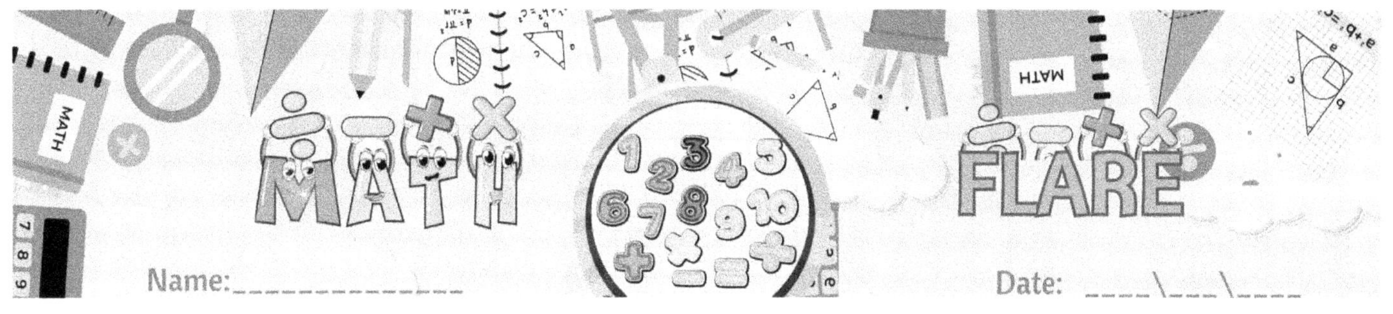

9) $8 = z \div 7$

10) $151 = 15k + 16$

11) $18 + 16m = 306$

12) $138 = 19y - 14$

13) $20 = m \div 5$

14) $m + 13 = 23$

15) $179 = 8 + 19m$

16) $13 - k = 6$

17) $28 = m \times 7$

18) $224 = 14 + 14k$

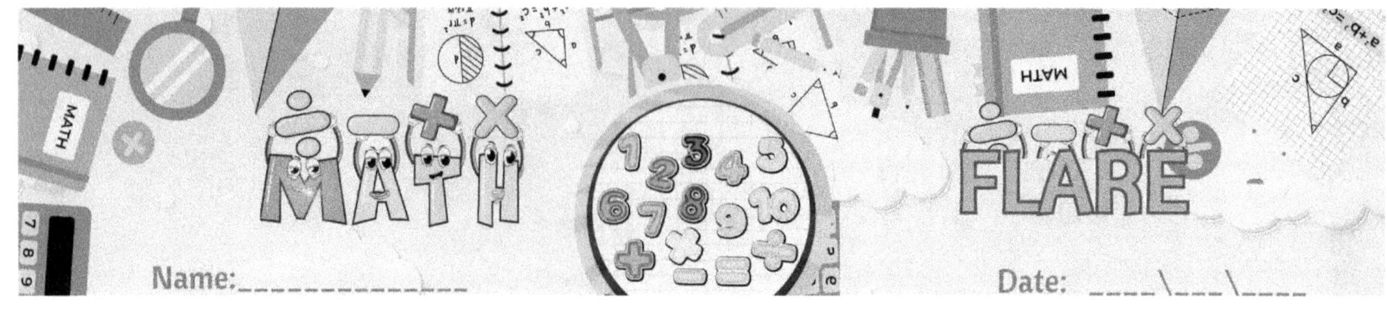

19) $170 = x \times 17$

20) $11 = m + 8$

21) $6 + y = 13$

22) $x \div 10 = 20$

23) $105 \div y = 7$

24) $14 = k - 2$

25) $66 = 3z + 18$

26) $4 = 48 - 4x$

27) $10 + 17z = 299$

28) $20 = 200 \div k$

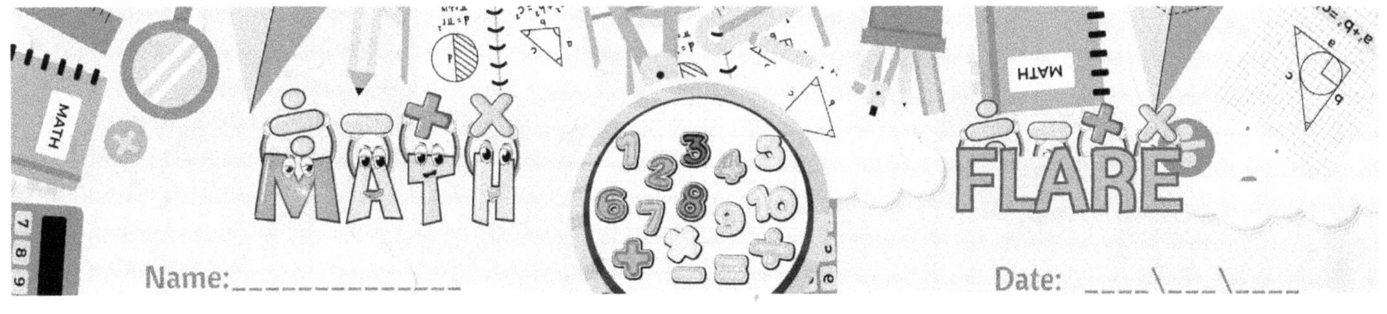

29) $14 = 154 \div k$

30) $15 = y + 2$

31) $k - 13 = 3$

32) $11 + z = 16$

33) $323 = y \times 19$

34) $310 - 16k = 6$

35) $23 = 12 + m$

36) $69 = 7x - 8$

37) $2 = 155 - 9z$

38) $8 = 15 - y$

76

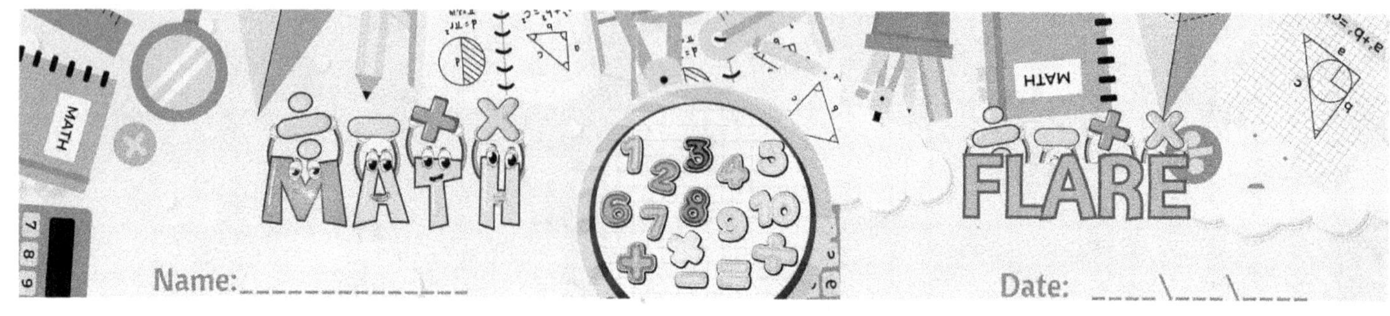# MathFlare

39) $216 - 19k = 7$

40) $242 = 14m + 4$

41) $k \times 2 = 2$

42) $106 = 7x - 20$

43) $8 = z \div 2$

44) $9 - z = 5$

45) $m - 4 = 7$

46) $8 + 14m = 64$

47) $14 - z = 2$

48) $8m - 18 = 22$

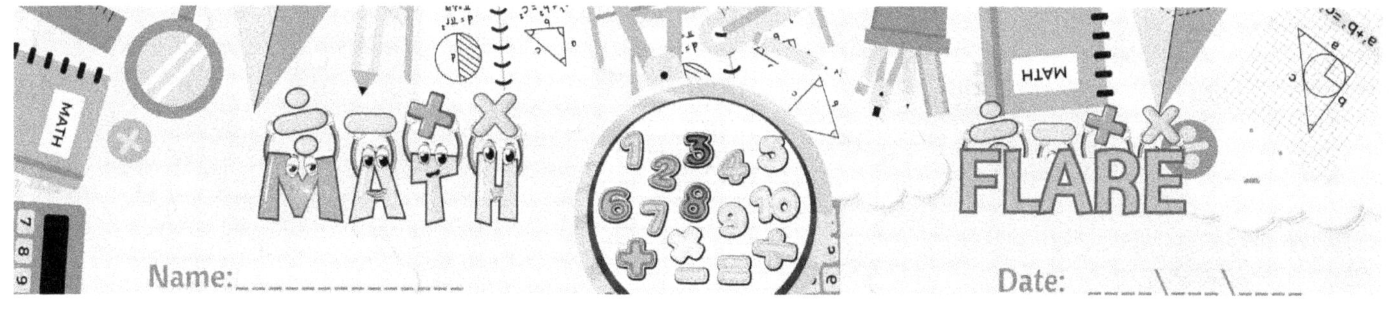

49) $k + 10 = 26$

50) $10 = 120 \div z$

51) $x \div 16 = 13$

52) $18k - 19 = 233$

53) $8 = k \div 13$

54) $17 \times y = 85$

55) $256 = k \times 16$

56) $72 = 5z - 8$

57) $24 = 3 \times y$

58) $z - 2 = 3$

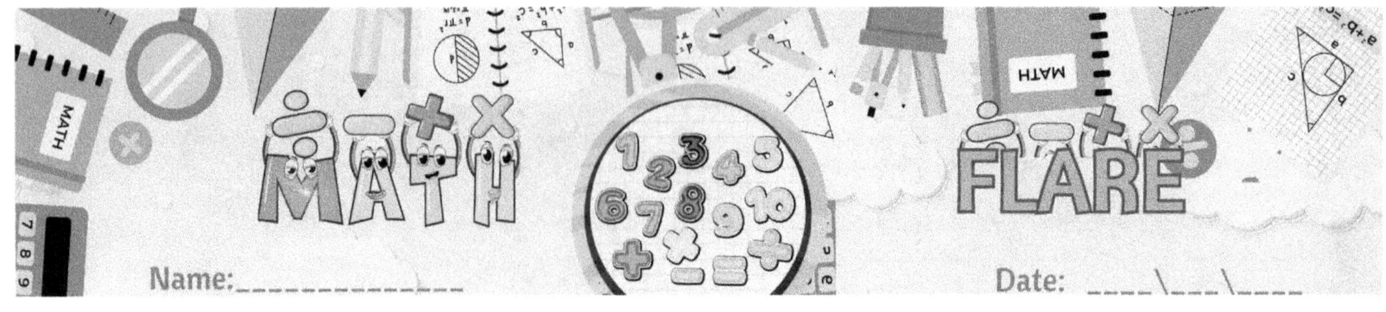

59) $18 = y \div 17$

60) $15y - 9 = 81$

61) $z \times 5 = 15$

62) $27 = k \times 3$

63) $9m + 19 = 127$

64) $3 \times m = 3$

65) $k + 20 = 32$

66) $0 = 15 - x$

67) $26 = 8 + z$

68) $13m - 6 = 254$

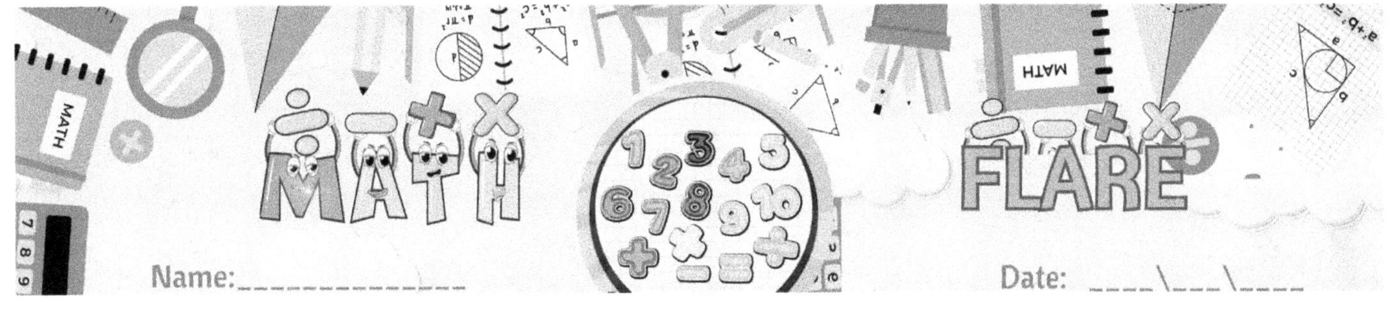

69) $19 = 5z + 9$

70) $18 = z \times 3$

71) $k \times 1 = 1$

72) $2 = 4 \div x$

73) $108 = 6z - 12$

74) $19 = m - 1$

75) $20m + 14 = 214$

76) $6 - k = 4$

77) $5 - y = 0$

78) $11y + 6 = 138$

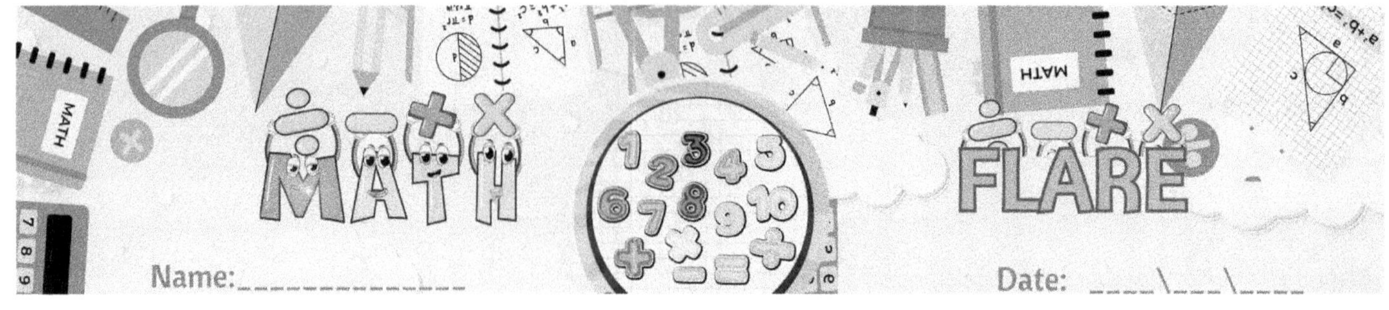

79) $7 + 14z = 77$

80) $78 \div y = 13$

81) $21 - 19x = 2$

82) $16 = 80 \div x$

83) $7 + 17z = 245$

84) $19k + 9 = 180$

85) $17 = m \div 9$

86) $z - 3 = 7$

87) $18 = 5 + y$

88) $10 = 1k - 3$

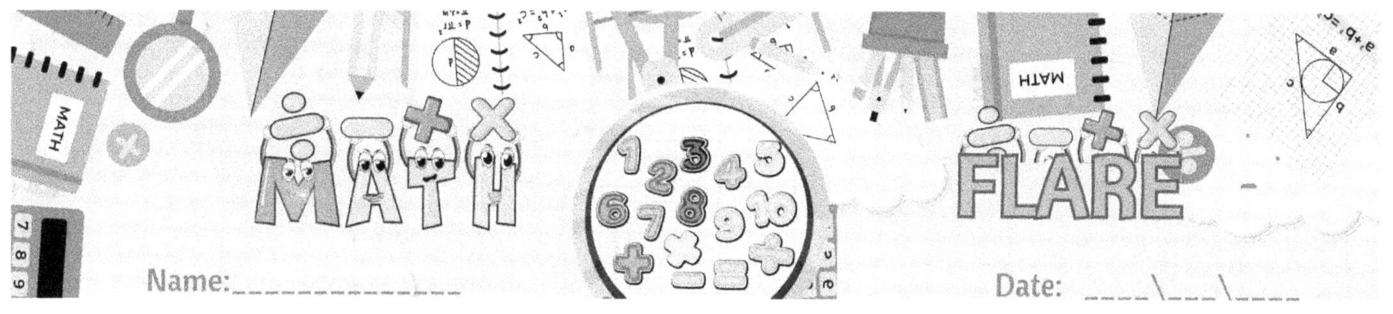

Equations (Two Steps)
Solve for the variable.

1) $2k + 8 = 6k + 4$

$$2k - 6k = 4 - 8$$
$$-4k = -4$$
$$k = \frac{-4}{-4}$$

2) $9 + 8x = 51 + x$

3) $6x + 5 = 20 + x$

4) $2 + x = 3x$

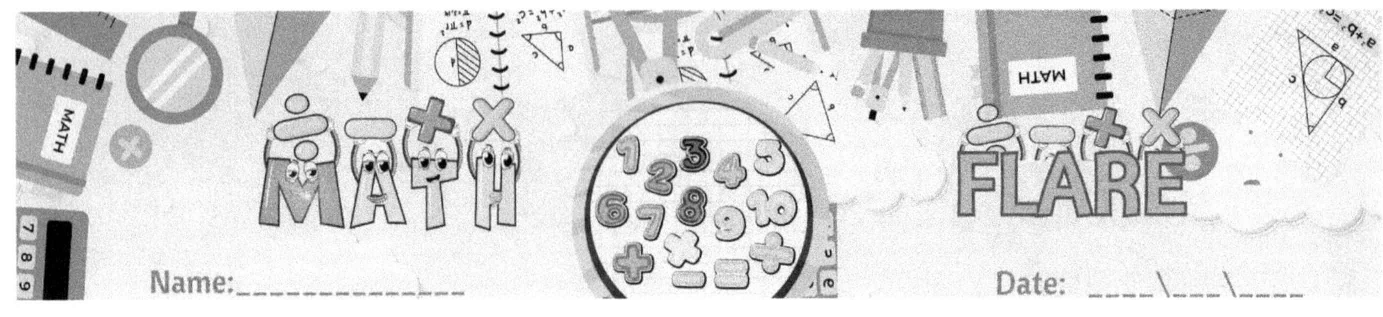

5) $15 - k = 2k$

6) $40 - z = 4z$

7) $13 - m = 2m + 1$

8) $6 - 2x = 3x + 1$

9) $6z = 15 + z$

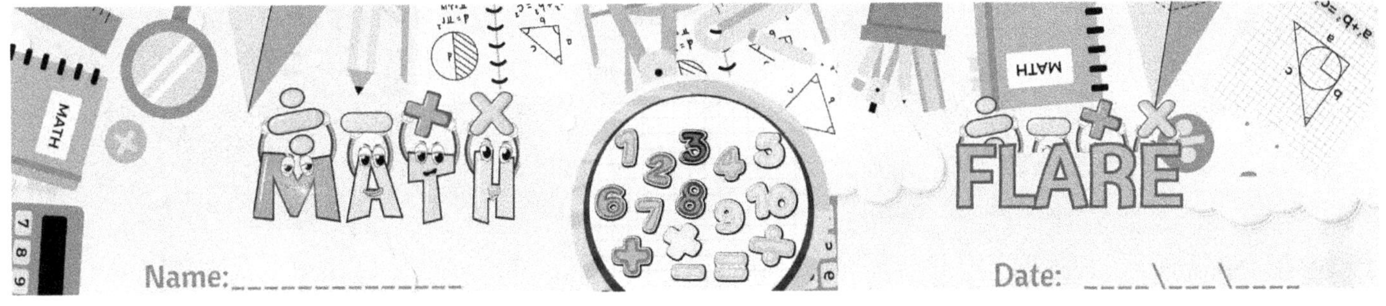

10) $9y + 8 = 8y + 13$

11) $8z = 72 - z$

12) $3m + 8 = 44 - m$

13) $3 + 8x + 8 = 64 + x + -4$

14) $7 + 7y = 37 + y$

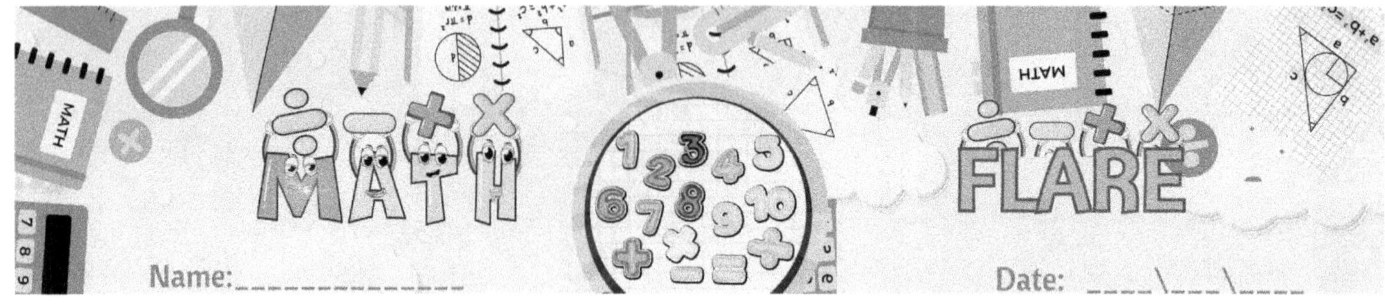

15) $130 - 7y = 2 + 9y$

16) $16 + z = 2z + 8$

17) $8z + 5 = 15 + 3z$

18) $7 + 3k + 4 = 19 + k + 2$

19) $3k + 9 = 19 + k$

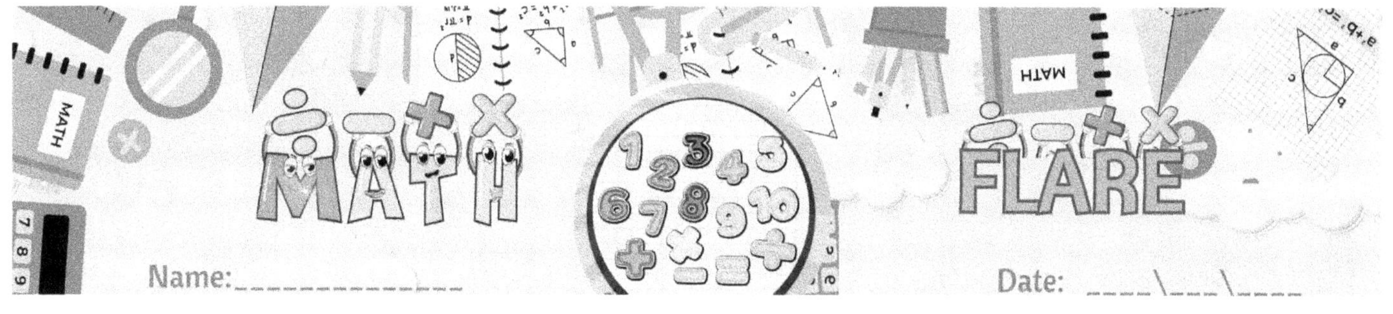

20) $15 - x + 7 = 2 + 2x + 5$

21) $45 - 4z = 9 + 5z$

22) $24 - x = 5x$

23) $3y = 32 - y$

24) $8 + 4m + 2 = 40 - m$

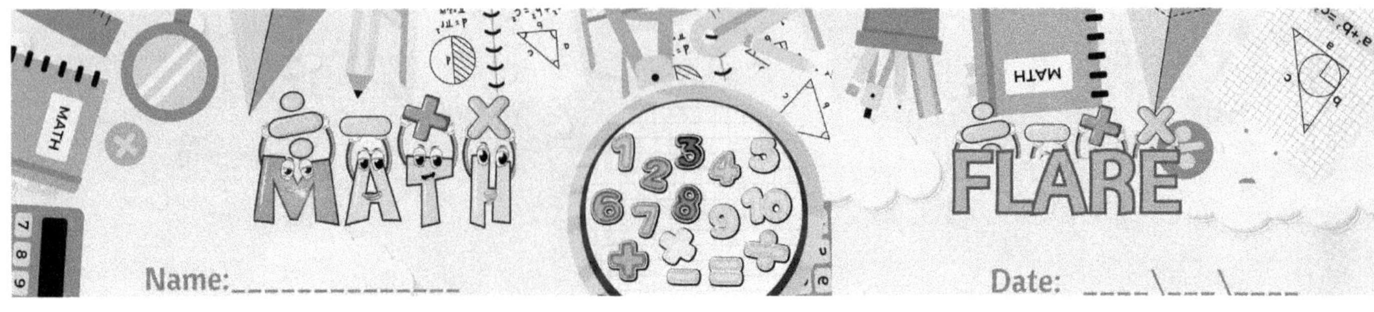

25) $1 + 4k + 4 = 25 + k + -2$

26) $20 - k = 3 + 5k + 5$

27) $9 - y = 2 + 6y$

28) $57 - 2y = 3 + 4y$

29) $6x + 3 = 59 - x$

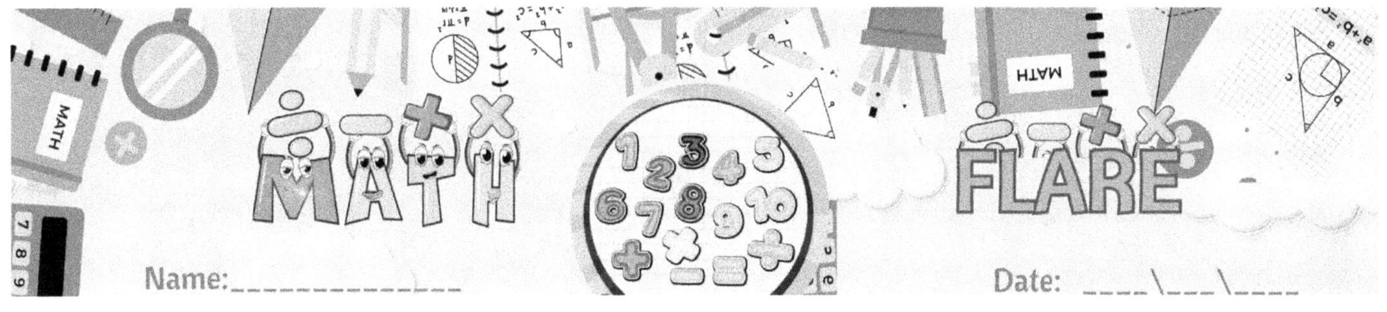

30) $30 - x = 2 + 3x$

31) $6 + 4x = 24 - 2x$

32) $16 + m = 7 + 7m + 3$

33) $14 - m = 6m$

34) $2z = 3 + z$

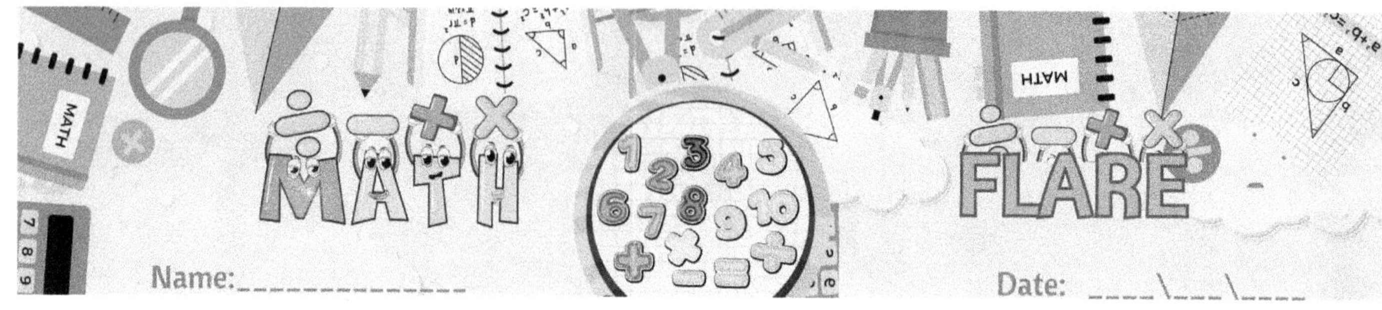

35) $8 + 2y + 6 = 10 - y + 7$

36) $23 - z = 4 + 4z + 9$

37) $3m + 2 = 10 - m$

38) $5 + 2y + 4 = 12 + y + 1$

39) $3 + 2k + 2 = 14 - k$

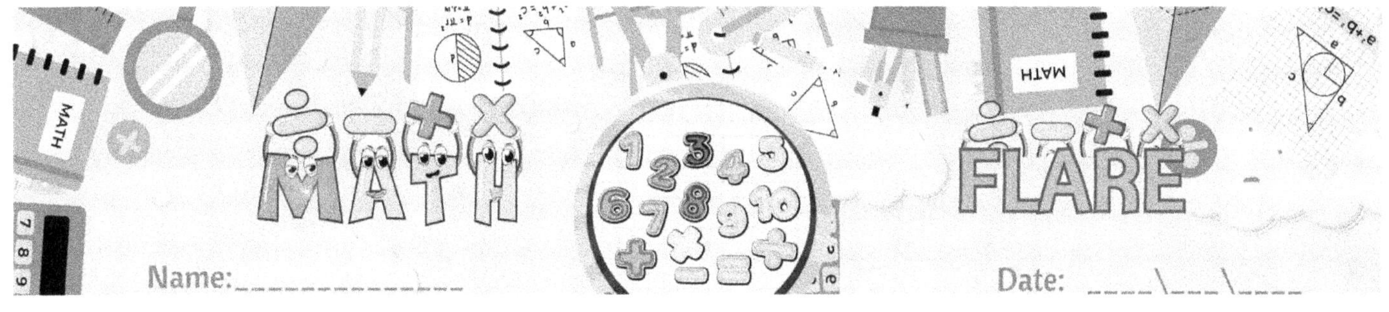

40) $5z = 36 + z$

41) $53 + m = 4 + 8m$

42) $68 - x + 14 = 6 + 8x + 4$

43) $7z + 2 = 38 - 2z$

44) $16 - m + 8 = 4 + 2m + 2$

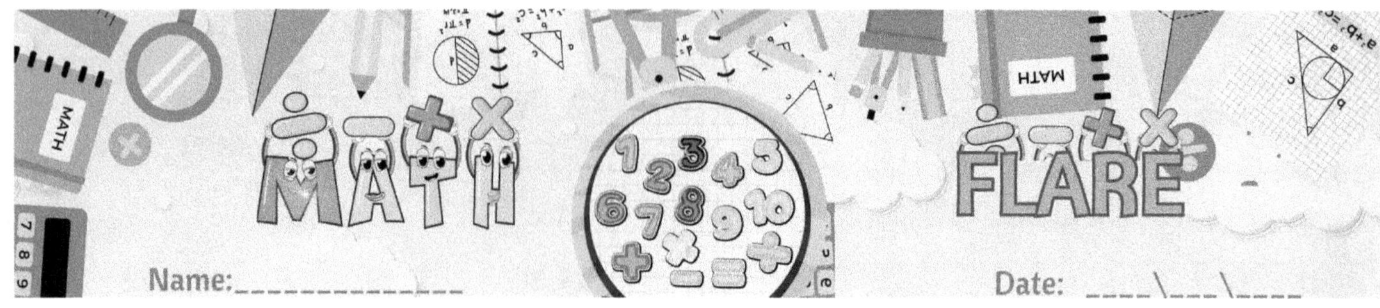

45) $49 + y = 8y$

46) $45 - z = 8z$

47) $3y = 16 + y$

48) $2m = 7 + m$

49) $48 - x = 5x$

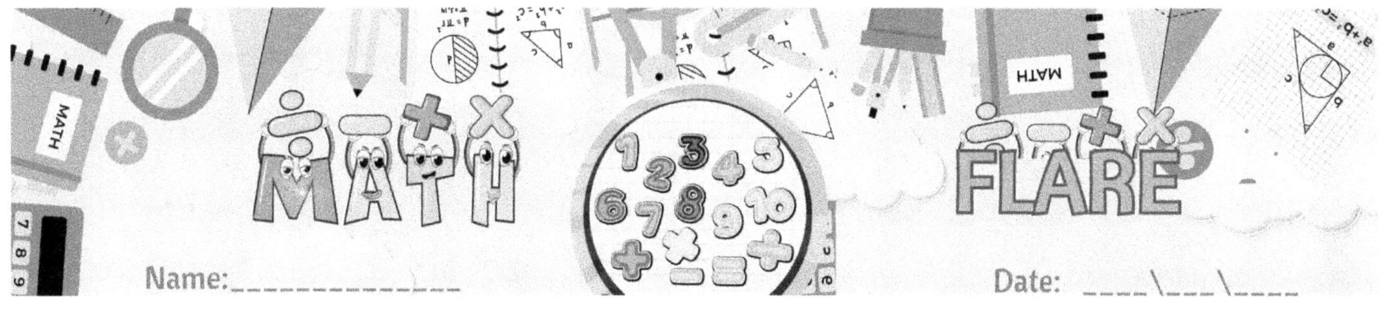

50) $14 + 8m = 8 + 9m$

51) $18 - k = 2k$

52) $5 + x = 6x$

53) $79 - y = 7y + 7$

54) $2 + 5m = 56 - m$

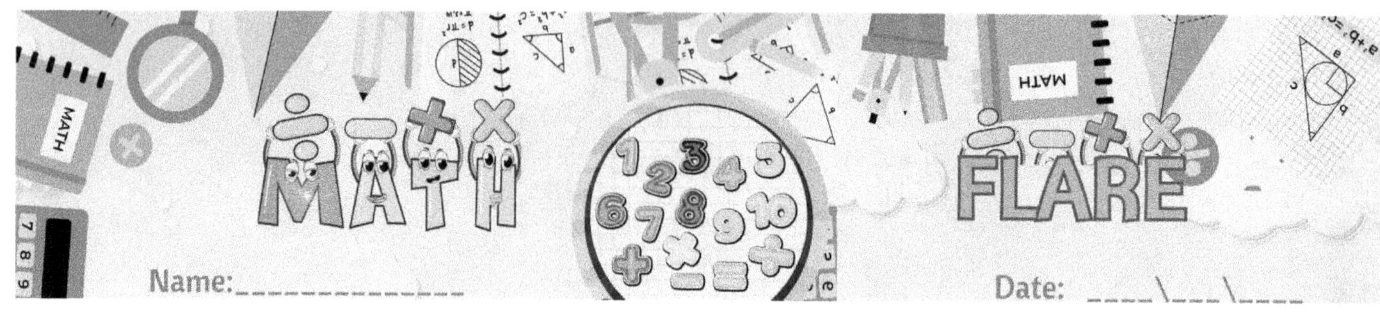

55) $2m + 29 = 8 + 9m$

56) $2y + 5 = 12 + y$

57) $1 + 8z + 4 = 41 + z + -1$

58) $12 - k = 5k$

59) $7 + x = 3x + 1$

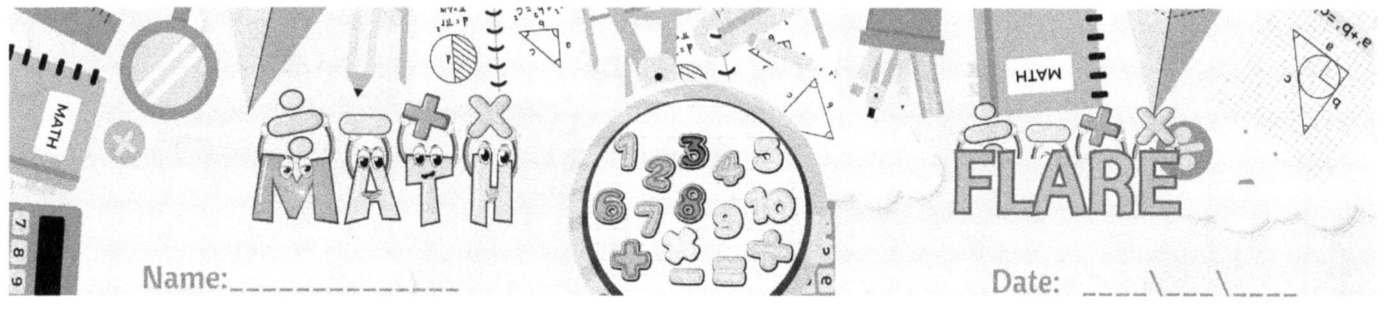

60) $13 + z = 2z + 7$

61) $5 + 6k = 25 + k$

62) $4 + 7y + 4 = 18 - y + 6$

63) $28 - 2z = 3z + 8$

64) $8 + 9m = 42 - 8m$

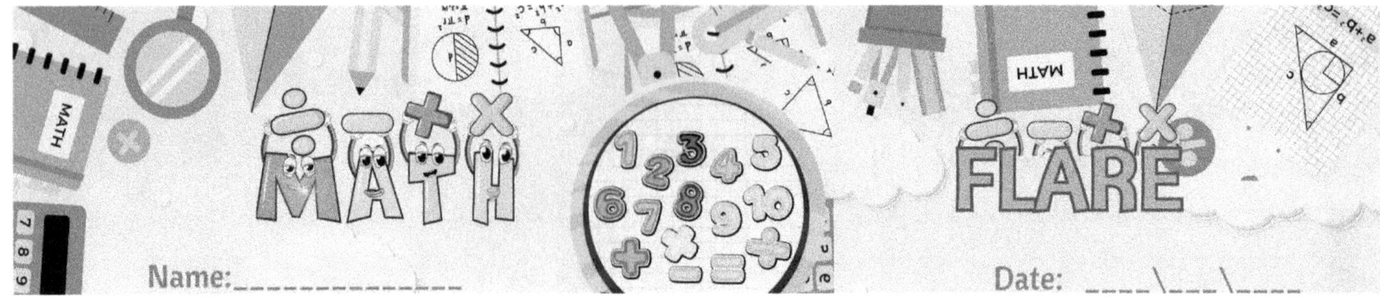

65) 9 - m = 8m

66) 4 + 8x + 4 = 89 - x

67) 5 + 2k = 11 + k

68) 9 + 4y = 44 - y

69) 30 - z = 5z

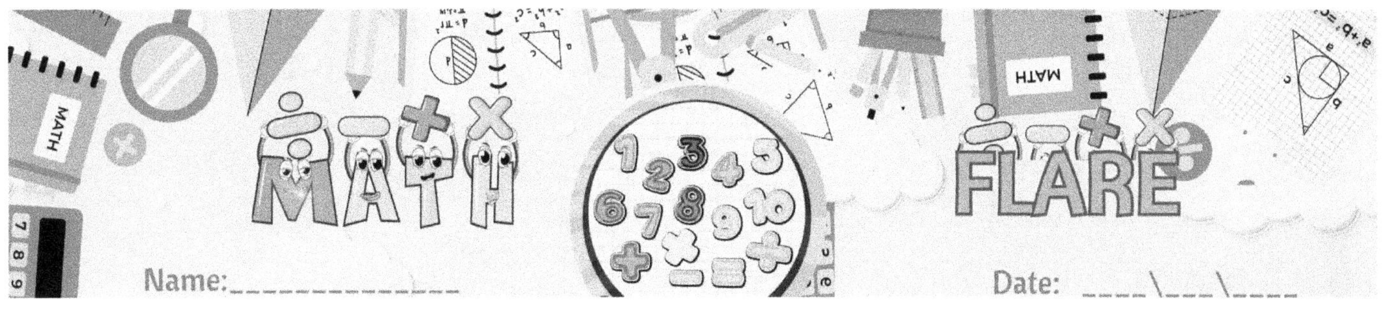

70) $72 + z = 8 + 8z + 1$

71) $6 + 6x = 60 - 3x$

72) $24 - m = 7m$

73) $6z = 7 - z$

74) $2k = 9 + k$

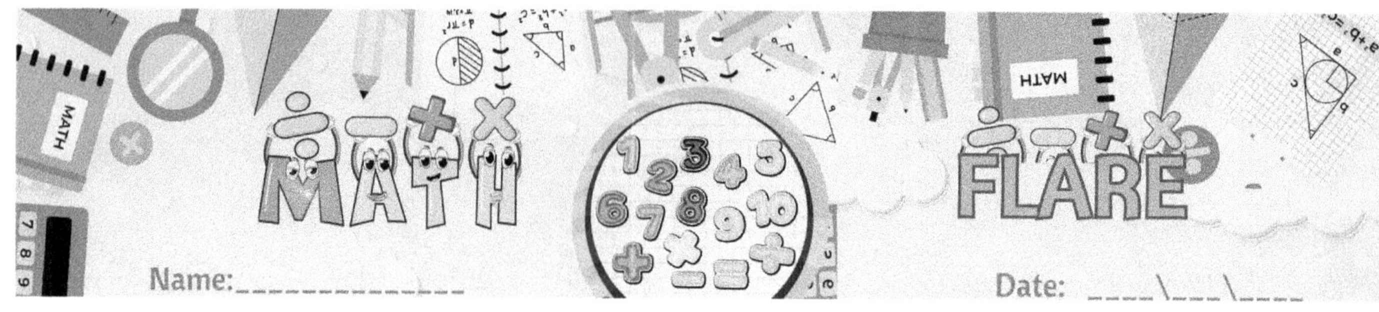

75) $63 - 6k = 9k + 3$

76) $28 - x = 3x$

77) $45 - y = 4y$

78) $24 - x = 7x$

79) $7y = 42 + y$

Chapter. 03

Cartesian Plane

Cartesian Coordinates

The Cartesian Coordinate System, also known as the x-y plane, provides a method for representing points on a graph using two perpendicular lines: the x-axis and the y-axis. At their intersection, denoted by the letter "O", lies the origin.

To plot a point on this system, we use coordinates, consisting of two numbers. The first number represents the horizontal movement from the origin (x-coordinate), while the second number represents the vertical movement (y-coordinate). These coordinates are written as an ordered pair (x, y).

For instance, let's plot these coordinates:

$$A = (1, 3) \quad B = (5, 0) \quad C = (8, 6)$$

$$D = (9, 5) \quad E = (1, 9) \quad F = (3, 1)$$

$$G = (0, 8) \quad H = (4, 6) \quad I = (4, 9)$$

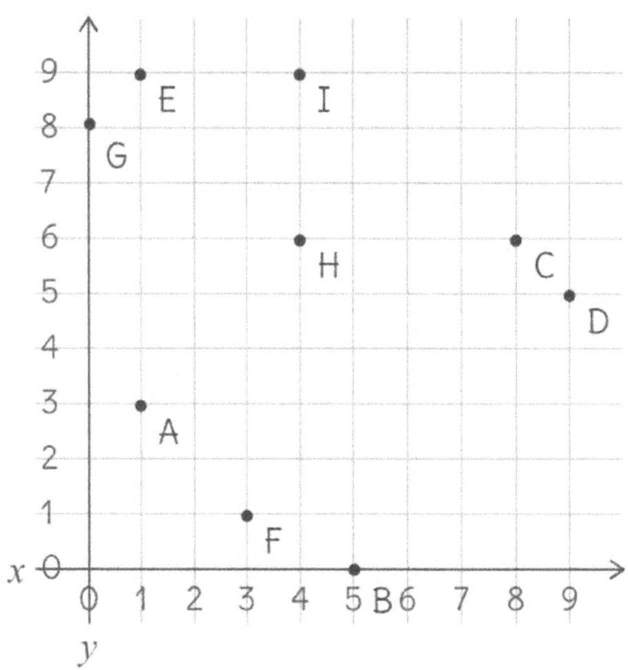

Cartesian Coordinates (Four Quadrants)

In a Cartesian coordinate system with four quadrants, there are two perpendicular number lines intersecting at the origin (0,0), dividing the plane into four quadrants.

To plot a point in this Cartesian coordinate system, we use an ordered pair (x, y), where x represents the distance from the y-axis, and y represents the distance from the x-axis.

For instance, let's plot these coordinates:

$$A = (-4, 1) \quad B = (2, 1) \quad C = (4, 2)$$

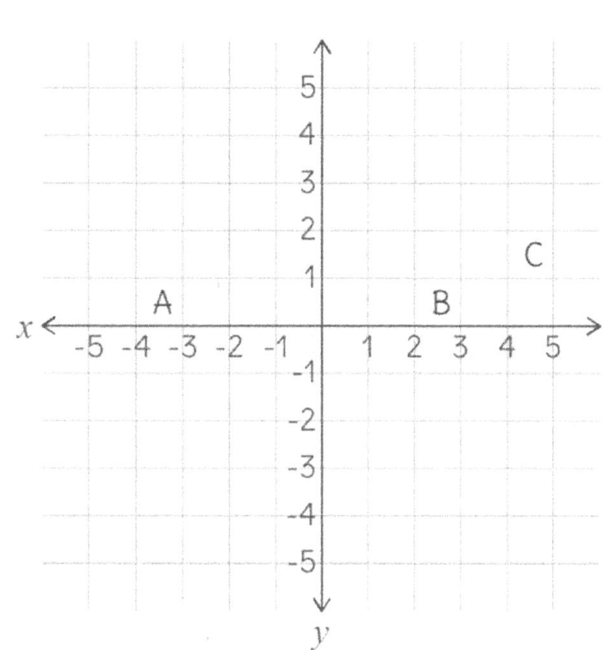

5
4
3
2
1
C
A
B
x
-5 -4 -3 -2 -1
1 2 3 4 5
-1
-2
-3
-4
-5
y

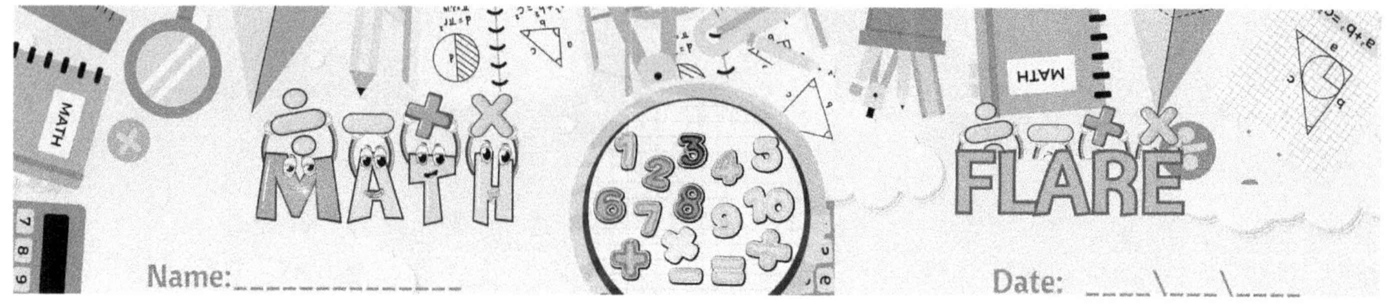

Cartesian Coordinates
Fill in as indicated.

1)
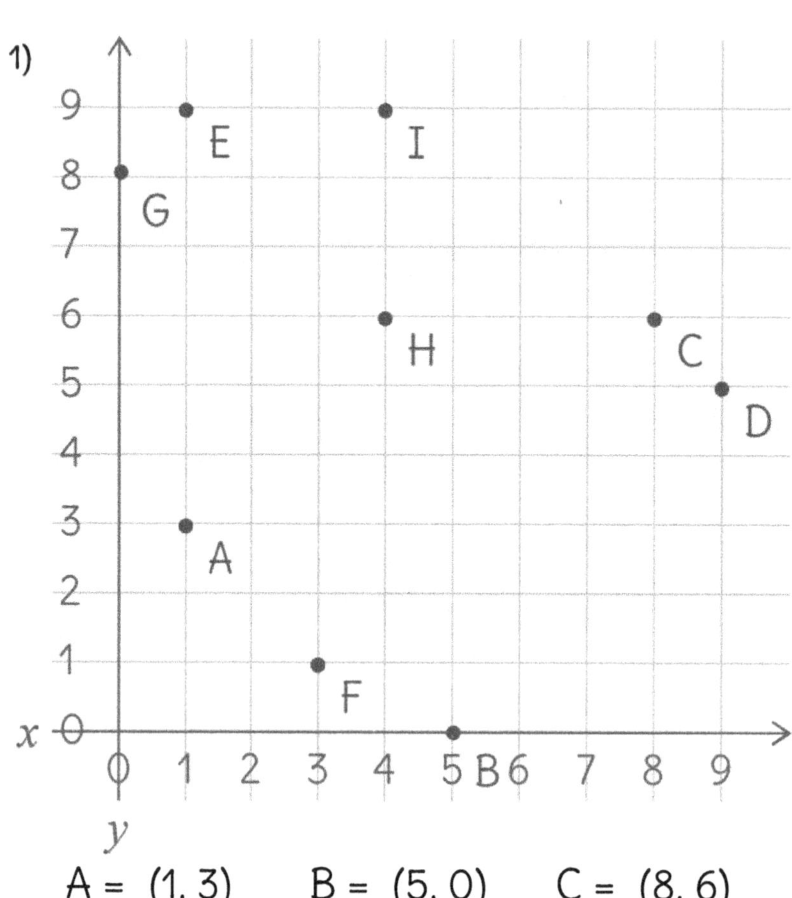

A = (1, 3)   B = (5, 0)   C = (8, 6)

D = (9, 5)   E = (1, 9)   F = (3, 1)

G = (0, 8)   H = (4, 6)   I = (4, 9)

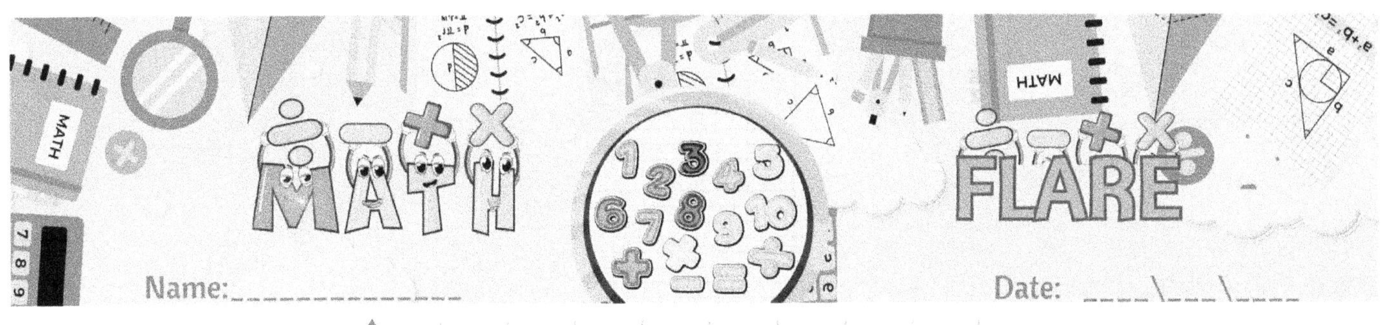

2)

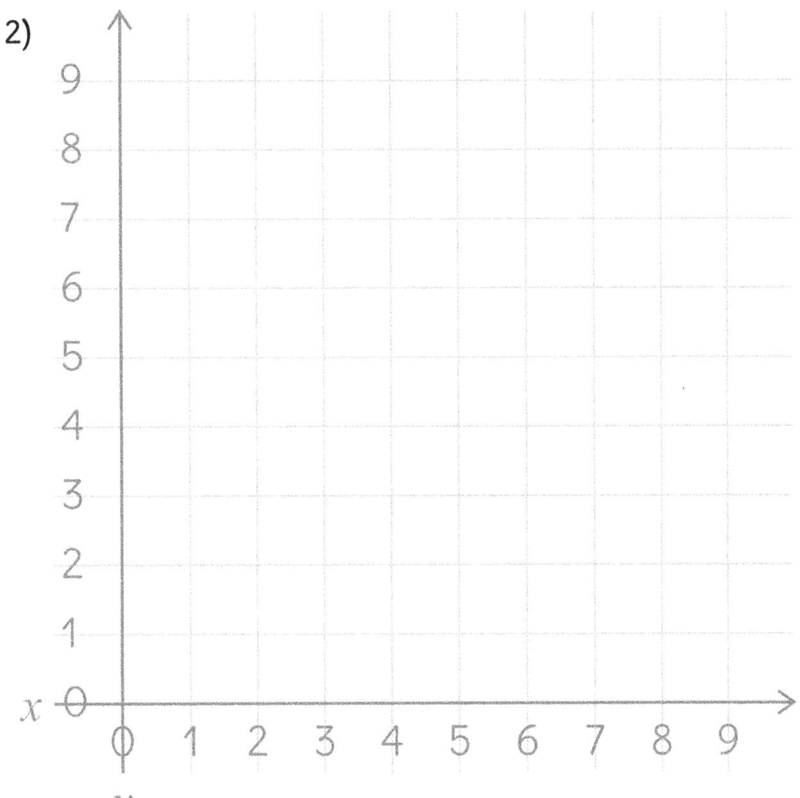

A = (1, 9)   B = (1, 3)   C = (6, 7)

D = (8, 5)   E = (5, 1)   F = (9, 8)

G = (4, 3)   H = (2, 6)   I = (4, 6)

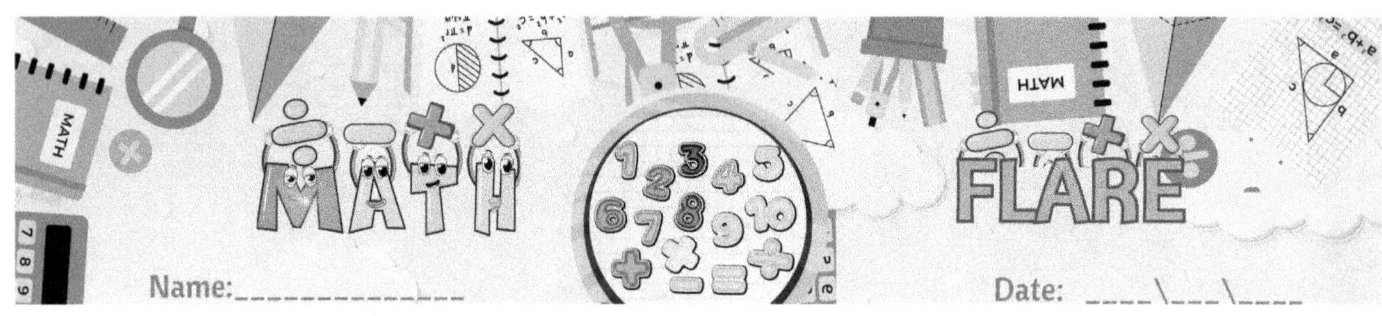

3)

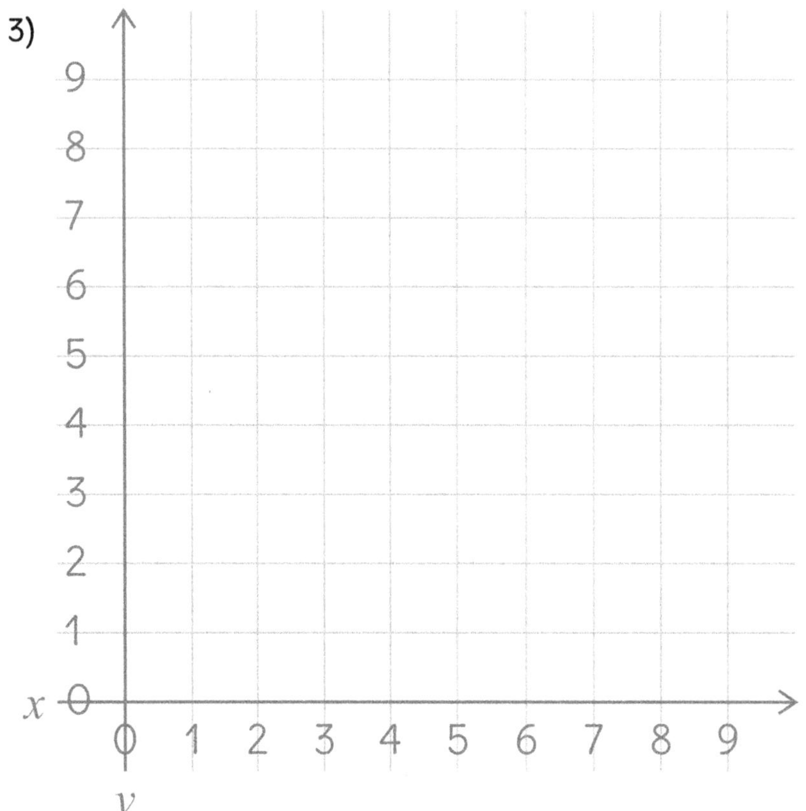

A = (7, 0)   B = (4, 8)   C = (0, 1)

D = (6, 9)   E = (2, 0)   F = (9, 3)

G = (7, 8)   H = (3, 5)   I = (5, 2)

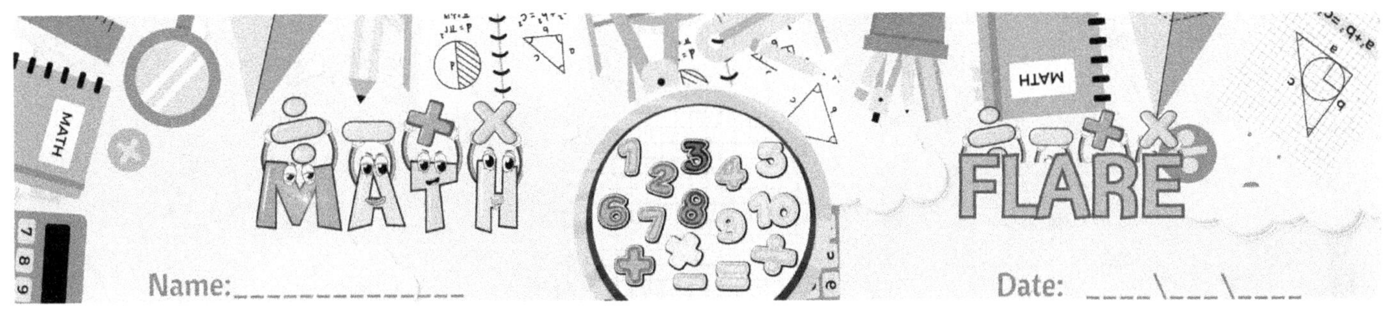

4)

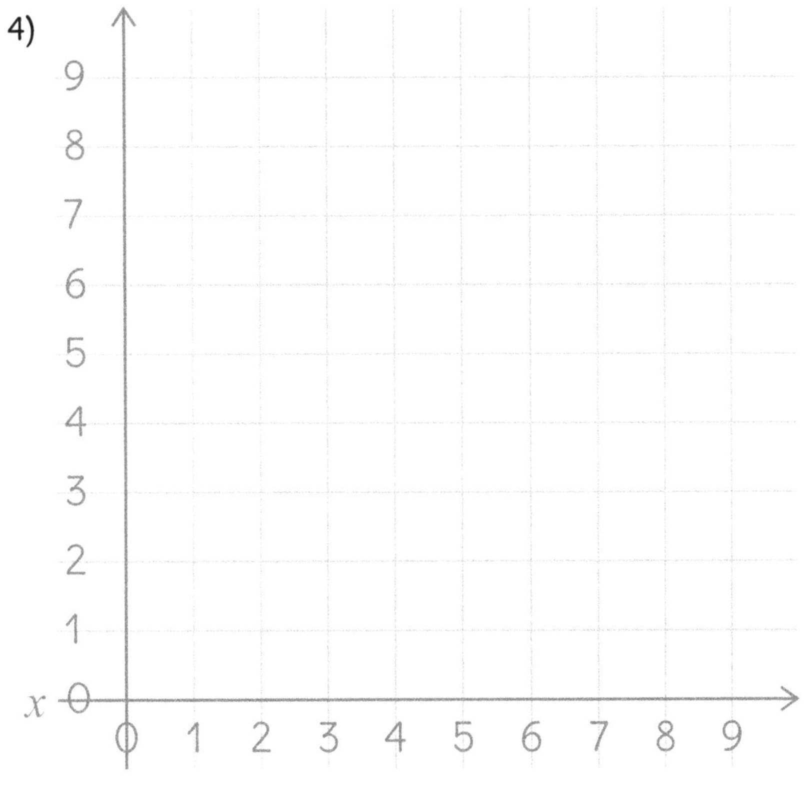

A = (2, 2)   B = (4, 4)   C = (4, 3)

D = (1, 7)   E = (5, 3)   F = (5, 0)

G = (9, 4)   H = (3, 8)   I = (8, 9)

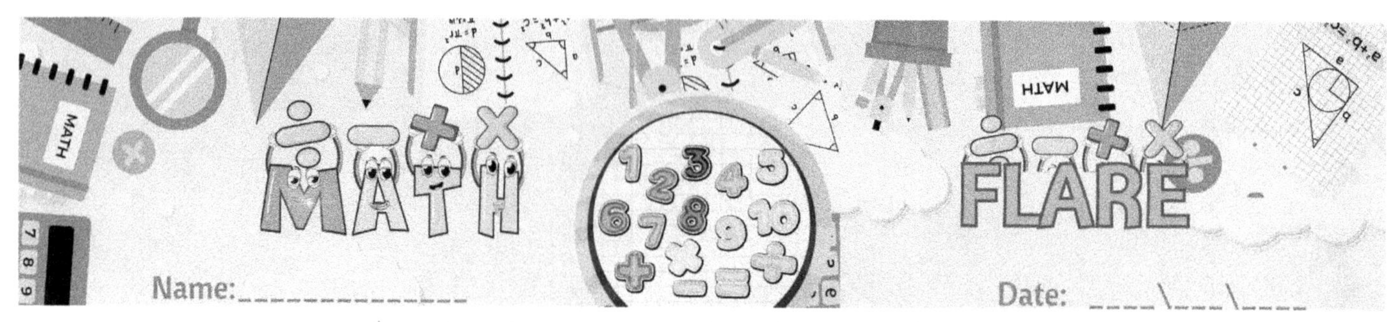

5)

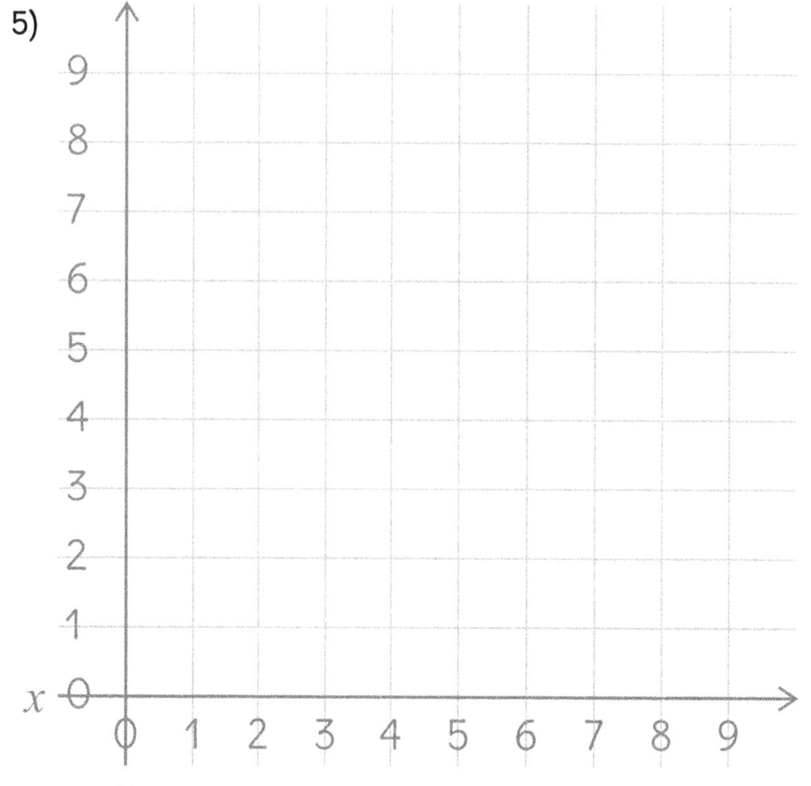

A = (6, 7)   B = (4, 7)   C = (5, 1)

D = (4, 1)   E = (4, 9)   F = (7, 9)

G = (3, 2)   H = (2, 2)   I = (5, 0)

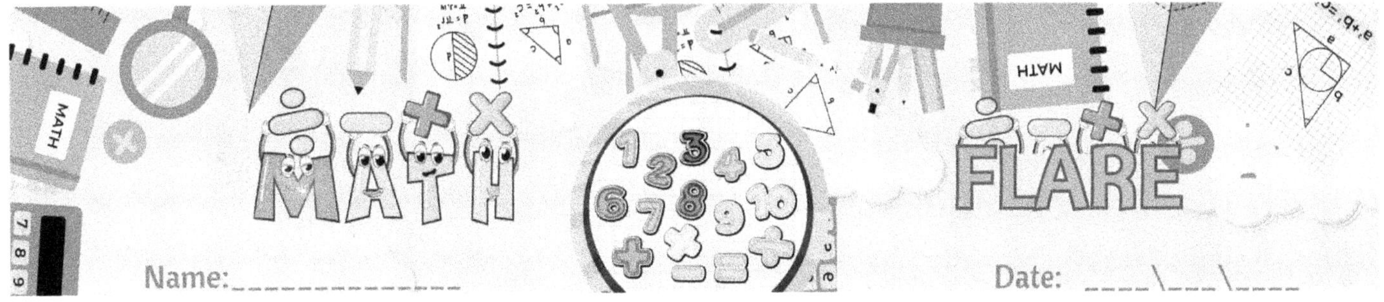

Name: ____________________   Date: _______________

Cartesian Coordinates

Fill in as indicated.

1)

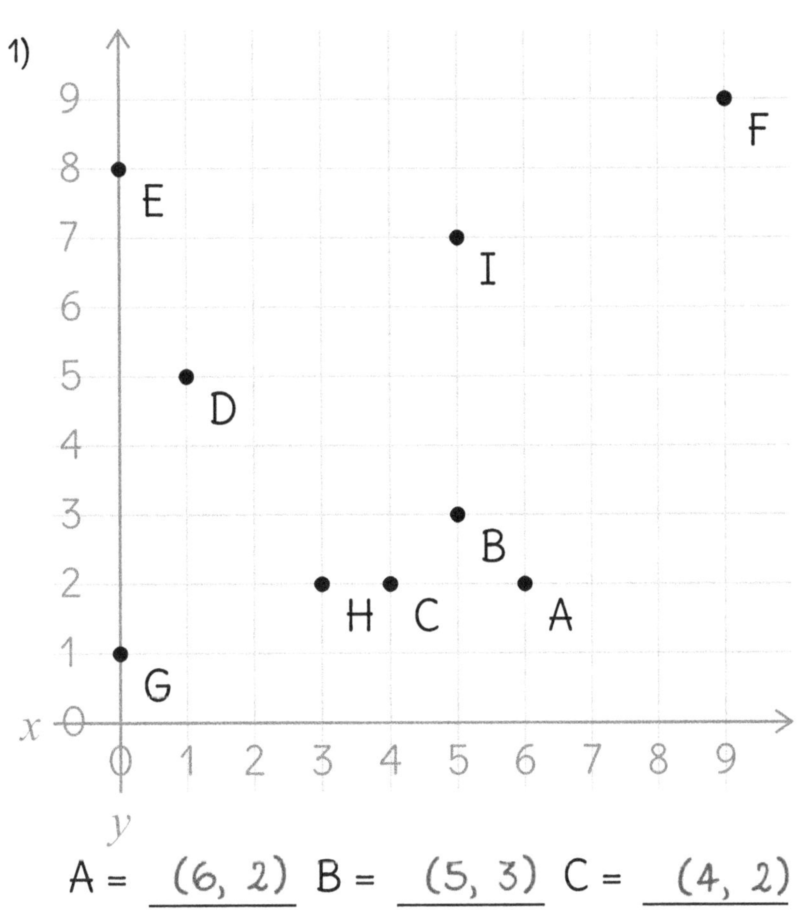

A = ___(6, 2)___ B = ___(5, 3)___ C = ___(4, 2)___

D = _______   E = _______   F = _______

G = _______   H = _______   I = _______

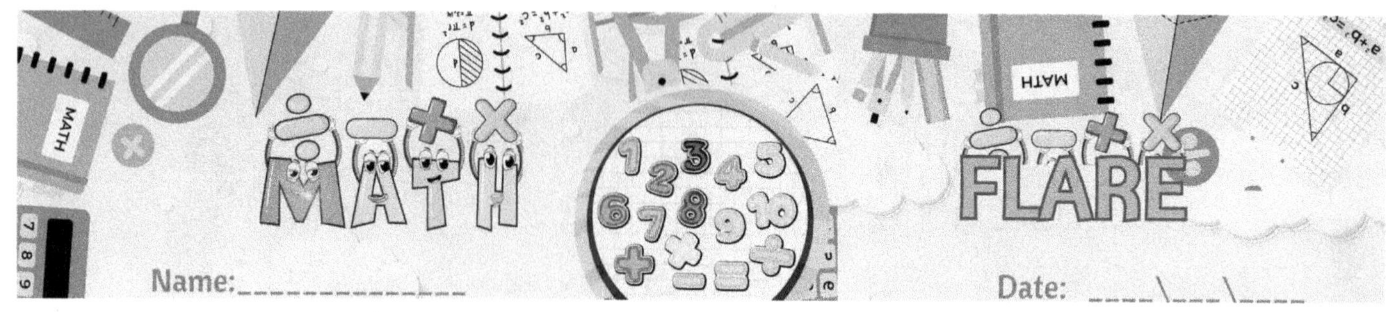

2)

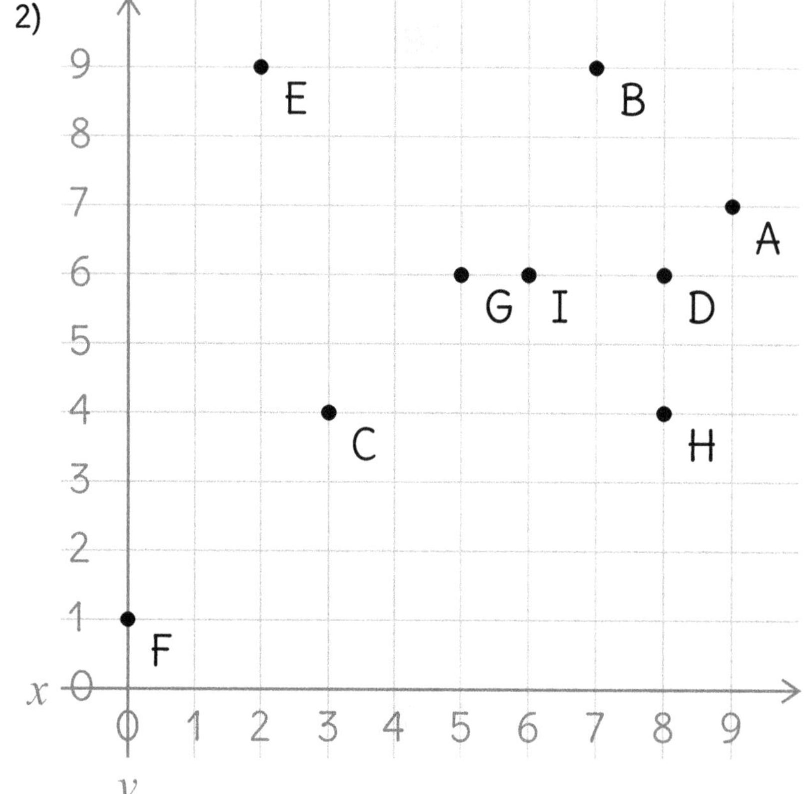

A = _______   B = _______   C = _______

D = _______   E = _______   F = _______

G = _______   H = _______   I = _______

3)

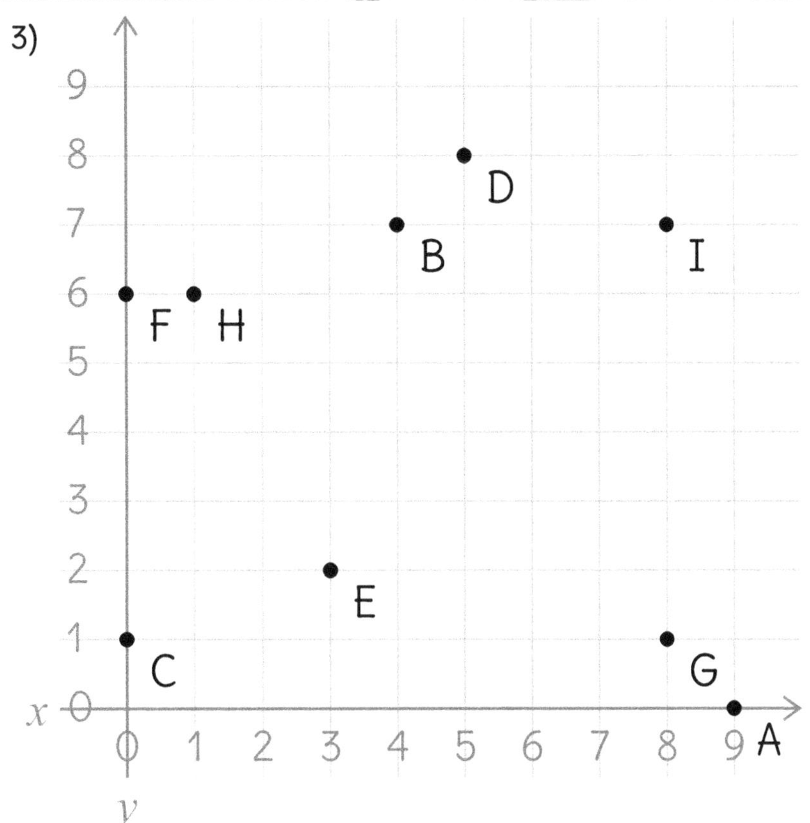

A = _______   B = _______   C = _______

D = _______   E = _______   F = _______

G = _______   H = _______   I = _______

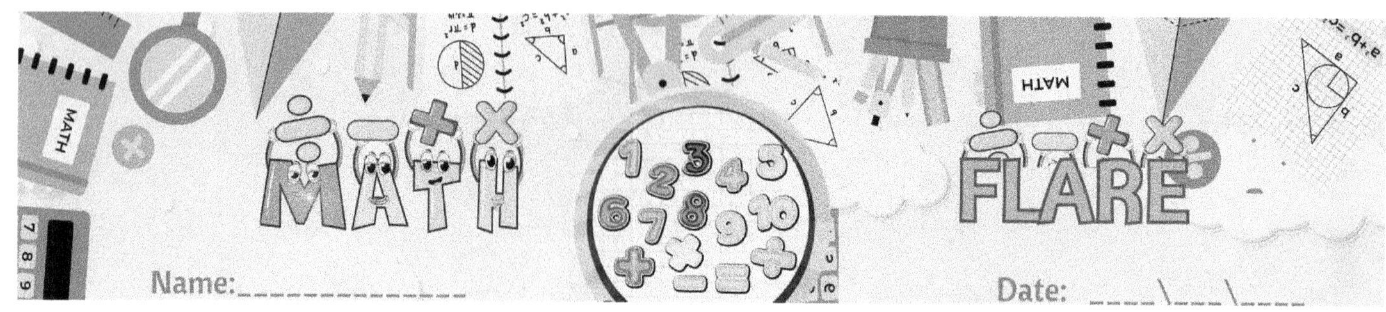

4)

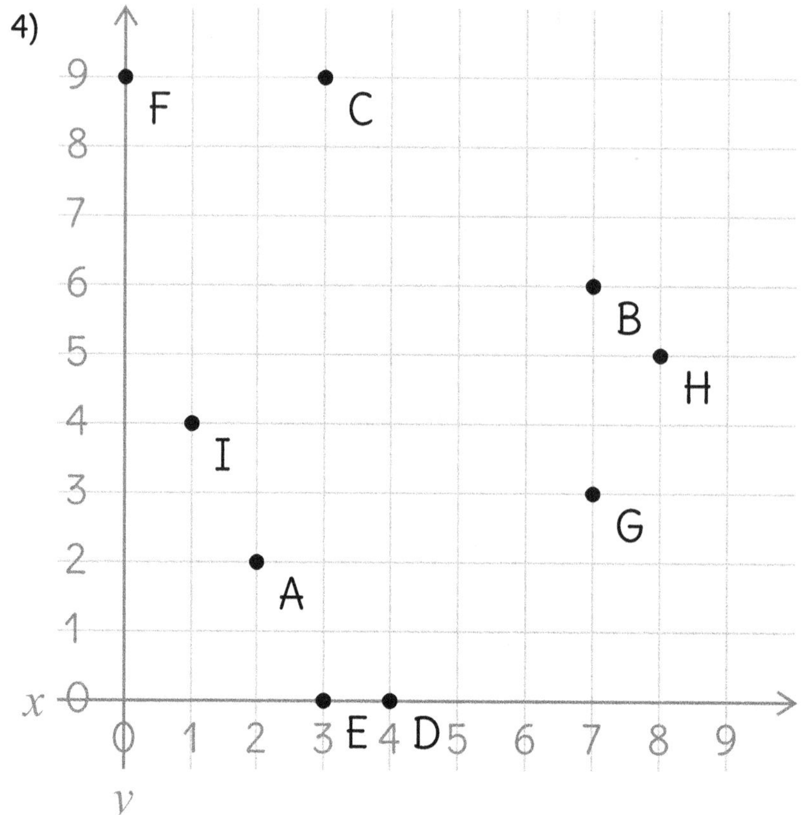

A = _______   B = _______   C = _______

D = _______   E = _______   F = _______

G = _______   H = _______   I = _______

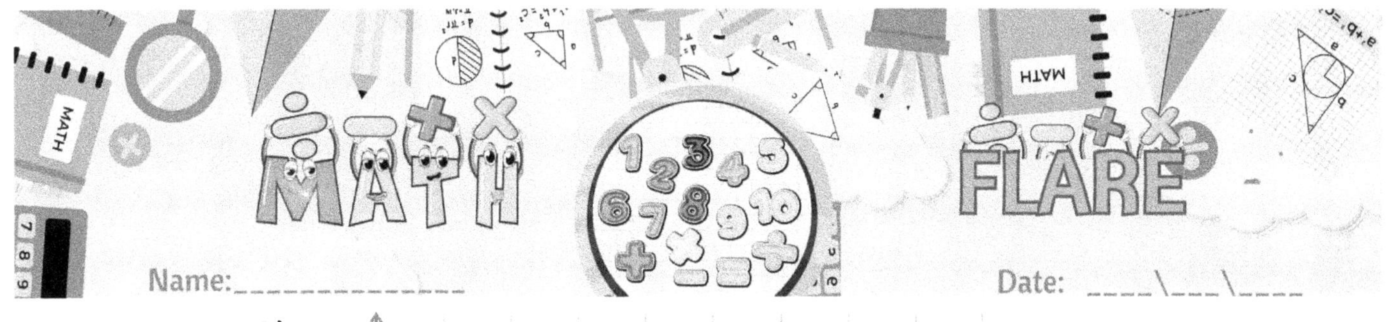

5)

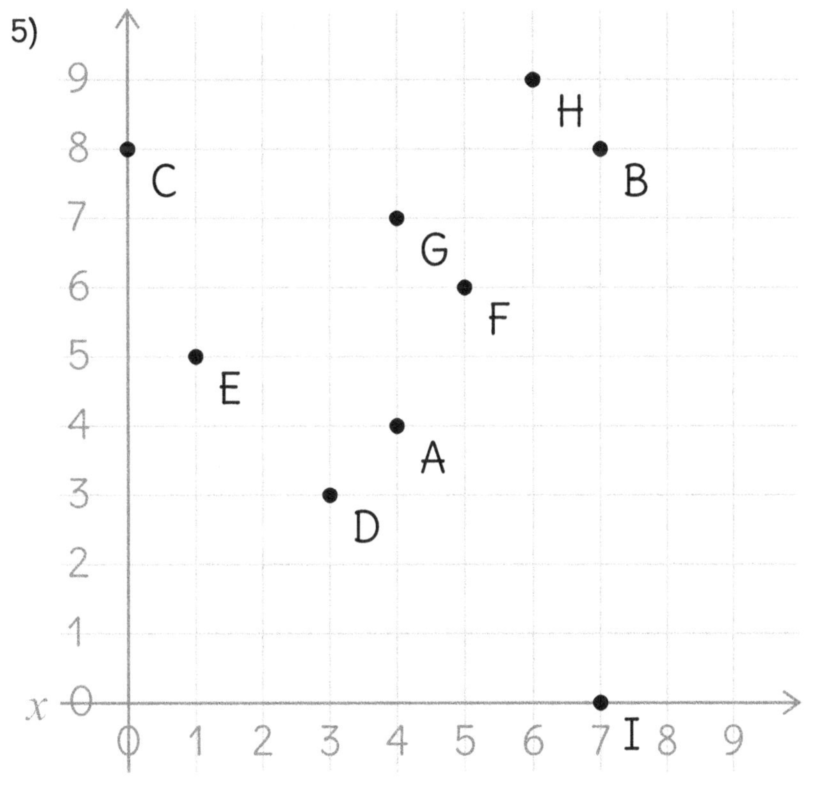

A = ______   B = ______   C = ______

D = ______   E = ______   F = ______

G = ______   H = ______   I = ______

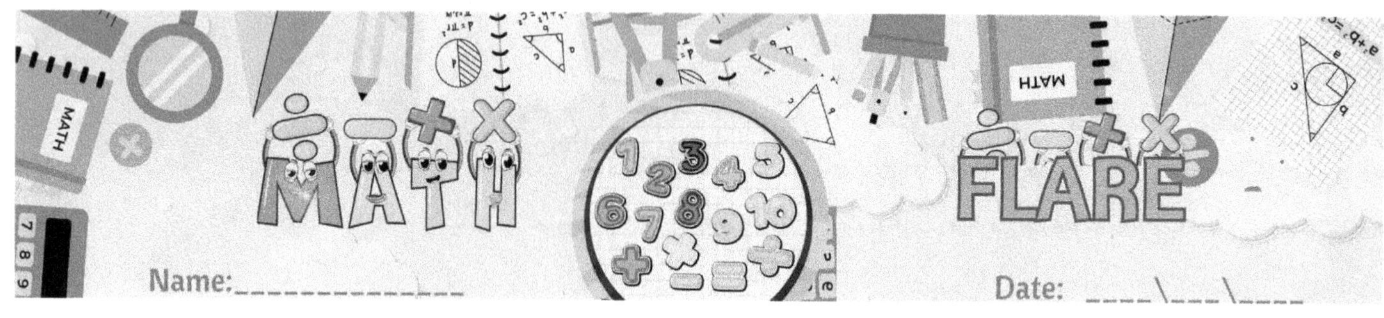

Cartesian Coordinates With Four Quadrants

Fill in as indicated.

1)

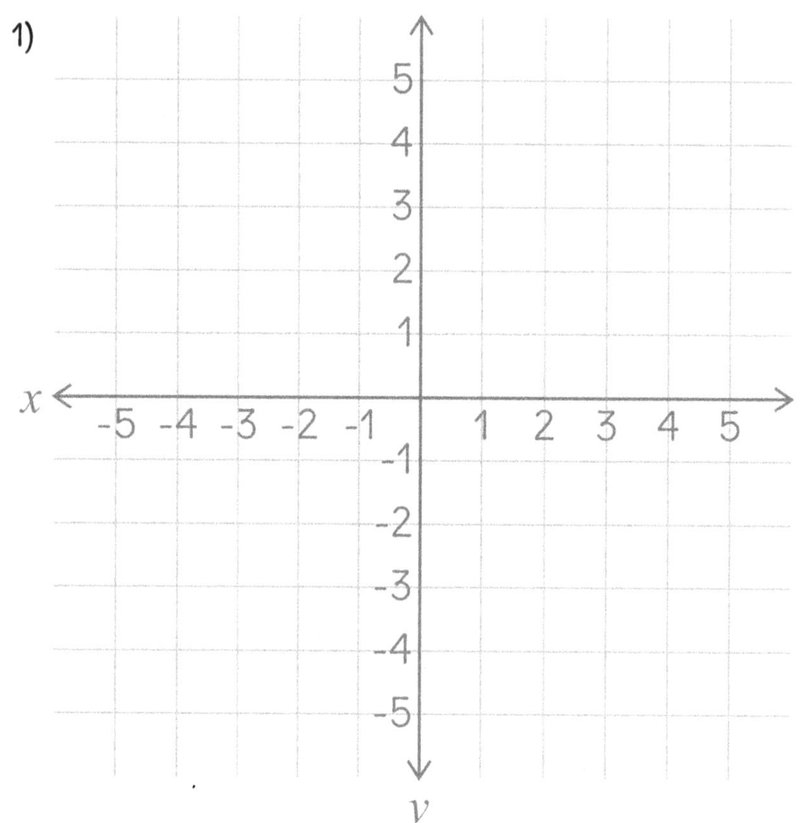

A = (-4, 1)   B = (2, 1)   C = (4, 2)

D = (-2, -4) E = (5, -5)   F = (1, -2)

G = (1, 0)   H = (0, 1)   I = (5, -2)

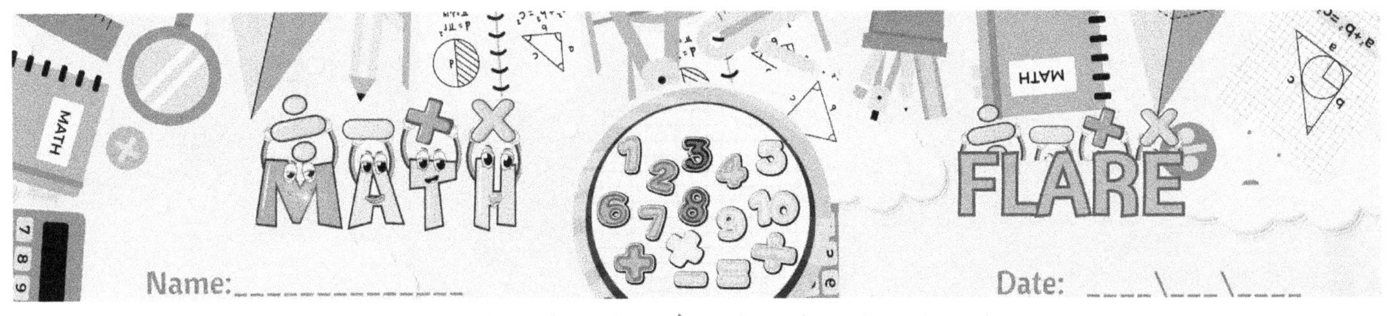

2)

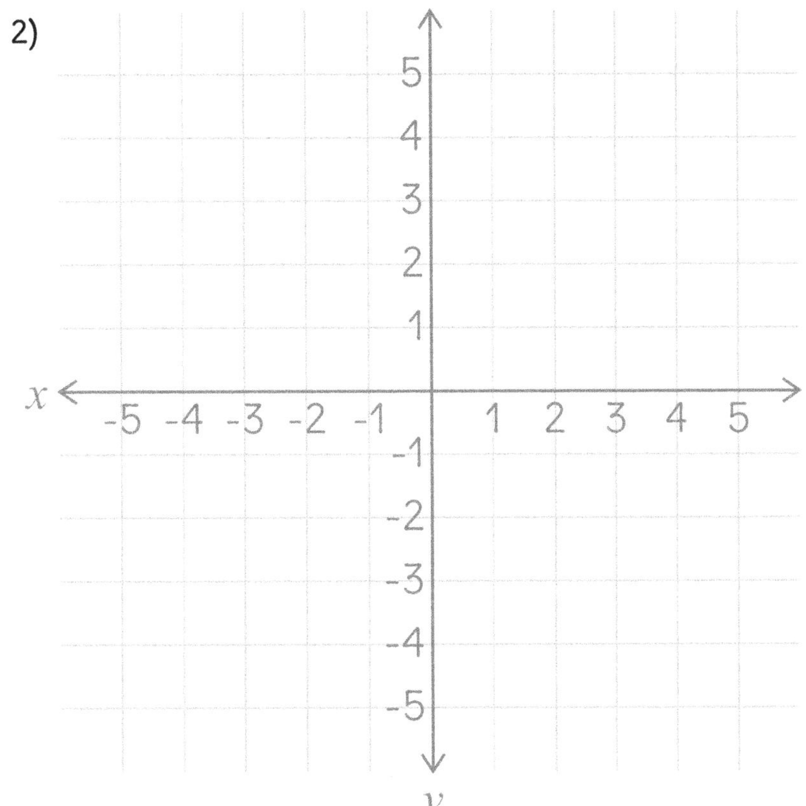

A = (4, 1)   B = (-3, 5)   C = (1, -3)

D = (-1, -1)   E = (-5, 1)   F = (0, 4)

G = (-5, -4)   H = (3, 0)   I = (-3, -5)

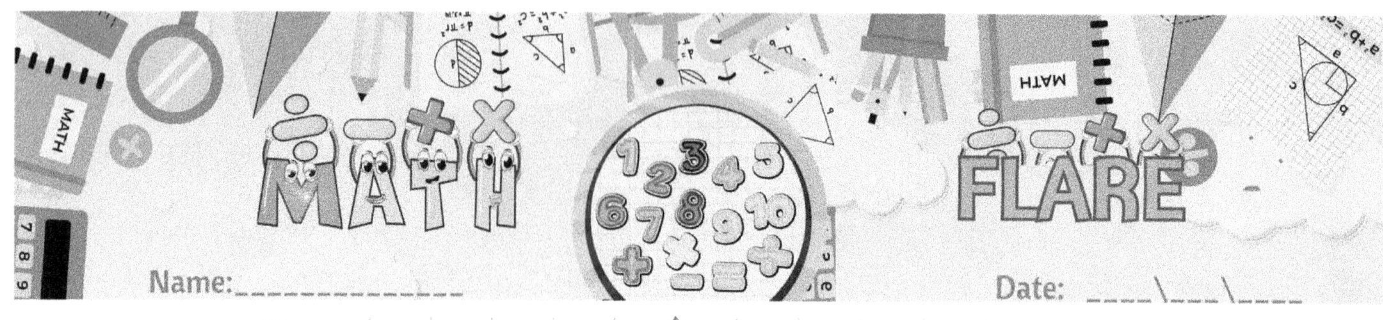

3)

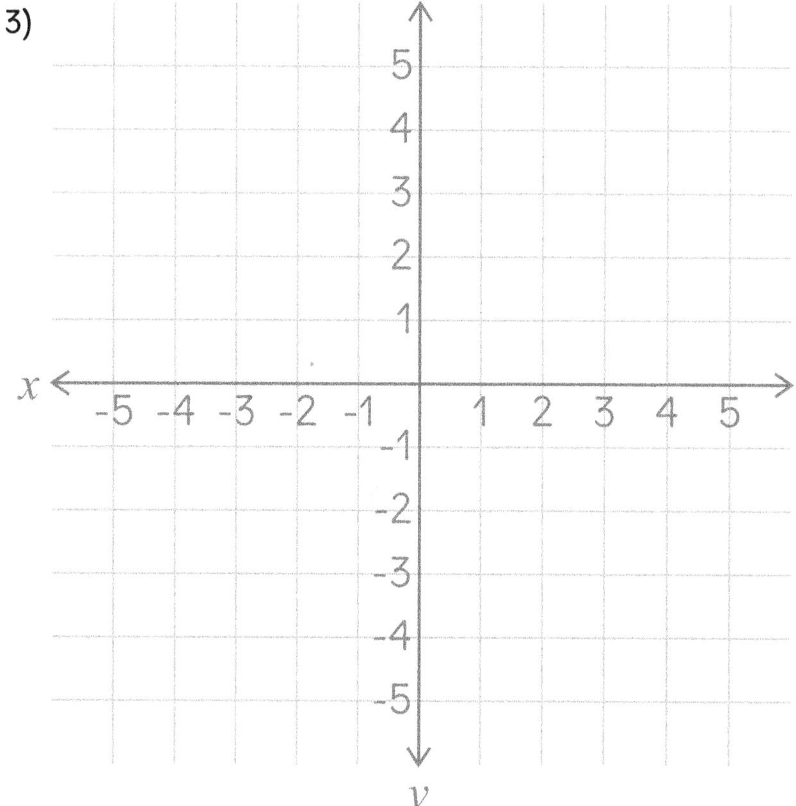

A = (-5, -1)   B = (-3, -1)   C = (2, 2)

D = (2, -4)   E = (0, -4)   F = (-2, -1)

G = (4, -5)   H = (2, 3)   I = (-5, -3)

4)

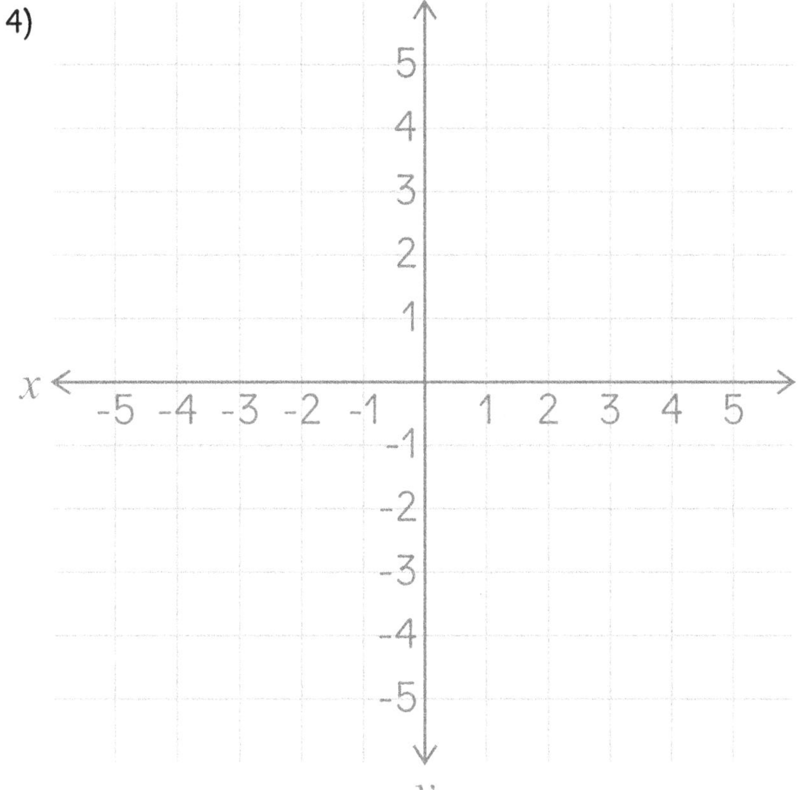

A = (-5, -2)   B = (-2, 5)   C = (-2, -3)

D = (-1, 0)   E = (-1, -4)   F = (-3, -4)

G = (4, -4)   H = (-4, 1)   I = (-2, 1)

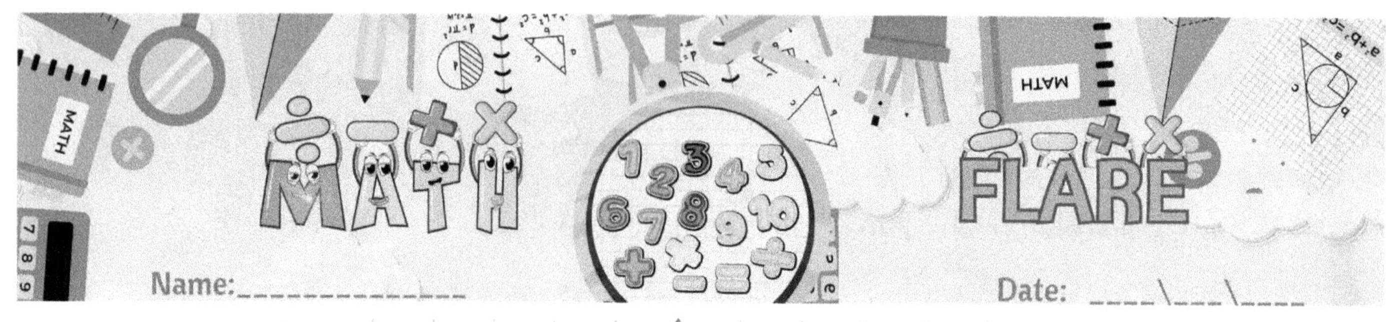

5)

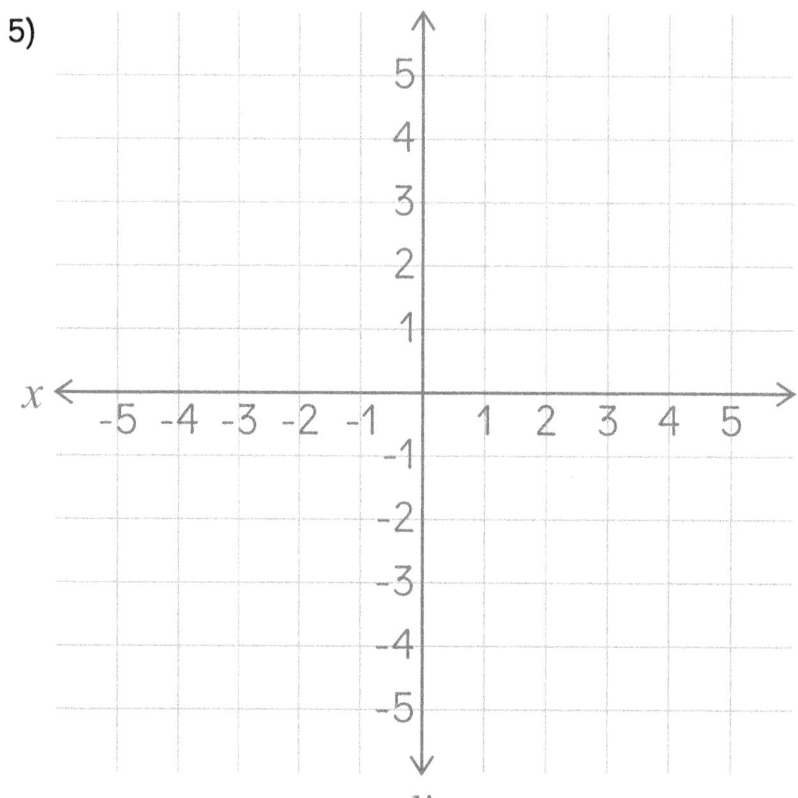

A = (1, -2)   B = (-4, 2)   C = (-1, -1)

D = (5, -4)   E = (-2, 5)   F = (-3, 2)

G = (0, -5)   H = (3, -5)   I = (-5, -1)

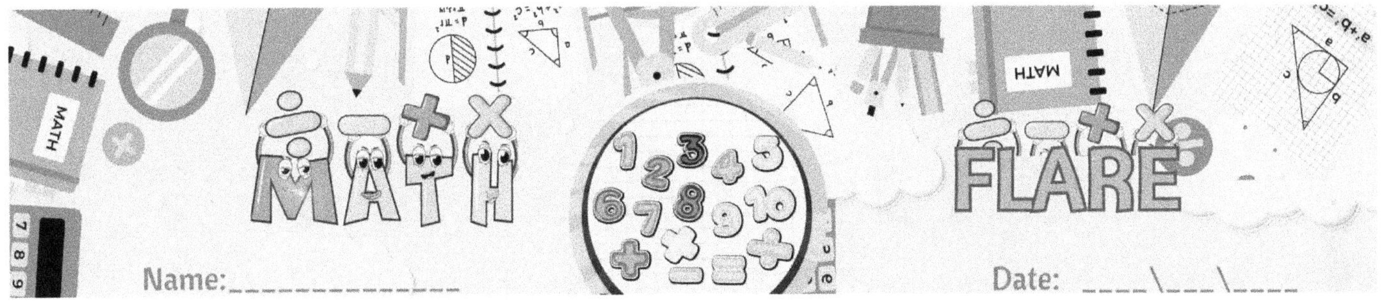

Cartesian Coordinates With Four Quadrants

Fill in as indicated.

1)

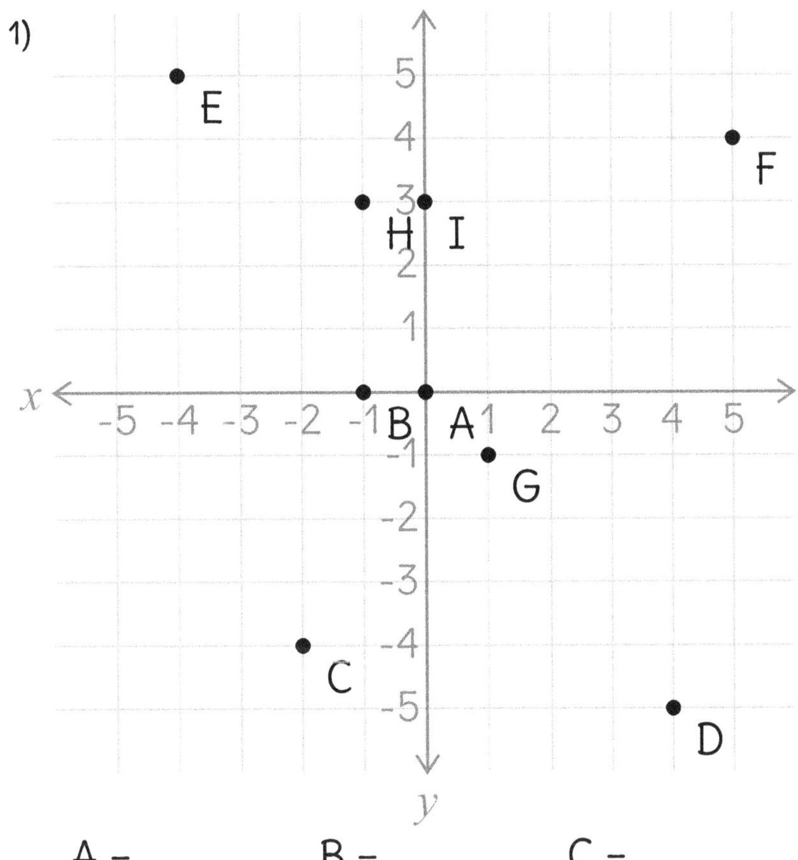

A = _______   B = _______   C = _______

D = _______   E = _______   F = _______

G = _______   H = _______   I = _______

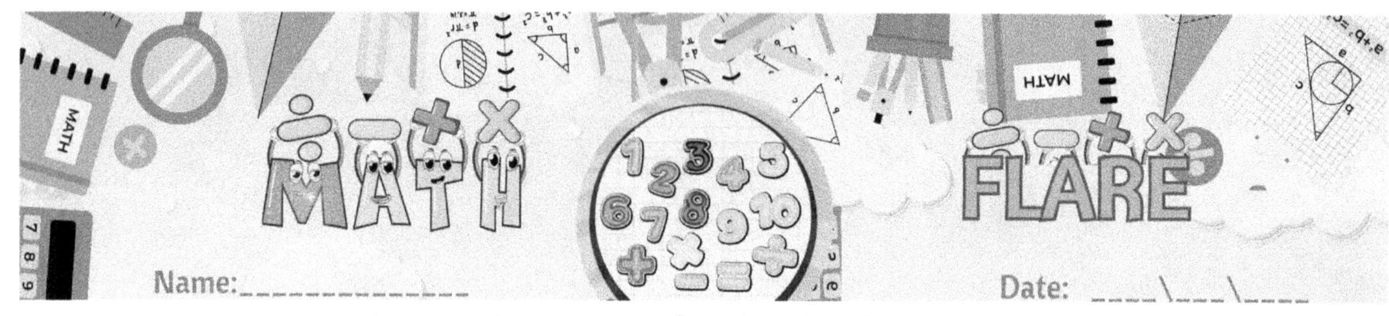

2)

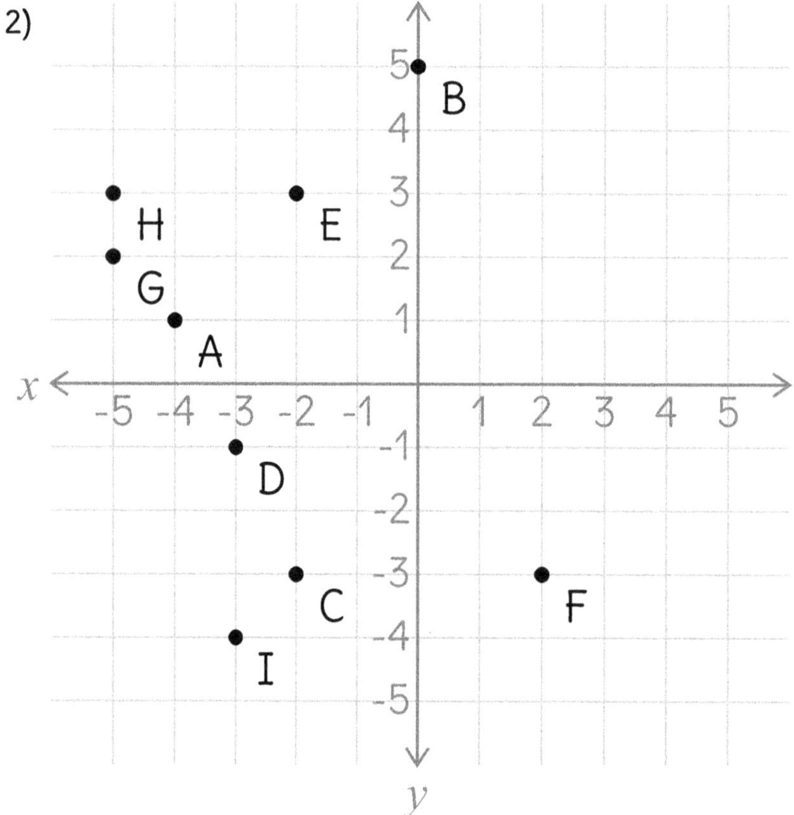

A = _______   B = _______   C = _______

D = _______   E = _______   F = _______

G = _______   H = _______   I = _______

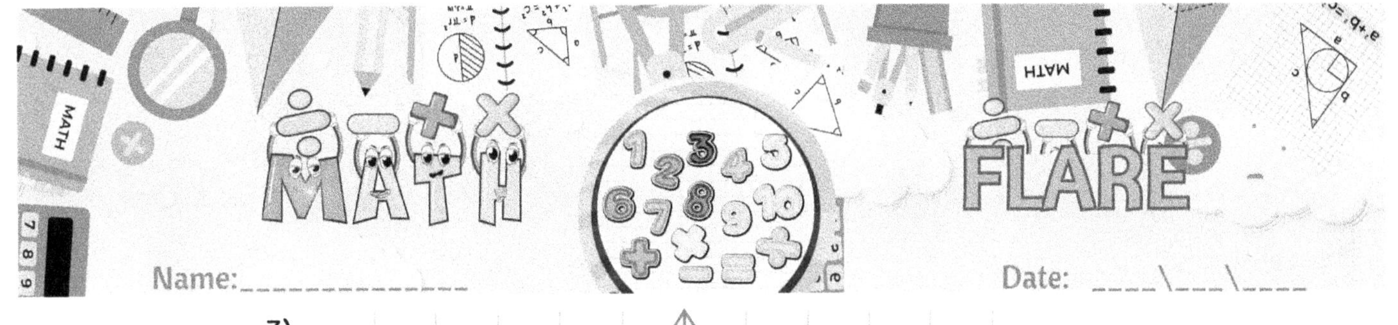

3)

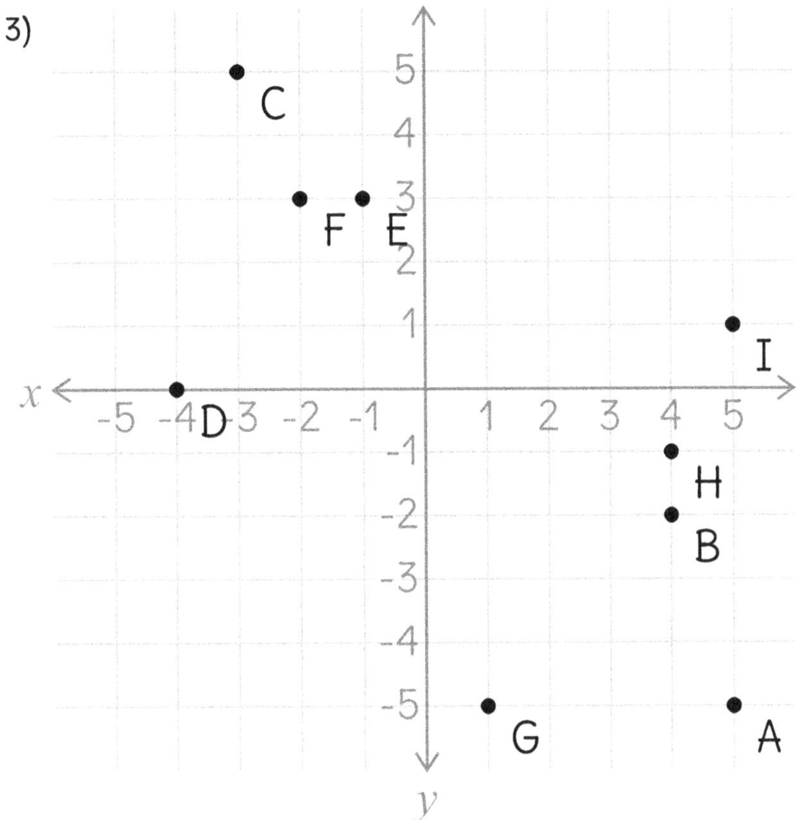

A = _______ B = _______ C = _______

D = _______ E = _______ F = _______

G = _______ H = _______ I = _______

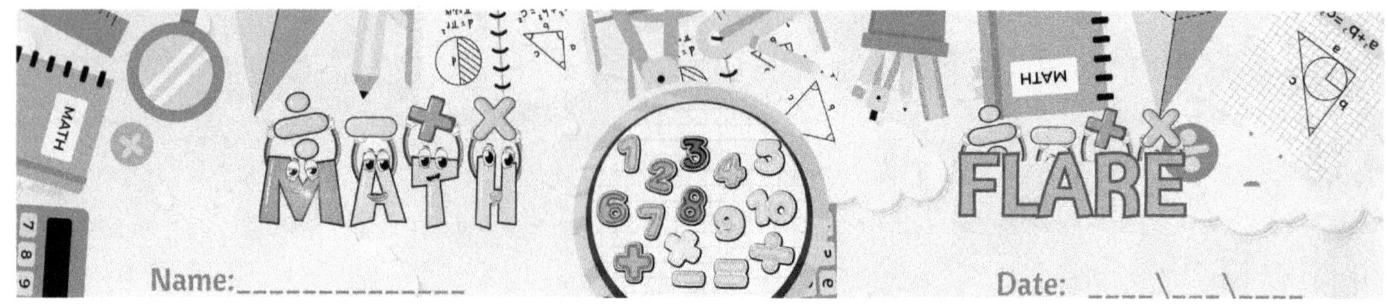

4)

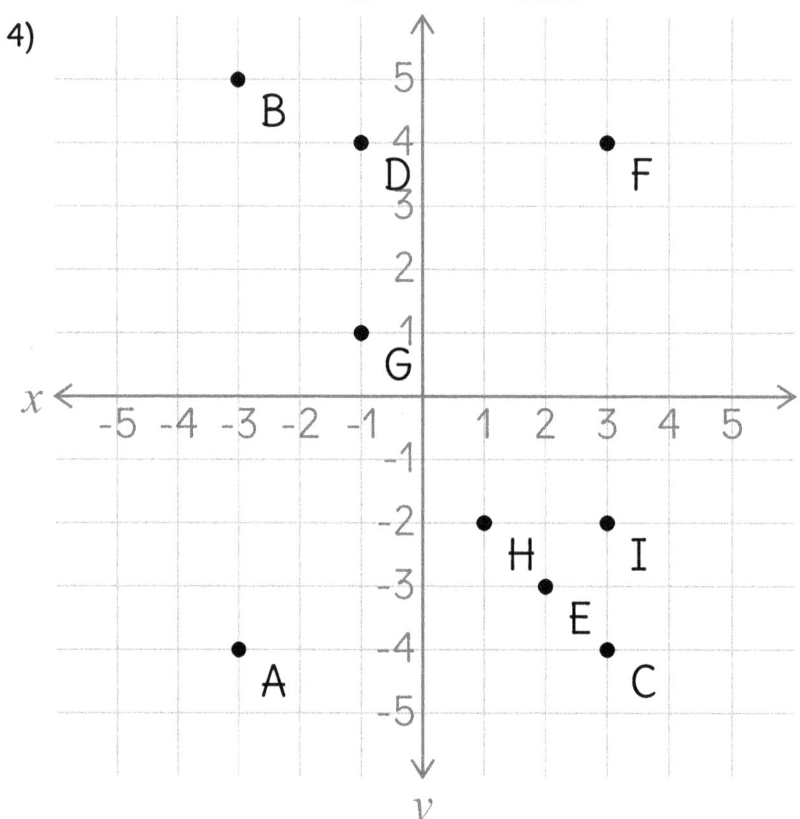

A = _______   B = _______   C = _______

D = _______   E = _______   F = _______

G = _______   H = _______   I = _______

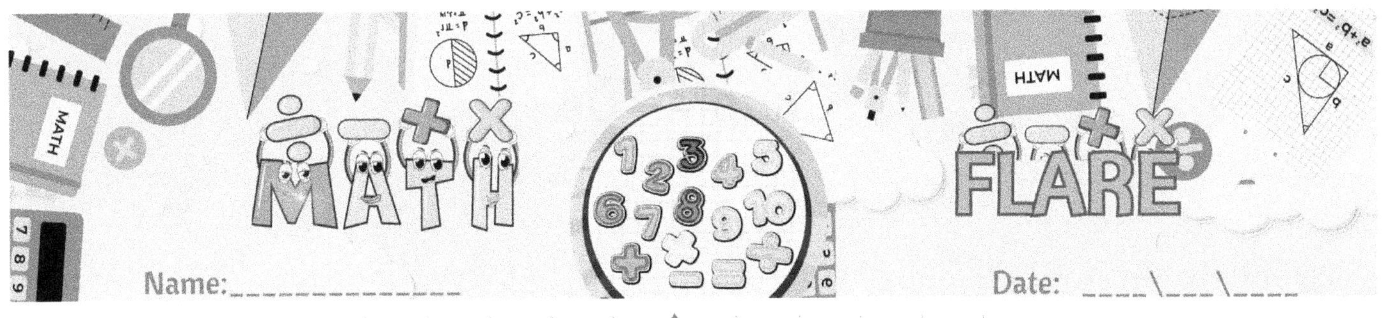

5)

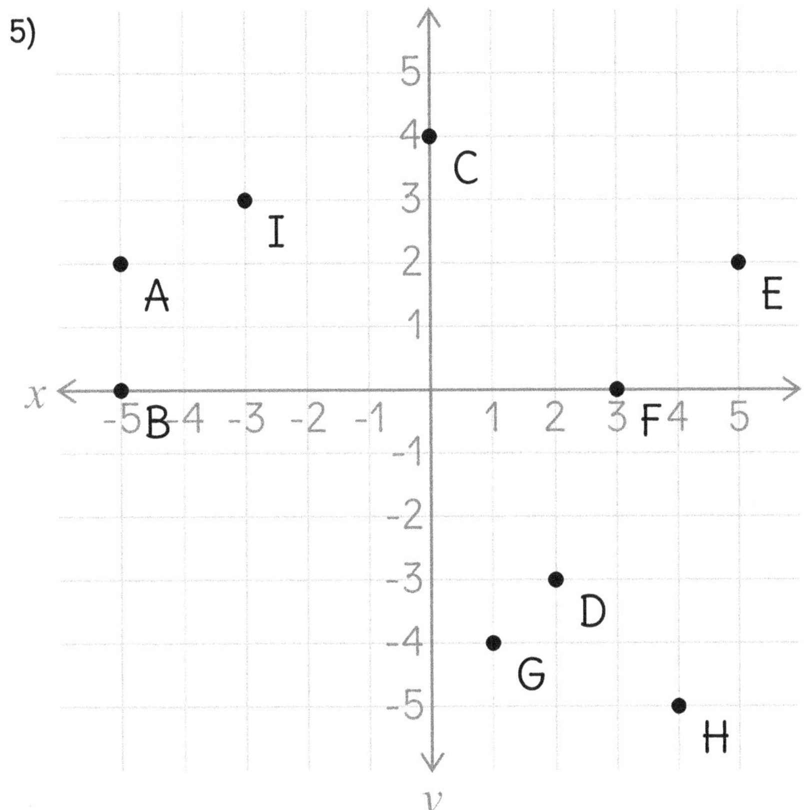

A = _______   B = _______   C = _______

D = _______   E = _______   F = _______

G = _______   H = _______   I = _______

Chapter. 04

Geometry

Area and Perimeter

The area of a shape represents the amount of space it occupies. The perimeter of a shape is the total distance around its outer edge.

Area of Rectangle

For a square, since all four sides are equal, we only need to know the length of one side to find its area. We can calculate the area of a square by multiplying the length of one side by itself (squared). So, if the length of one side of the square is 's', then the area (A) is given by:

$$A = s \times s$$

4 in

4 in

$$A = 4 \times 4$$

$$A = 16$$

Perimeter of Rectangle

For a square, since all four sides are equal, we can find the perimeter by adding up the lengths of all four sides. If 's' represents the length of one side, then the perimeter (P) is given by:

$$P = 4 \times s$$

$$P = 4 \times 4$$

$$P = 16$$

Area of Triangle:

The area of a triangle represents the amount of space enclosed within its three sides. The formula for calculating the area of a triangle depends on the type of triangle. For a general triangle, we use the formula:

$$A = \frac{1}{2} \times base \times height$$

Where:

- *A* represents the area of the triangle.

- The base is the length of any one side of the triangle.

- The height is the perpendicular distance from the base to the opposite vertex.

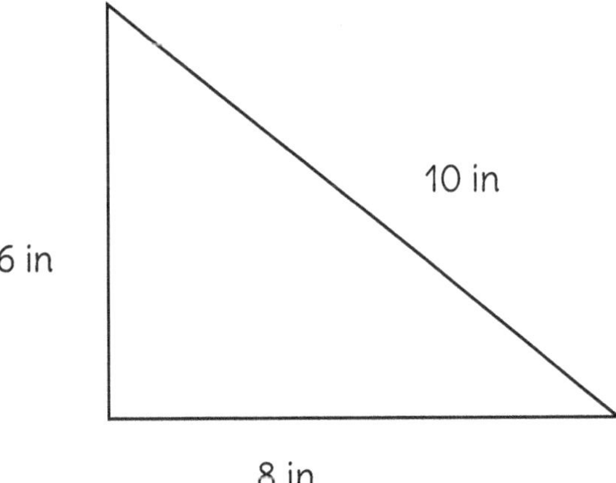

$$A = \frac{1}{2} \times base \times height$$

$$A = \frac{1}{2} \times 6 \times 8$$

$$A = \frac{1}{2} \times 48$$

$$A = 24$$

Perimeter of Triangle:

The perimeter of a triangle is the total length of its three sides. To find the perimeter, we simply add the lengths of all three sides together:

$$P = side1 + side2 + side3$$

$$P = 6 + 8 + 10$$

$$P = 24$$

Equilateral Triangle

An equilateral triangle is a triangle in which all three sides are equal in length. To find the area and perimeter of an equilateral triangle, we can use the following formulas:

- Area (A): $\frac{\sqrt{3}}{4} \times a^2$ where a is the length of one side of the equilateral triangle.

- Perimeter (P): $P = 3a$ where a is the length of one side of the equilateral triangle.

Let's solve a problem:

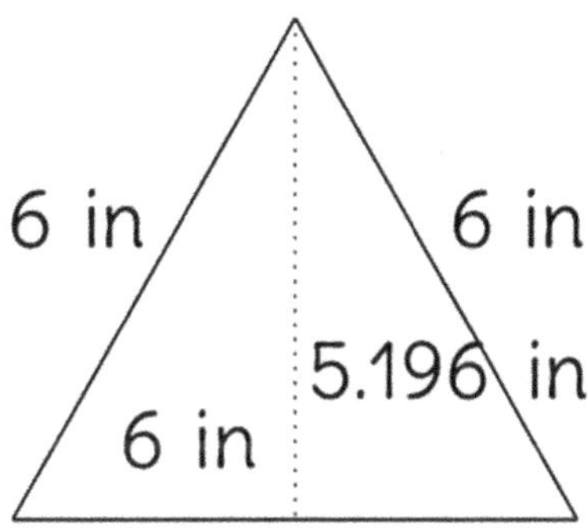

Area of Equilateral Triangle:

$$\text{Area (A): } \frac{\sqrt{3}}{4} \times (6)^2$$

$$\text{Area (A): } \frac{\sqrt{3}}{4} \times 36$$

$$\text{Area (A): } \frac{36\sqrt{3}}{4}$$

$$\text{Area (A): } \frac{36(1.73)}{4}$$

$$\text{Area (A): } \frac{62.35}{4}$$

$$\text{Area (A): } 15.59 \text{ in}^2$$

Perimeter of Equilateral Triangle:

$$P = 3a$$

$$P = 3(6) = 18$$

Isosceles Triangle

An isosceles triangle is a triangle with at least two sides of equal length. The angles opposite the equal sides are also equal.

Area of Isosceles Triangle

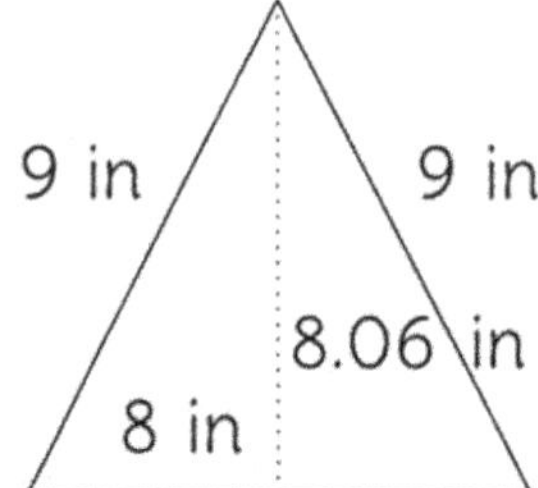

$$A = \frac{1}{2} \times base \times height$$

$$A = \frac{1}{2} \times 8 \times 8$$

$$A = \frac{1}{2} \times 64$$

$$A = 32$$

Perimeter of Isosceles Triangle

The perimeter of a triangle is the total length of its three sides. To find the perimeter, we simply add the lengths of all three sides together:

$$P = side1 + side2 + side3$$

$$P = 9 + 9 + 8$$

$$P = 26$$

Scalene Triangle

A scalene triangle is a triangle with no equal sides and no equal angles. The formula for finding various properties of a scalene triangle is as follows:

Area (A): The area of a scalene triangle can be calculated using Heron's formula, which is given by:

$$A = \sqrt{s(s-a)(s-b)(s-c)}$$

where s is the semi-perimeter of the triangle,

and a, b, and c are the lengths of its three sides.

Perimeter (P): The perimeter of a scalene triangle is the sum of the lengths of its three sides.

$$P = side1 + side2 + side3$$

Let's find the Area and Perimeter of a Scalene Triangle:

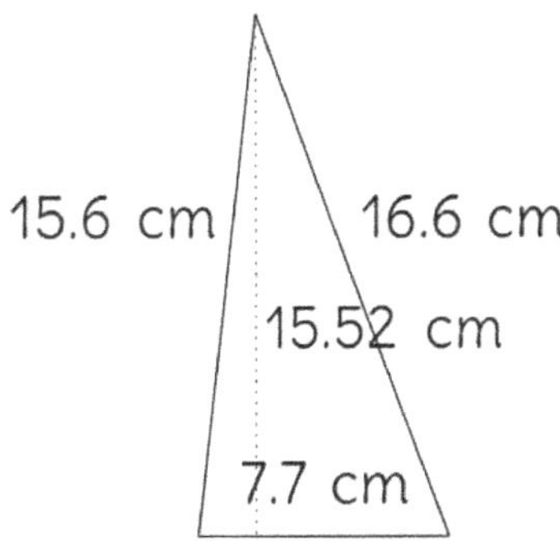

Area (A): First, we calculate the semi-perimeter (s):

$$S = \frac{a+b+c}{2} = \frac{15.6 + 16.6 + 7.7}{2} = \frac{39.8}{2} = 19.9 \text{ cm}$$

Heron's formula to find the area:

$$A = \sqrt{s(s-a)(s-b)(s-c)}$$

$$A = \sqrt{19.9\,(19.9-15.6)(19.9-16.6)(19.9-7.7)}$$

$$A = \sqrt{19.9 \times 4.3 \times 3.3 \times 12.2}$$

$$A = \sqrt{3445} \approx 59$$

Perimeter (P):

$$P = side1 + side2 + side3$$

$$P = 15.6 + 16.6 + 7.7$$

$$P = 39.8$$

Area and Perimeter of an L-shape

The L-shaped figure typically consists of two rectangles joined together to form an L-shape. To find the area and perimeter of an L-shaped figure, we will need to calculate the areas and perimeters of each rectangle and then combine them.

Area=Area of Rectangle 1 + Area of Rectangle 2

Perimeter=Perimeter of Rectangle 1 + Perimeter of Rectangle 2

Let's find the Area and Perimeter of an L-shape:

10.92 cm

4.38 cm

11.28 cm

6.78 cm

Area of L-Shape

$$\text{Area 1} = 4.38 \times 4.5 = 19.7 \text{ cm}^2$$

$$\text{Area 2} = 11.28 \times 6.54 = 73.7 \text{ cm}^2$$

$$\text{Area} = 19.7 + 73.7$$

$$\text{Area} = 93.481 \text{ cm}^2$$

Perimeter of L-Shape

$$P = 11.28 + 6.54 + 6.78 + 4.38 + 4.5 + 10.92$$

$$P = 44.4 \text{ cm}$$

Area and Perimeter of U-shape

U-shape is basically composed of three rectangles, we'll need to calculate the area and perimeter of each rectangle separately and then sum them up.

Area of the U-shape:

The total area (A) of the U-shape is the sum of the areas of the three rectangles:

$$A = A1 + A2 + A3$$

Perimeter of the U-shape: The total perimeter (P) of the U-shape is the sum of the perimeters of the three rectangles:

$$P = P1 + P2 + P3$$

Let's find the area and perimeter of the following U-shape:

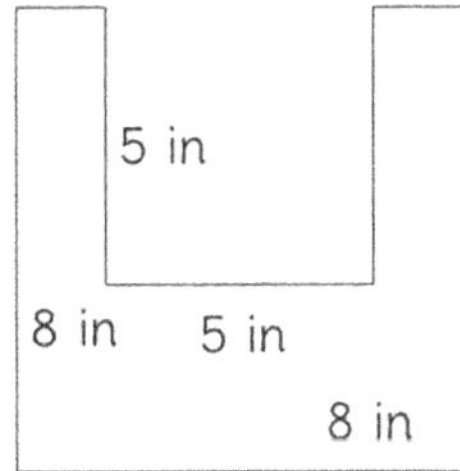

Area:

$$A1 = 8 \times 1.5 = 12 + A2 = 3 \times 5 = 15 + A3 = 8 \times 1.5 = 12$$

$$= 12 + 15 + 12$$

$$= 39 \text{ in}^2$$

Perimeter:

$$2 \times 8 + 2 \times 5 + 2 \times 8$$

$$= 16 + 10 + 16$$

$$= 42$$

Pythagorean Theorem

The Pythagorean Theorem is a fundamental principle in geometry that relates the lengths of the sides of a right triangle. It states that in any right triangle, the square of the length of the hypotenuse (the side opposite the right angle) is equal to the sum of the squares of the lengths of the other two sides.

$$a2 + b2 = c2$$

Let's use the Pythagorean Theorem to find the length of the hypotenuse (c) when a=44 and b=78.

$$c^2 = 44^2 + 78^2$$
$$c^2 = 1936 + 6084 \qquad c = \sqrt{8020}$$
$$c^2 = 8020 \qquad c \approx 89.554$$

Volume and surface Area

Volume refers to the amount of space occupied by a three-dimensional object. For shapes like cubes or rectangular prisms, we calculate volume by multiplying their length, width, and height.

To find the volume V of a rectangular prism, we use the formula:

$$Volume = length \; x \; width \; x \; height$$

Surface Area represents the total area covering all the faces of a three-dimensional object. For shapes like cubes or rectangular prisms, we find the surface area by summing the areas of all its faces.

The formula for surface area SA of a cube or rectangular prism is:

$$Surface\ Area = 2lw + 2lh + 2wh$$

Where: l is the length, w is the width, and h is the height of the object.

For example: Let's find the Volume and Surface Area of following rectangular prisms:

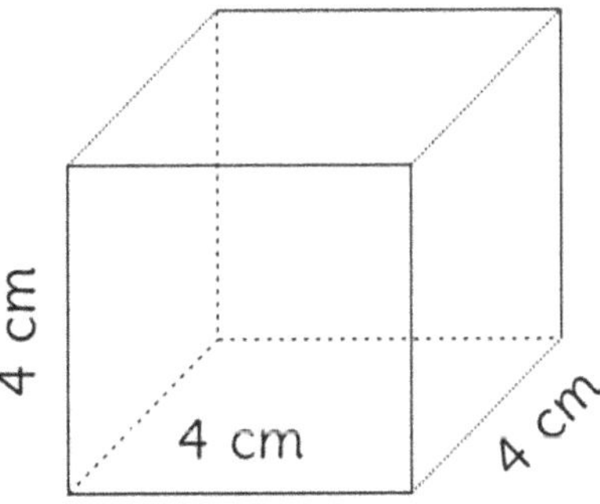

$$Volume = length \times width \times height$$

$$= 4 \times 4 \times 4$$

$$= 64 \text{ cm}^2$$

$$Surface\ Area = 2lw + 2lh + 2wh$$

$$= 2(4 \times 4) + 2(4 \times 4) + 2(4 \times 4)$$

$$= 32 + 32 + 32$$

$$= 96\ cm2$$

Different 3D objects have unique formulas for finding their volume and surface area. Here are some common ones:

1. **Cube:**

   - Volume: $V = s^3$ (where s is the length of one side of the cube)

   - Surface area: $SA = 6s^2$

2. **Sphere:**

   - Volume: $V = (\frac{4}{3})\pi r^3$ (where r is the radius of the sphere)

   - Surface area: $SA = 4\pi r^2$

3. **Cone:**

   - Volume: $V = (\frac{1}{3})\pi r^2 h$ (where r is the radius of the base and h is the height of the cone)

   - Surface area: $SA = \pi r^2 + \pi r \sqrt{(r^2 + h^2)}$

4. **Cylinder:**

   - Volume: $V = \pi r^2 h$ (where r is the radius of the base and h is the height of the cylinder)

   - Surface area: $SA = 2\pi r^2 + 2\pi rh$

5. Pyramid:

- Volume: $V = (\frac{1}{3})Bh$ (where B is the area of the base and h is the height of the pyramid)

- Surface area: $SA = B + \frac{1}{2}Pl$ (where P is the perimeter of the base and l is the slant height of the pyramid)

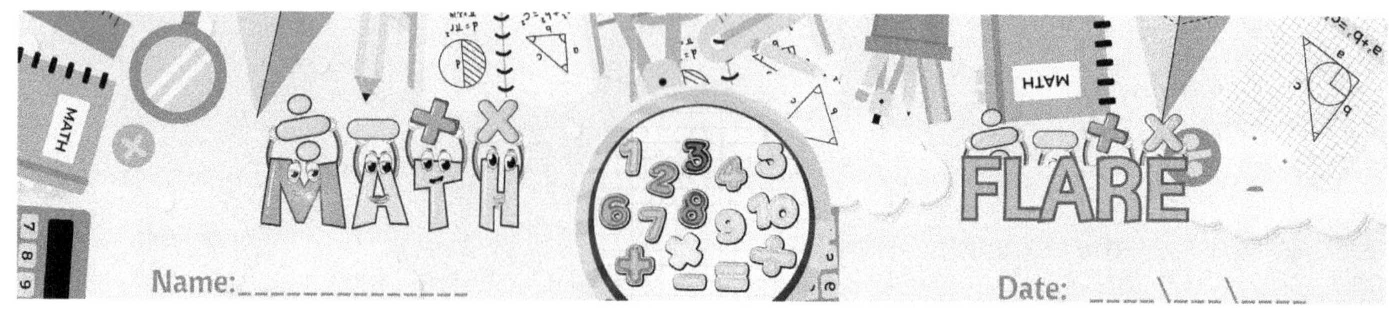

Area and Perimeter

1) 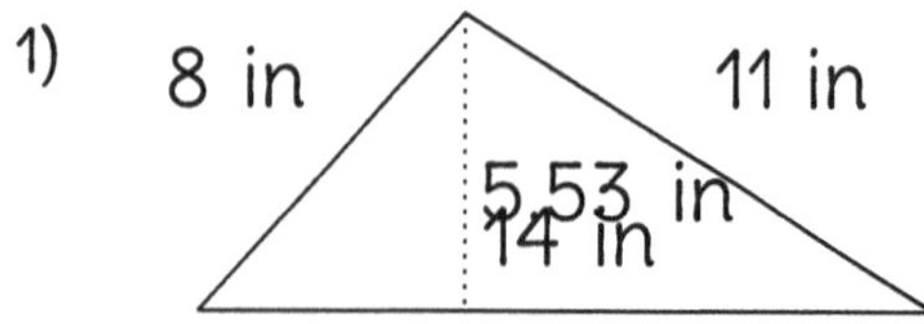

2) 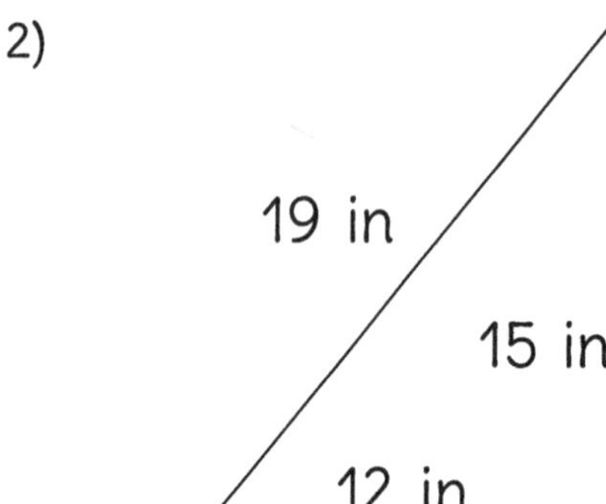

3)

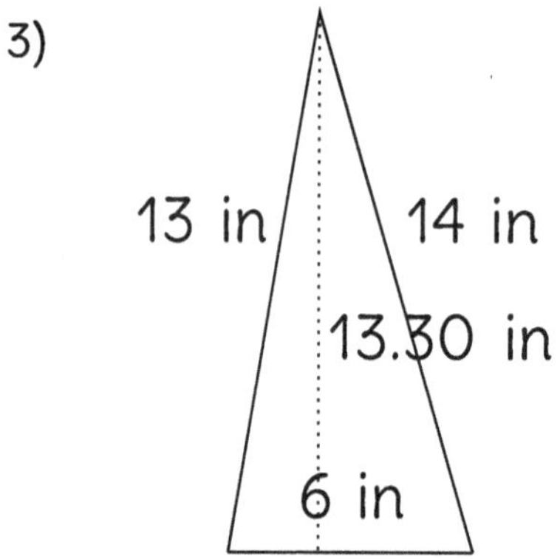

4) 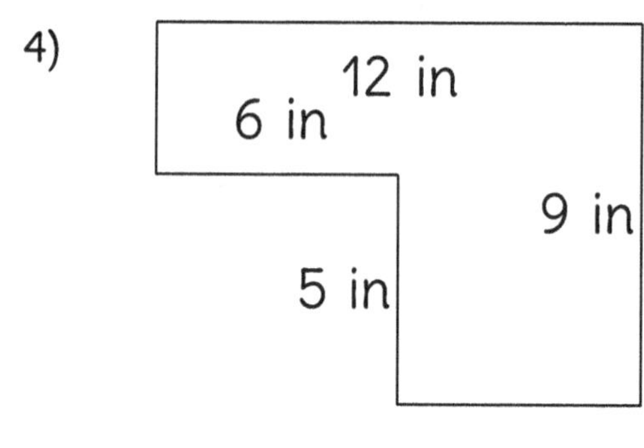

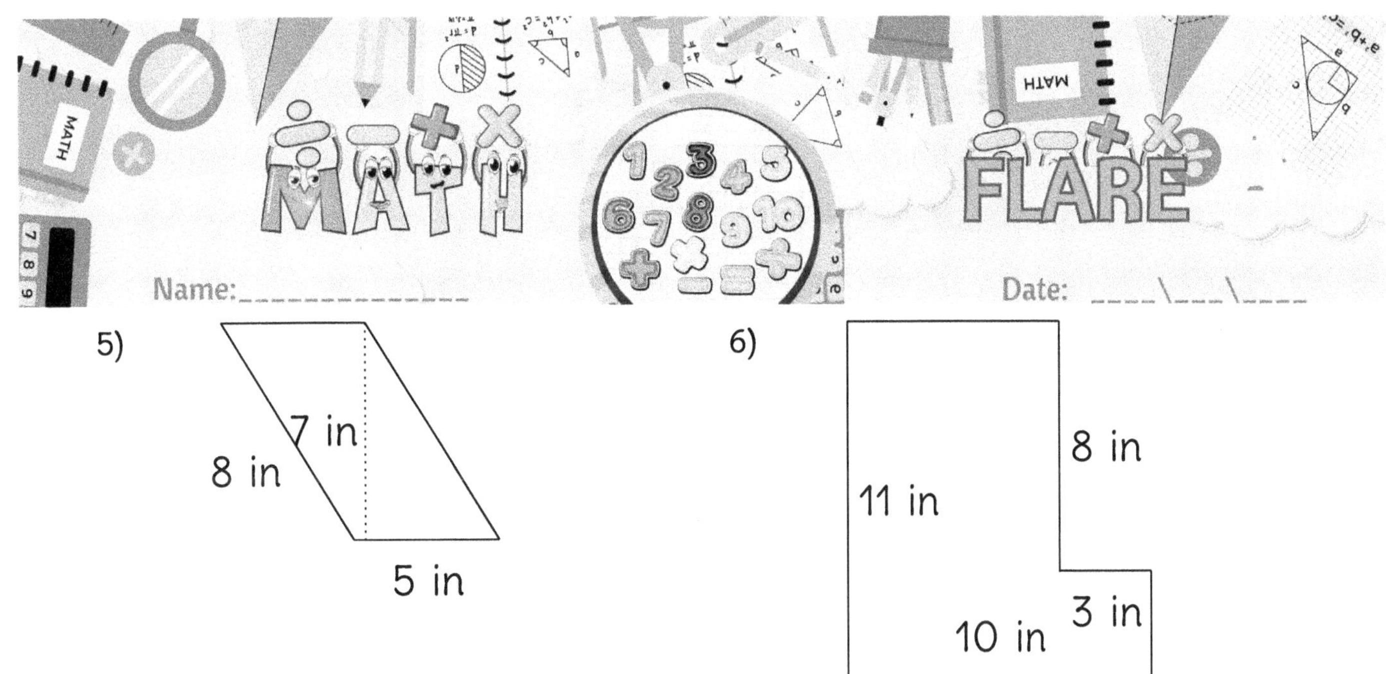

7)

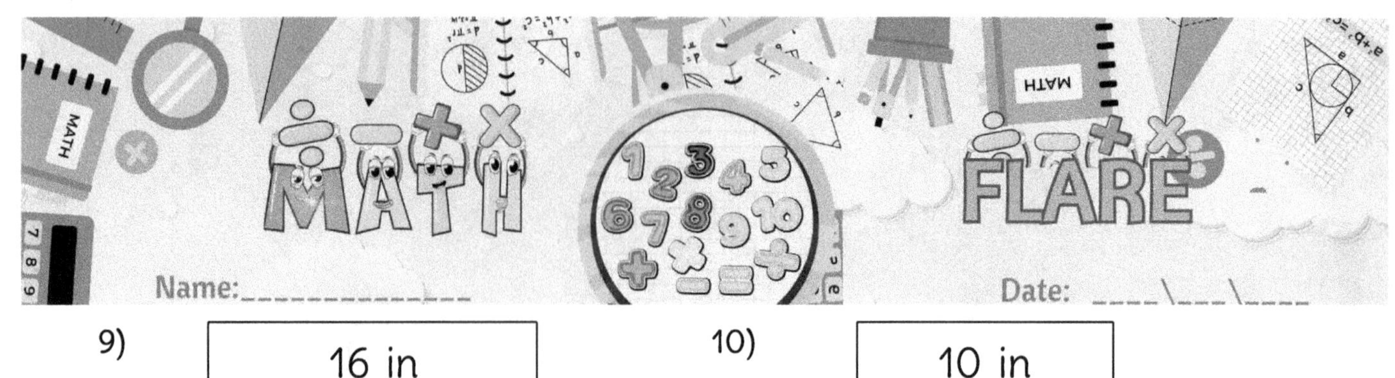

9)

16 in
6 in
17 in
7 in

10)

10 in
7 in   12 in
5 in

11)

11 in
8 in
4 in
0 in

12)

17 in   8 in
8.28 in
17 in

MATH FLARE
Name:
Date:

13)

14 in
10 in
13 in
5 in

14)

4 in
4 in
5 in

15)

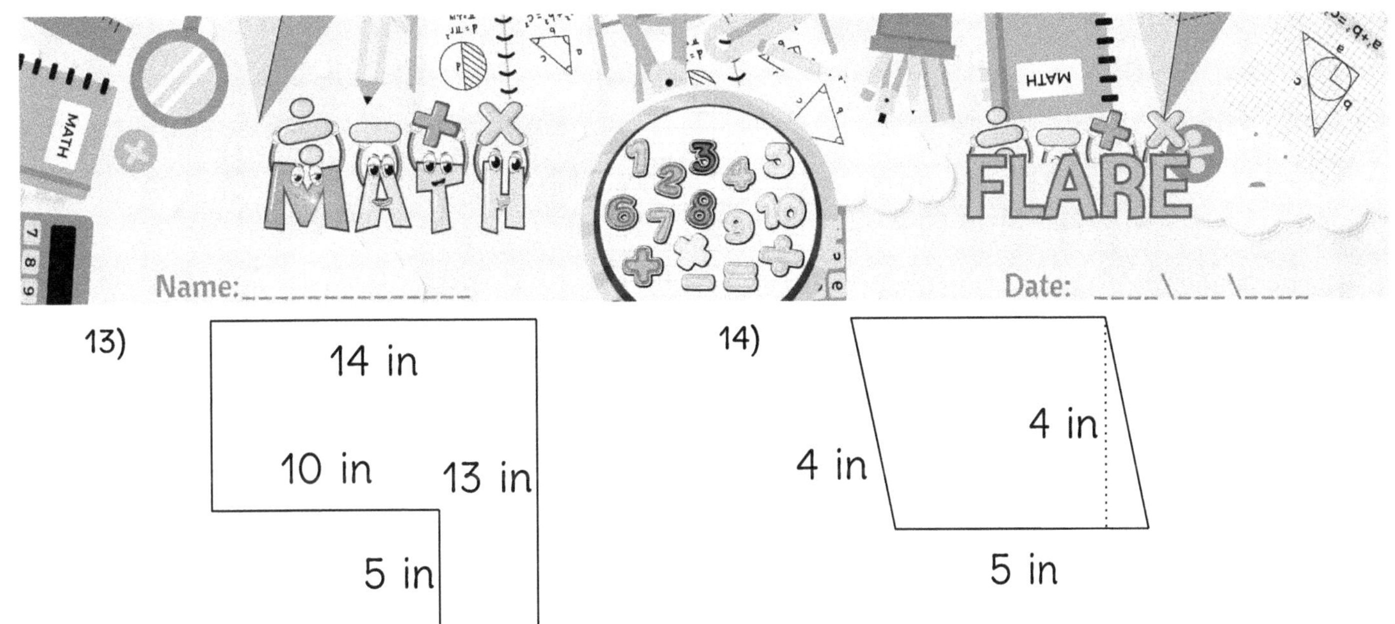

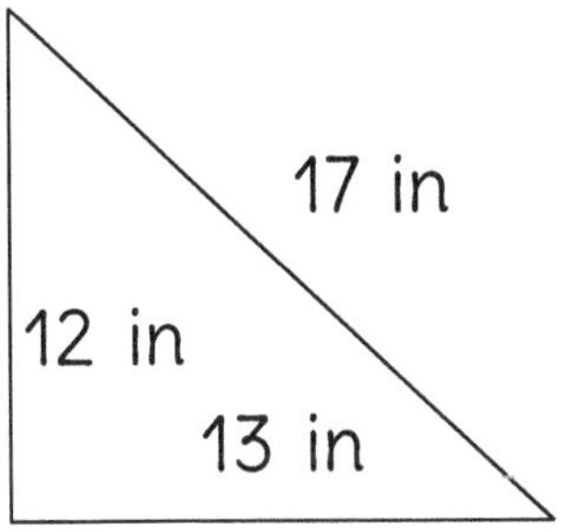
17 in
12 in
13 in

16)

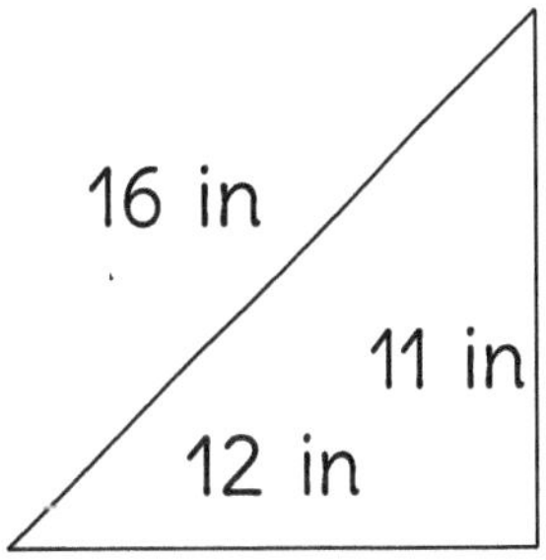
16 in
11 in
12 in

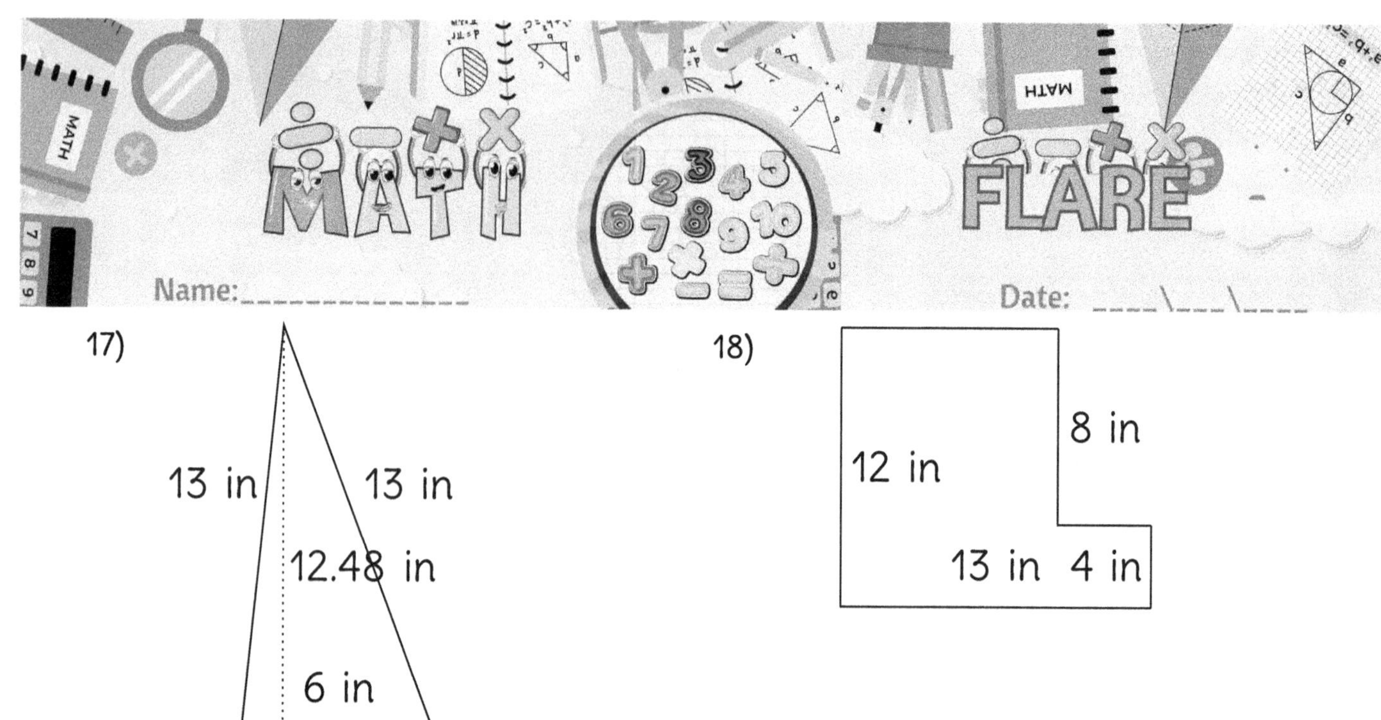

Name:
Date:
17)
13 in
13 in
12.48 in
6 in
18)
8 in
12 in
13 in
4 in

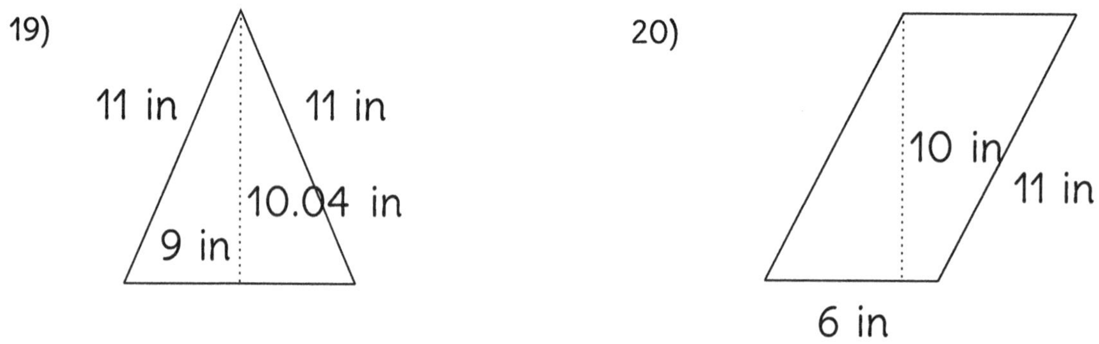

19)
11 in
11 in
10.04 in
9 in
20)
10 in
11 in
6 in

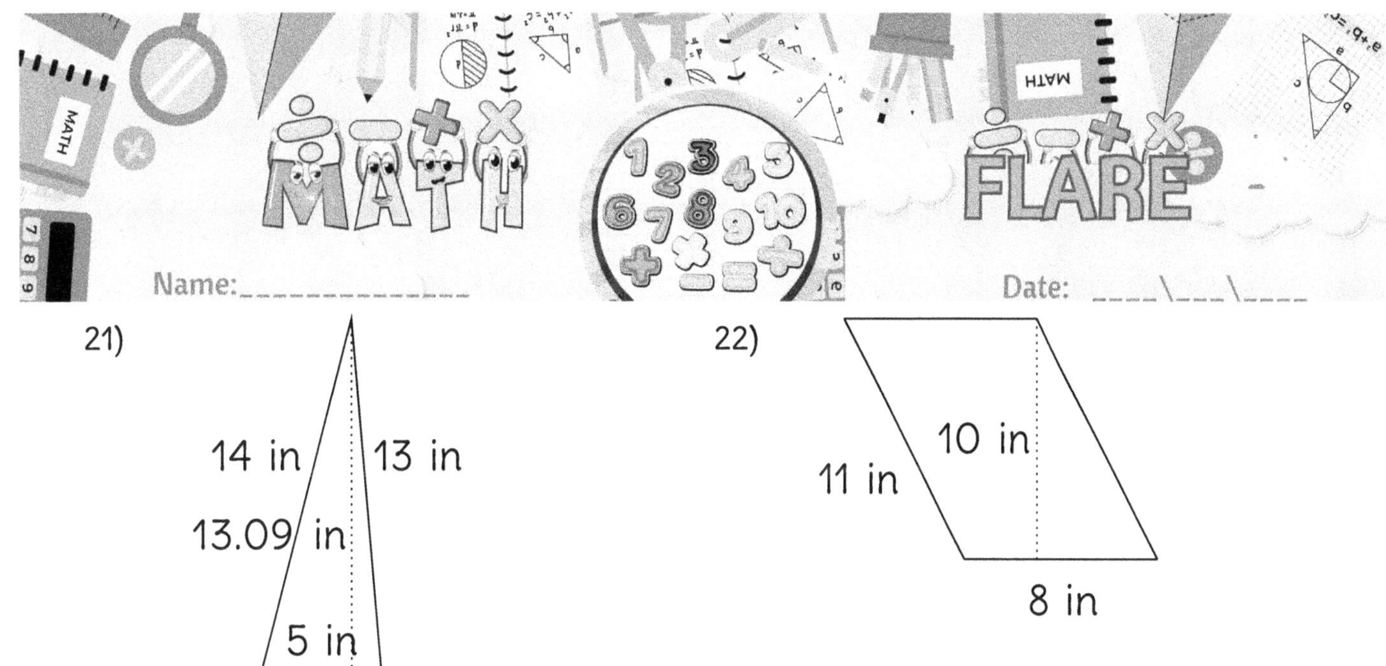

21)

22)

23)

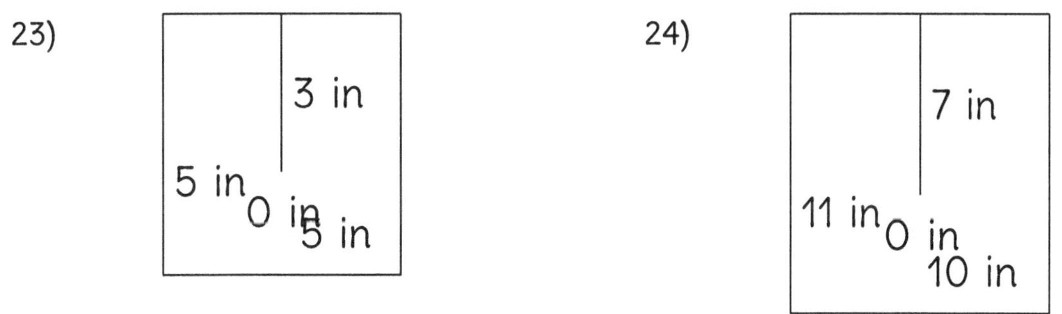

Name:
Date:

14 in
13 in
13.09 in
5 in

10 in
11 in
8 in

3 in
5 in
0 in
5 in

7 in
11 in
0 in
10 in

24)

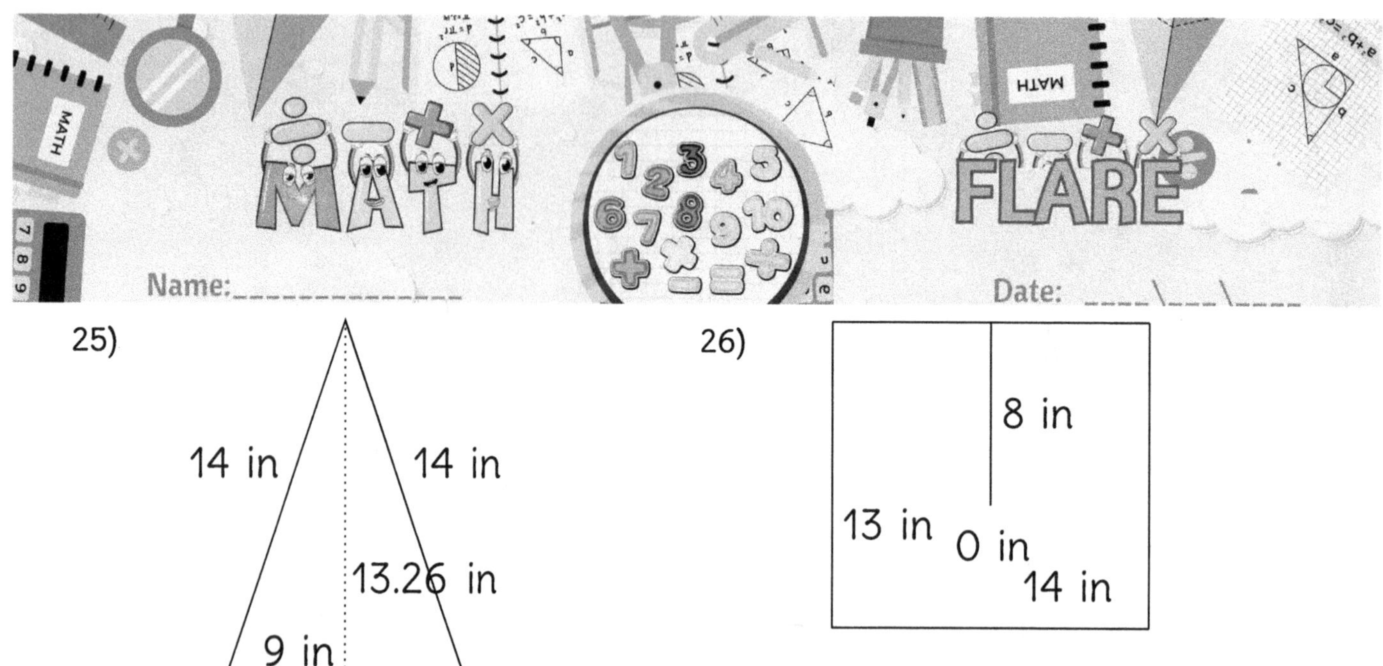

25)

26)

27)

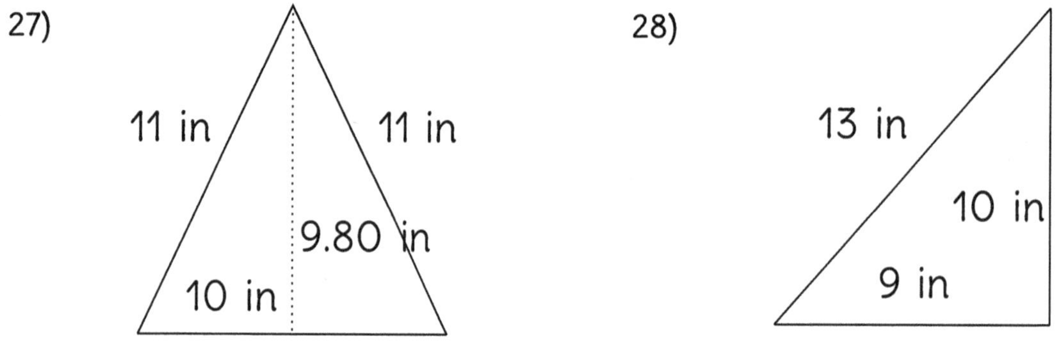

28)

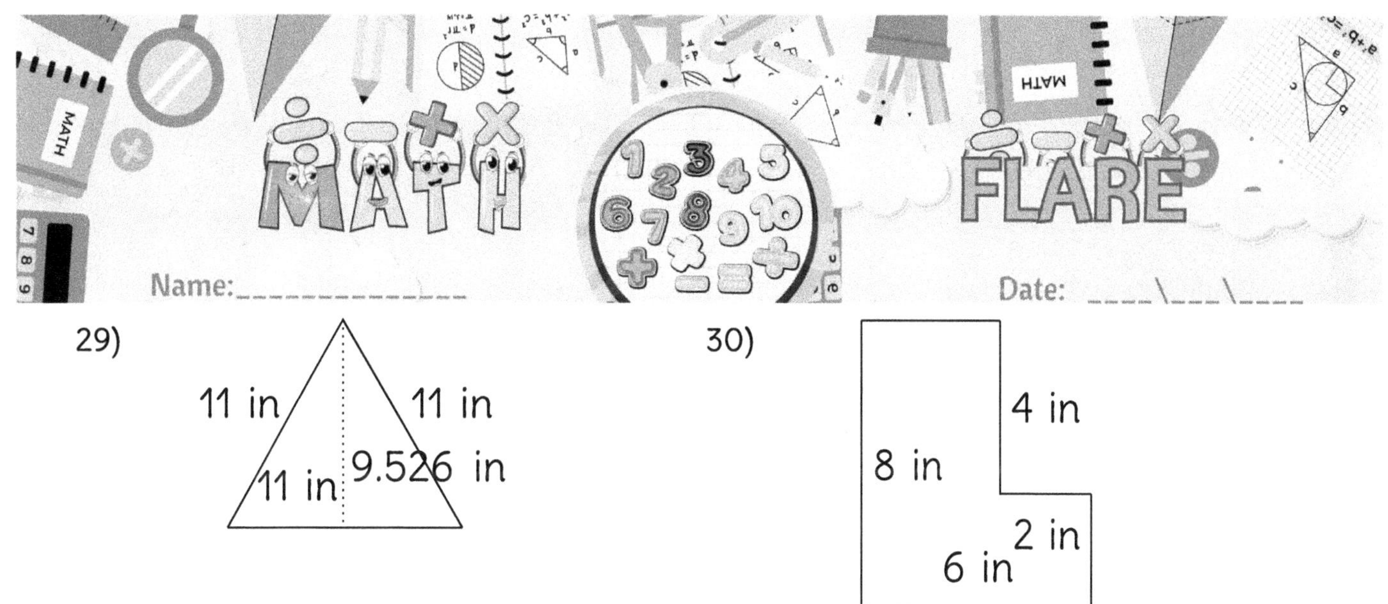

29)

30)

31) 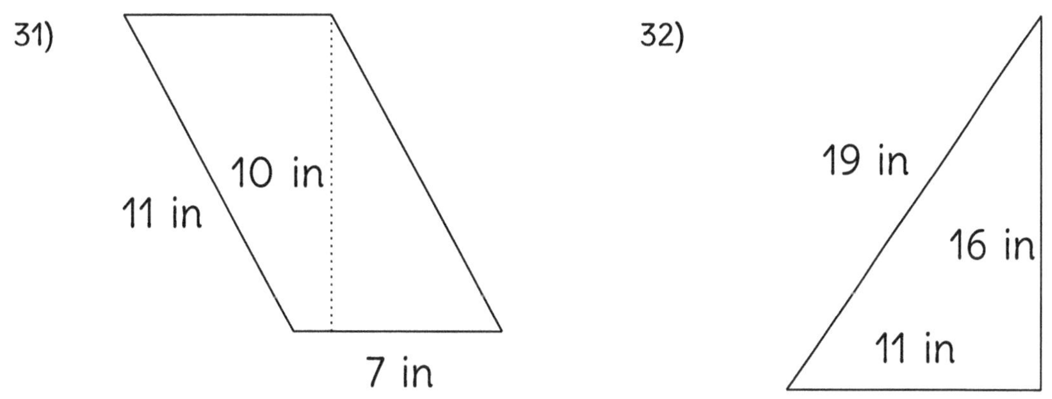

32)

125

Name:
Date:

33)

11 in
11 in
5 in
0 in

34)

5 in
2 in
6 in
4 in

35)

7 in
7 in
6.54 in
5 in

36)

12 in
13 in
12.00 in
6 in

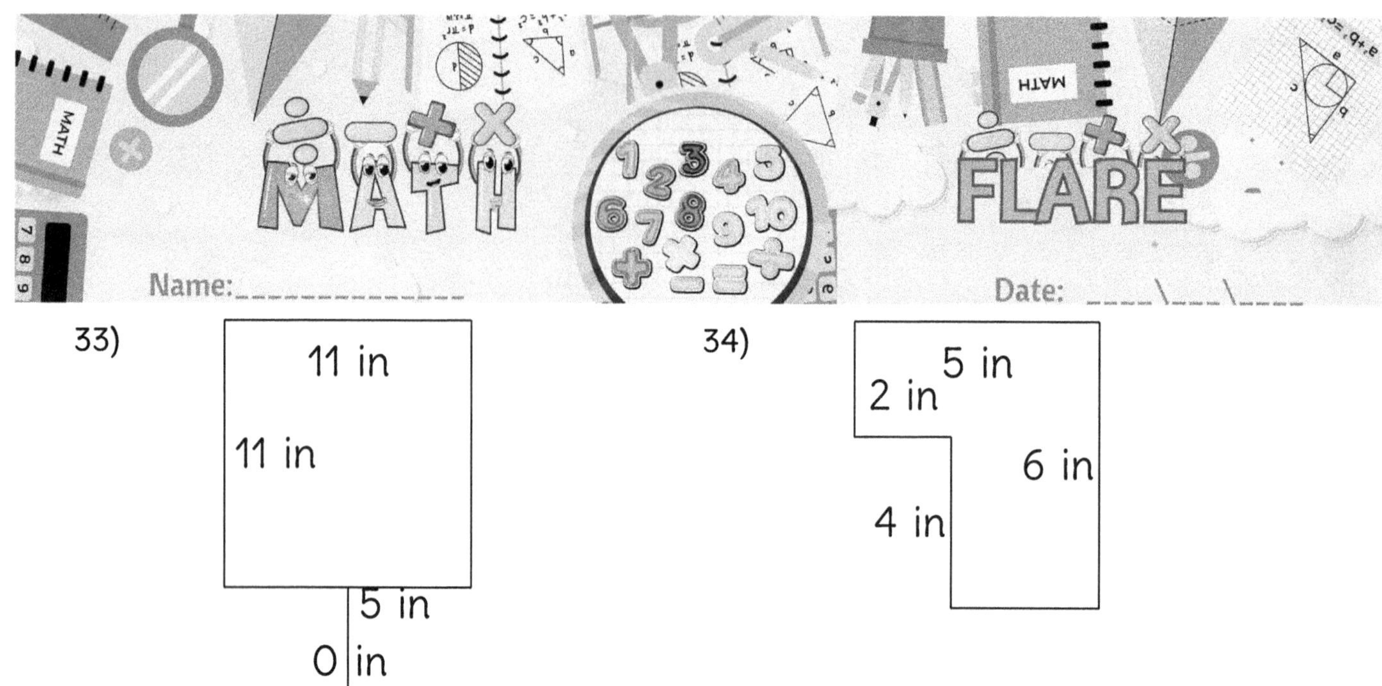

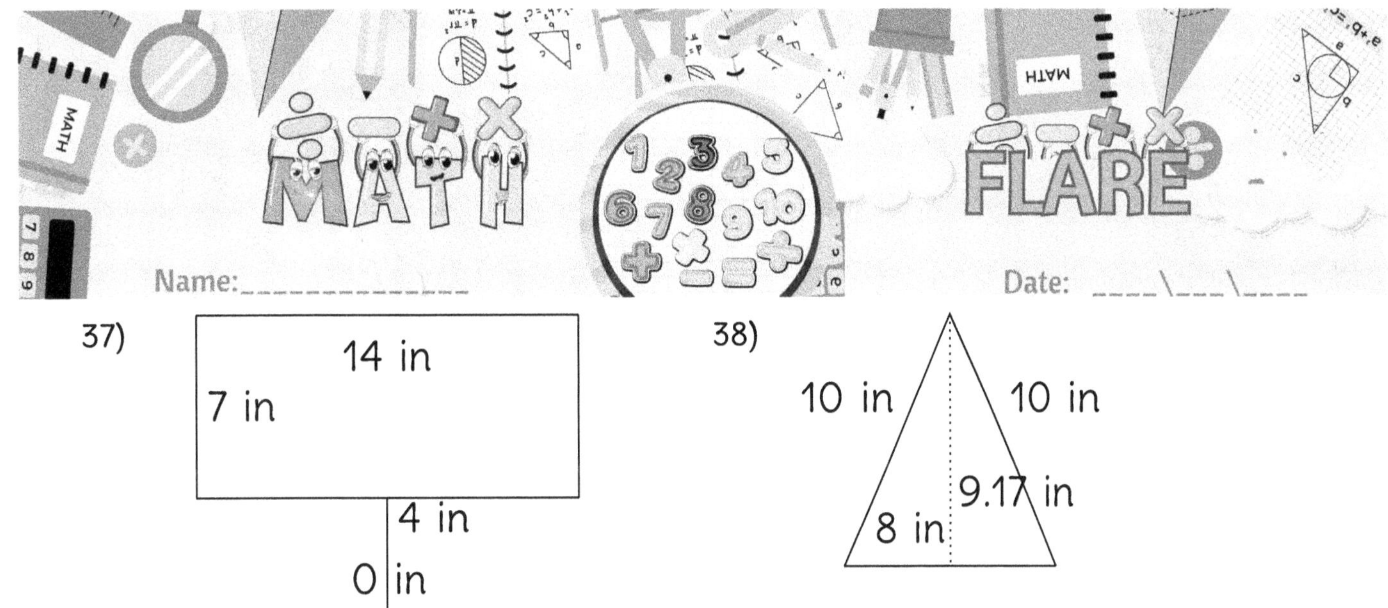

37)

38)

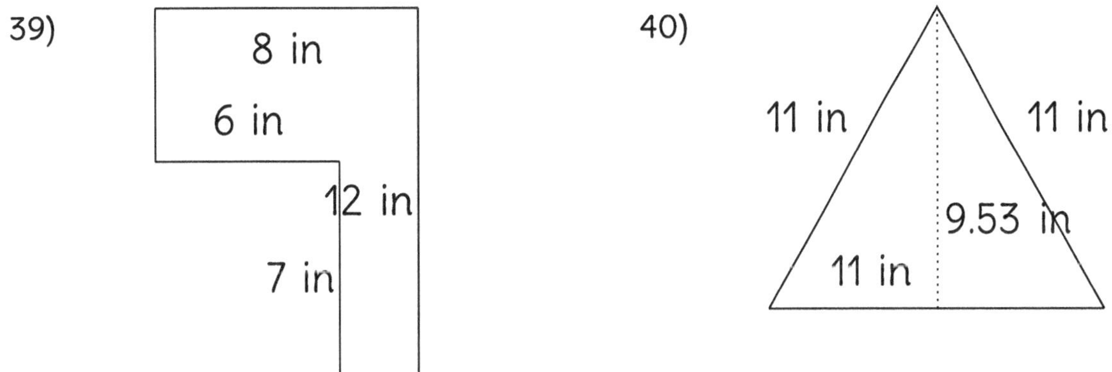

39)

40)

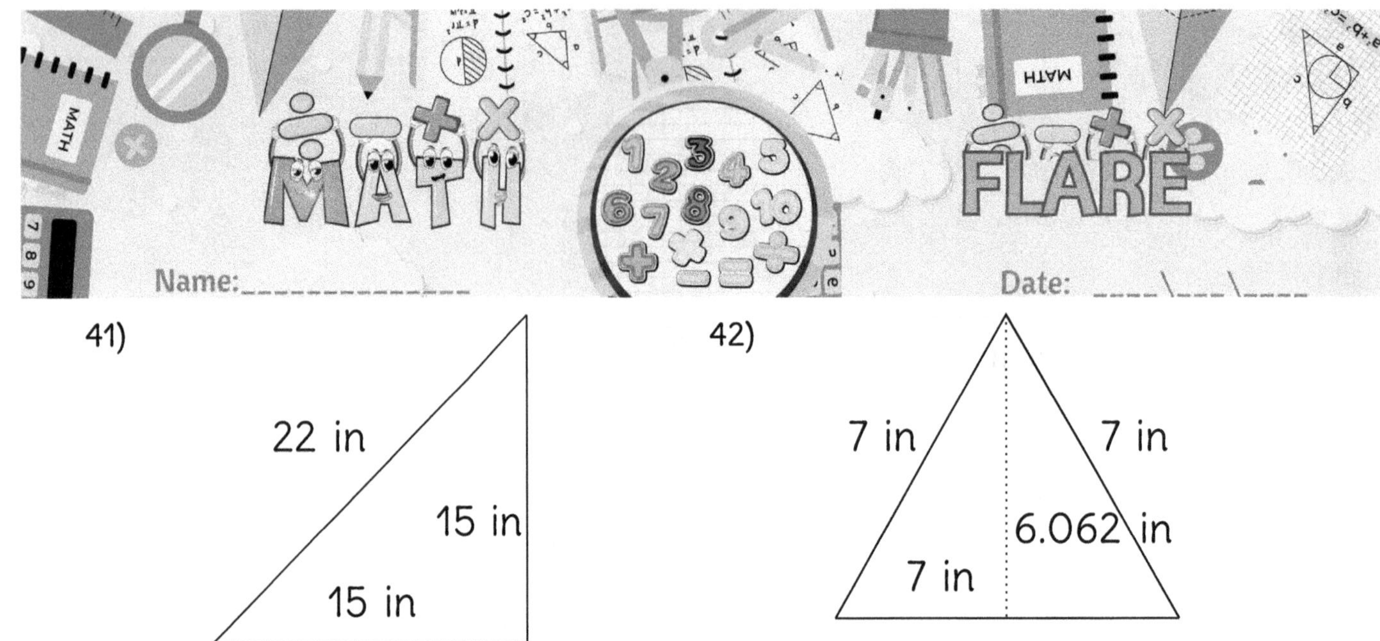

41)

42)

43)

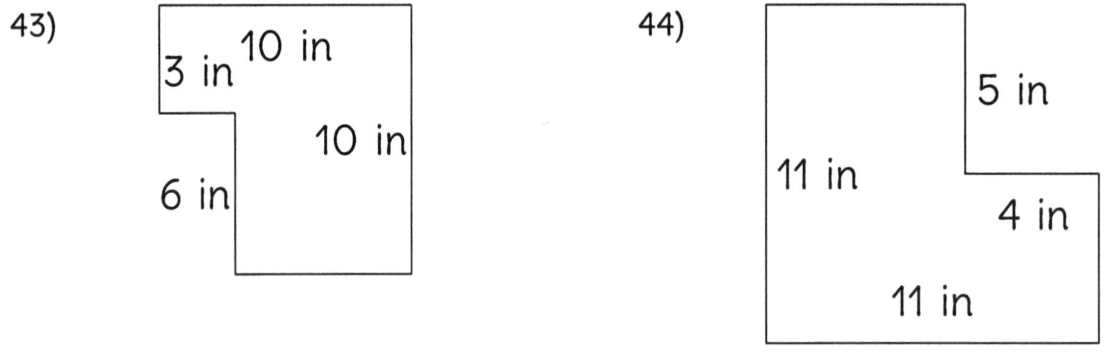

44)

128

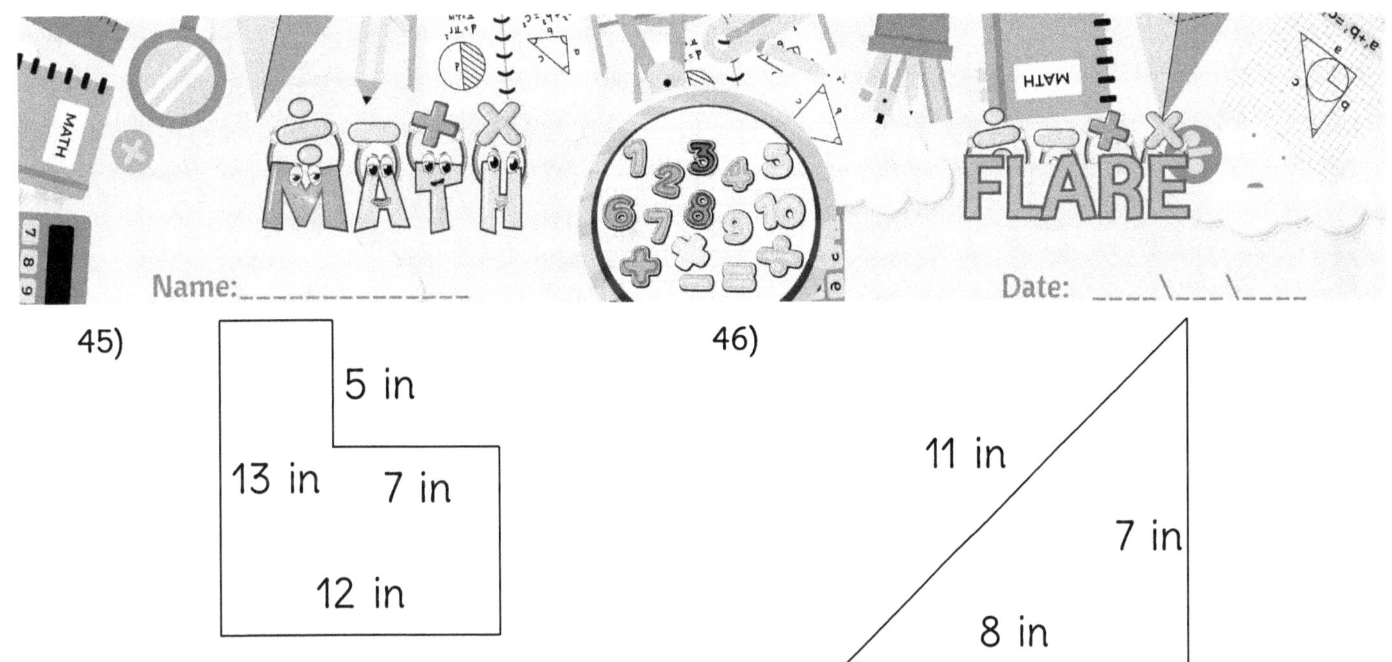

45)

46)

47) 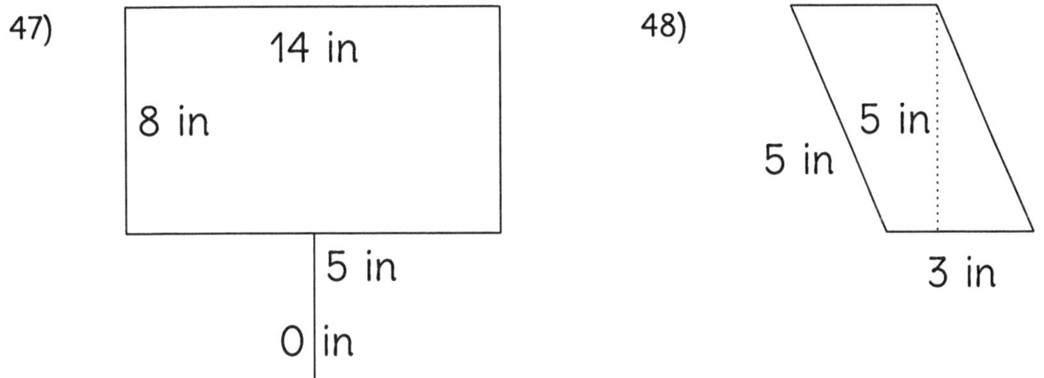

48)

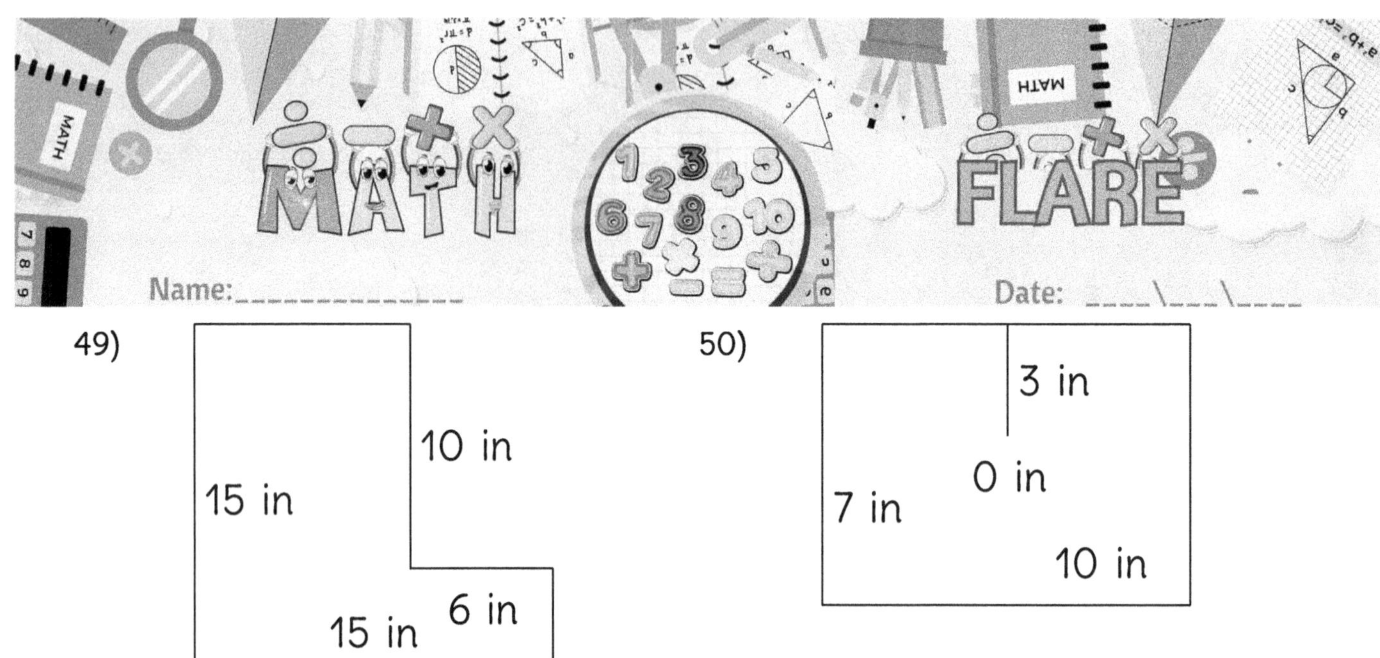

49)

50)

51)
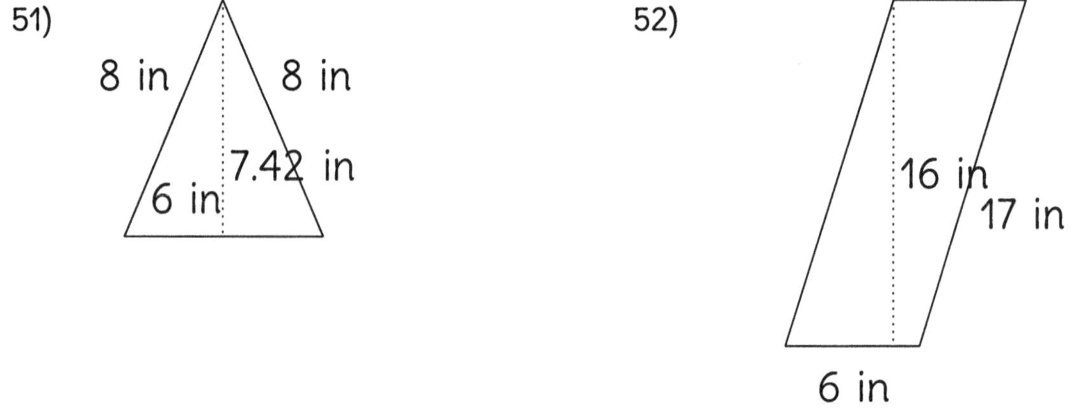

52)

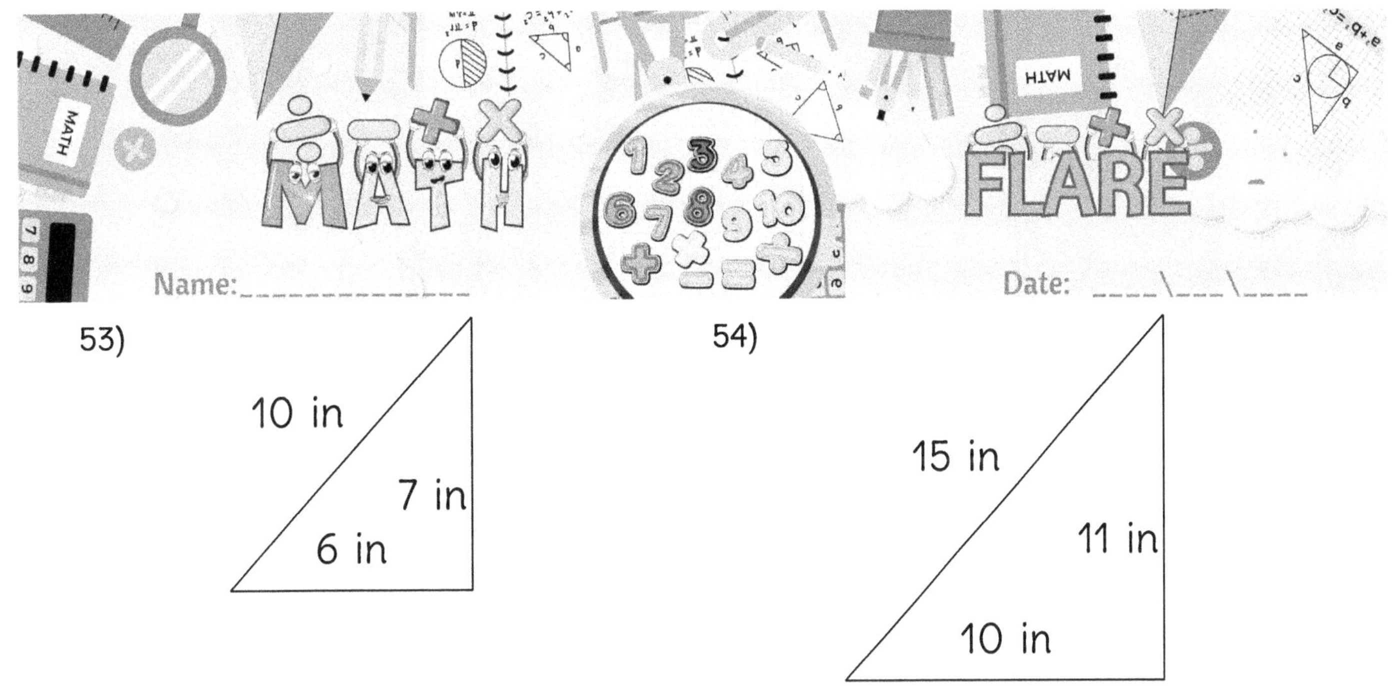

53)

10 in
7 in
6 in

54)

15 in
11 in
10 in

55) 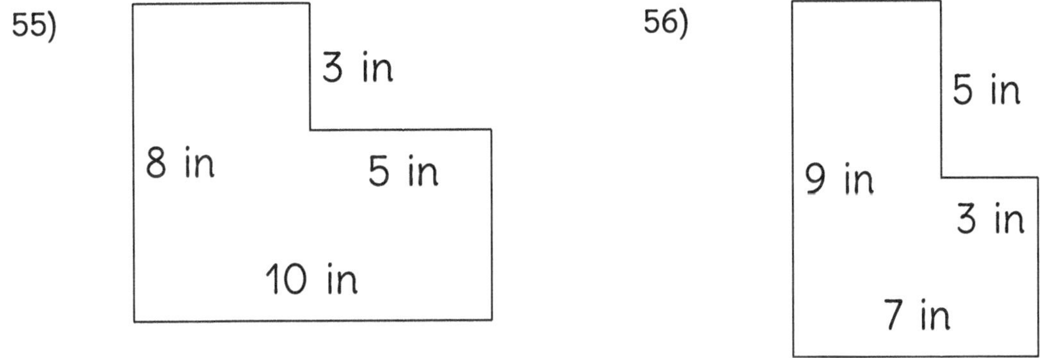

3 in
8 in
5 in
10 in

56)

5 in
9 in
3 in
7 in

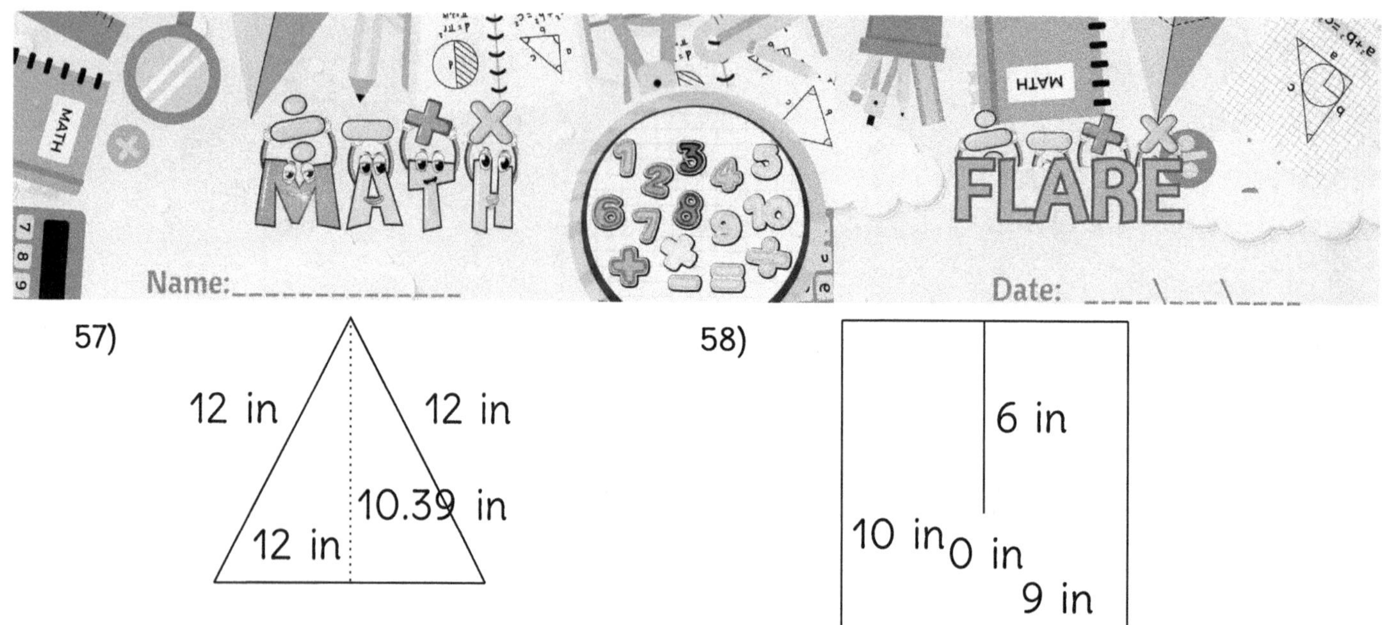

57)

58)

59)

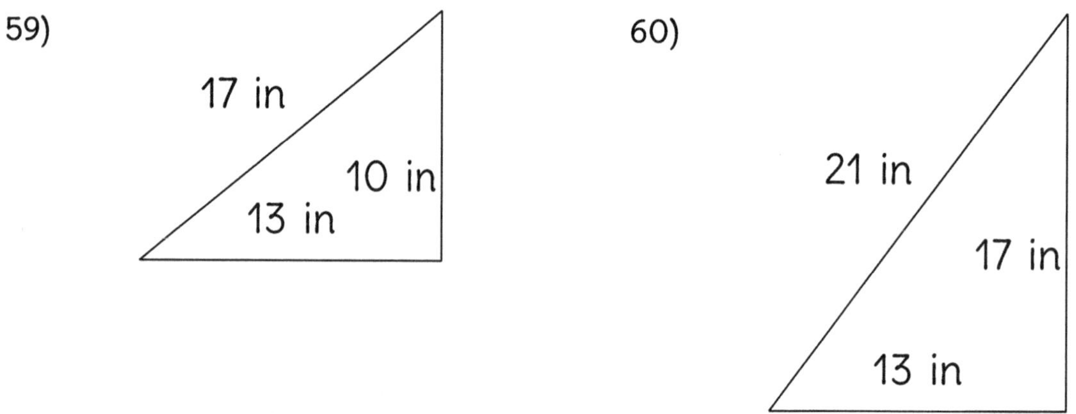

60)

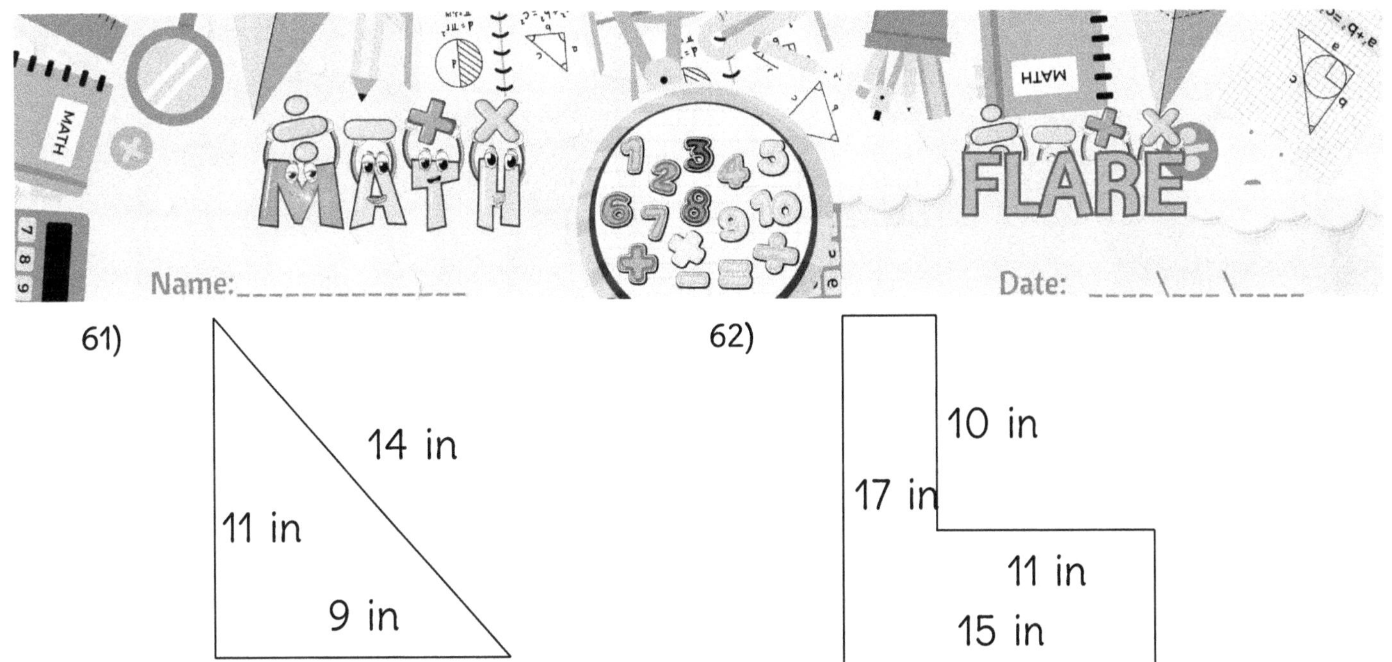

61)

62)

63)

64)

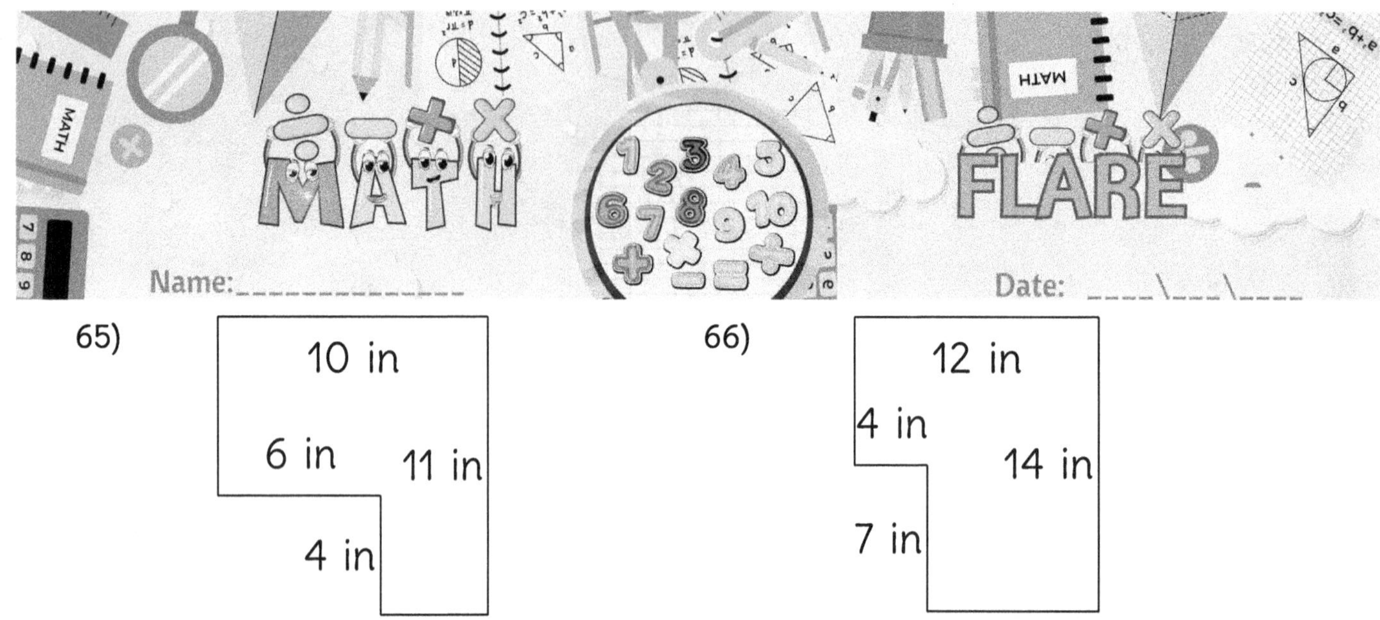

65)

66)

67)

68)
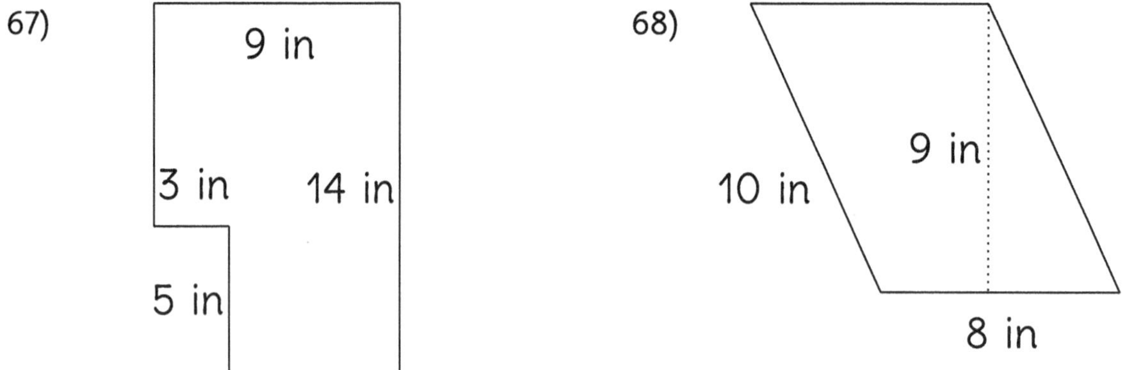

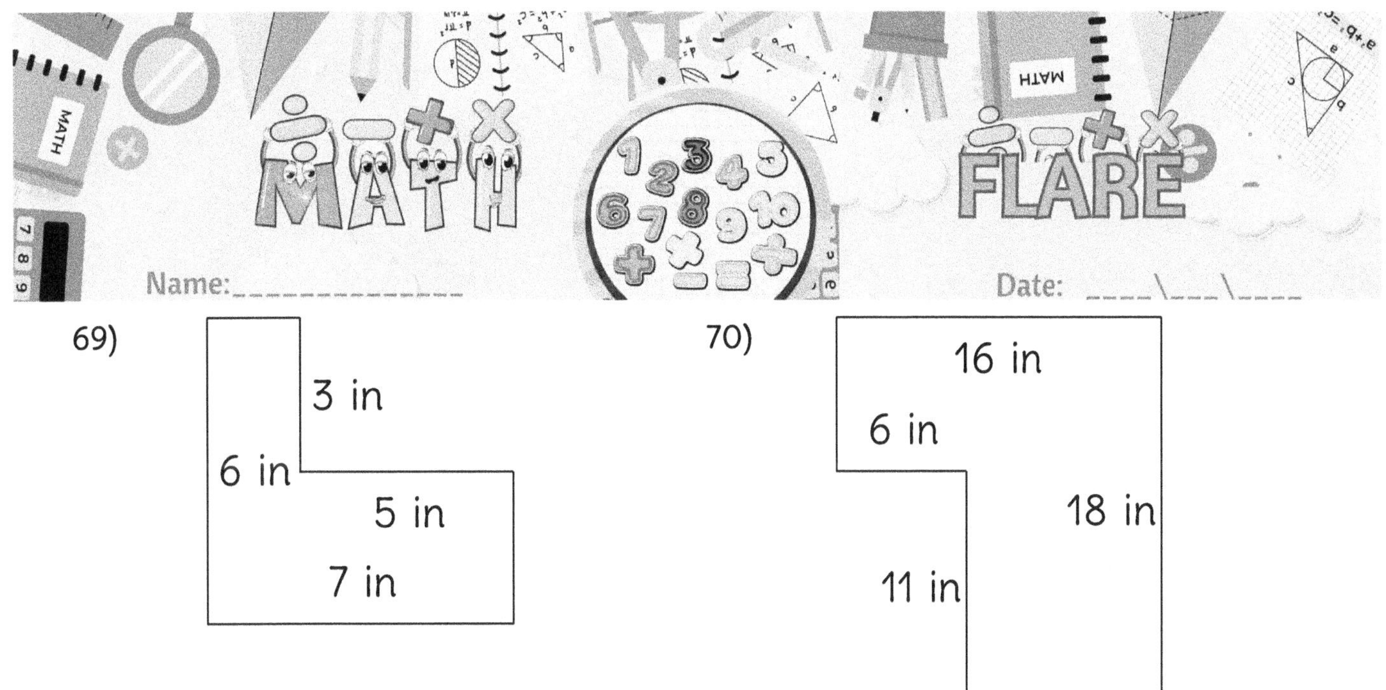

69)

70)

71)

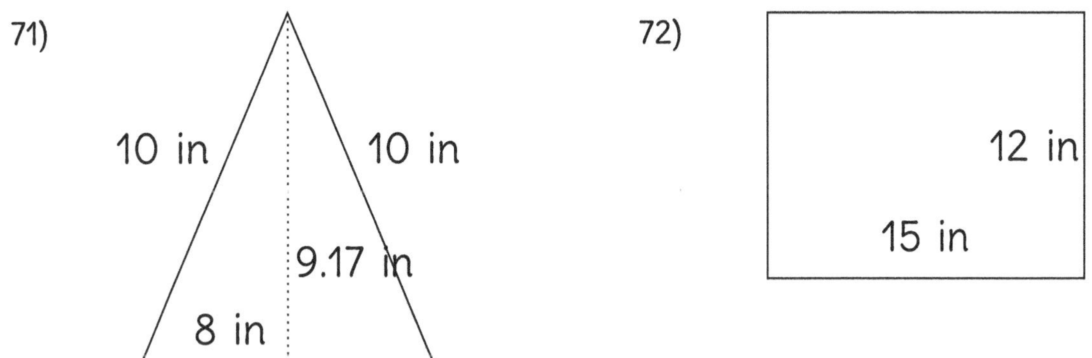

72)

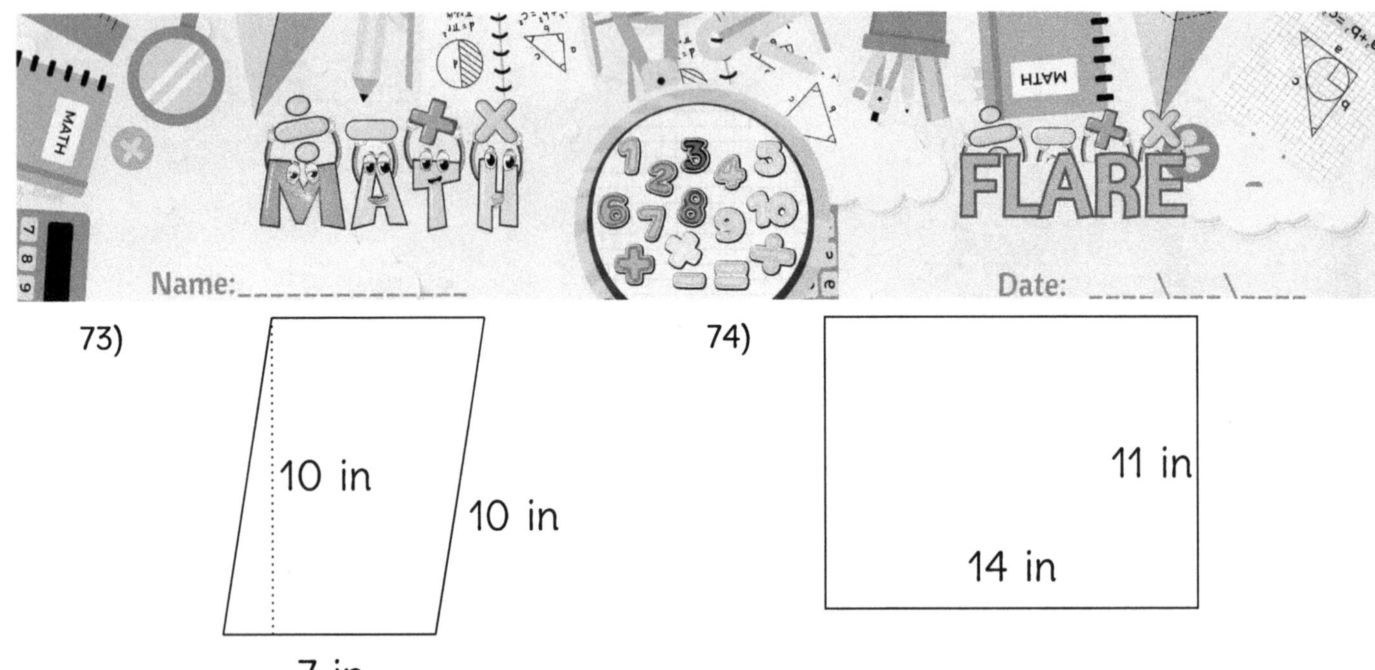

73)

74)

75)
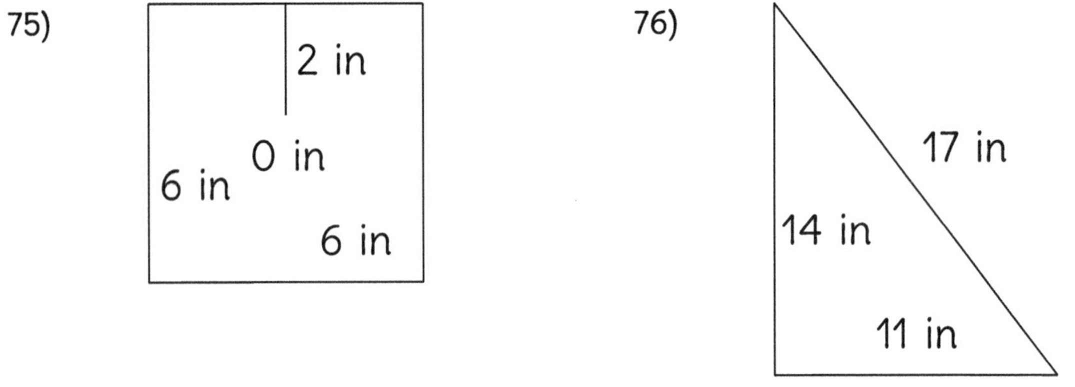

76)

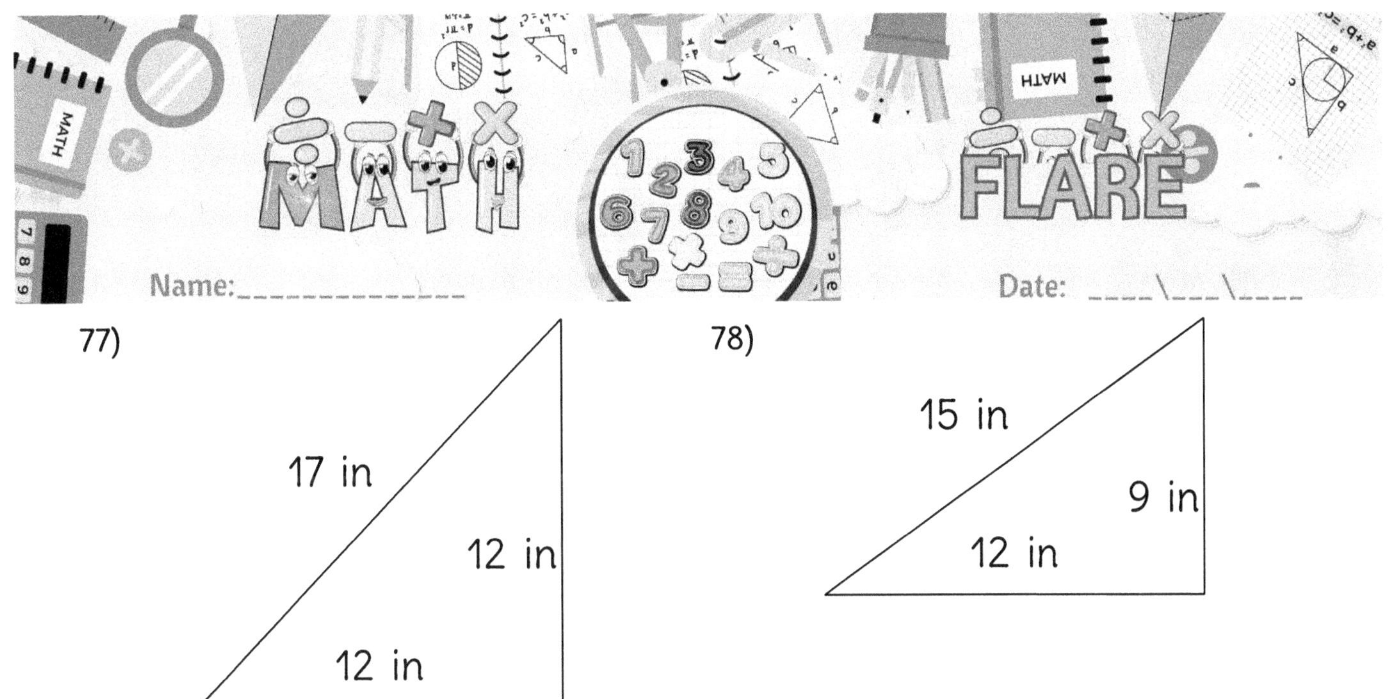

77)

78)

79)

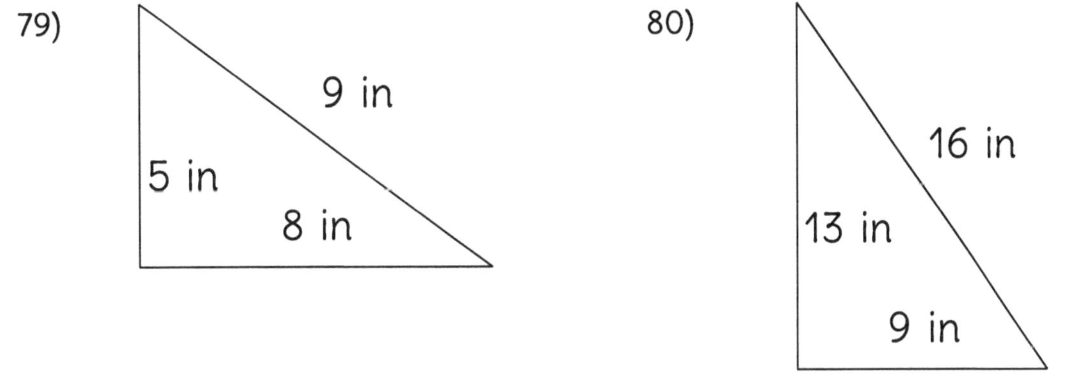

80)

Pythagorean Theorem
Find the length of the side.

1)
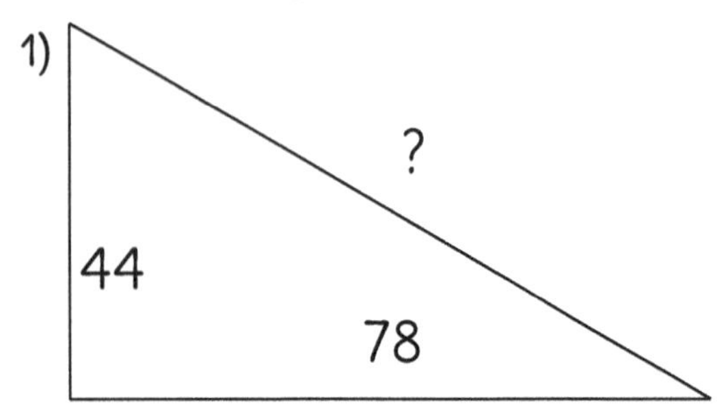

S = 89.554

$c^2 = 44^2 + 78^2$

$c^2 = 1936 + 6084$ $c = \sqrt{8020}$

$c^2 = 8020$ $c \approx 89.554$

2)
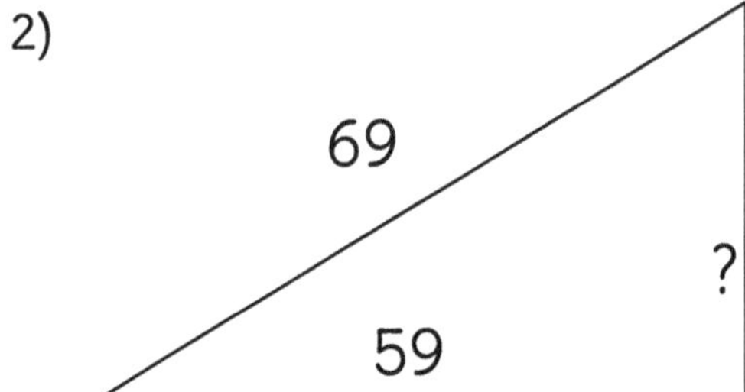

3)
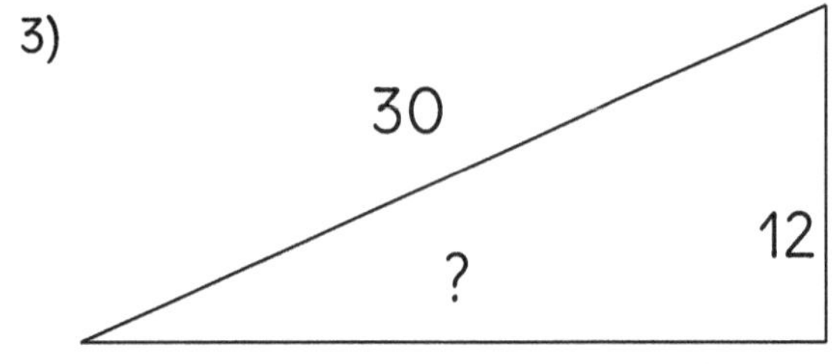

4)
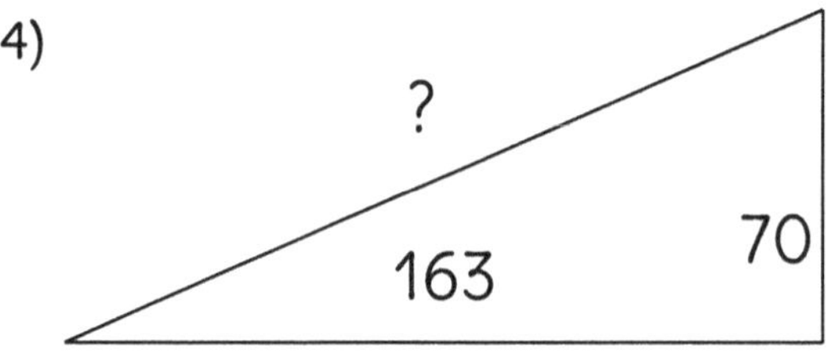

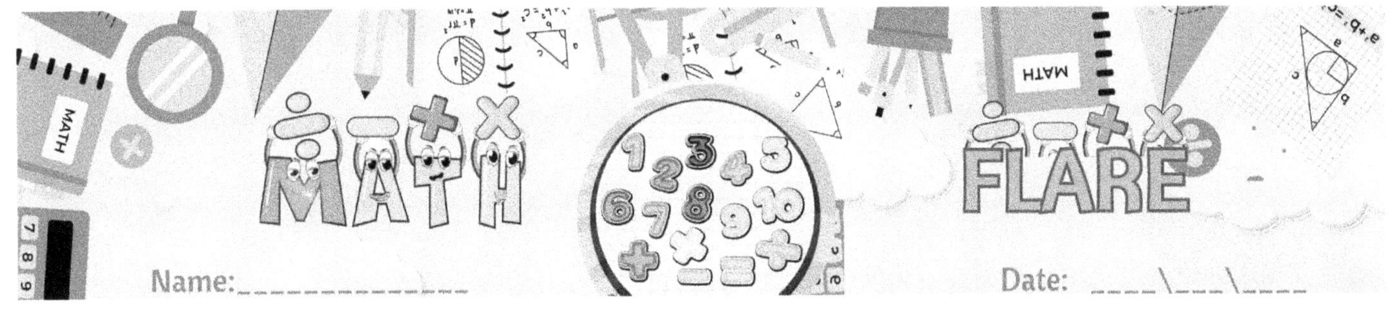

5)

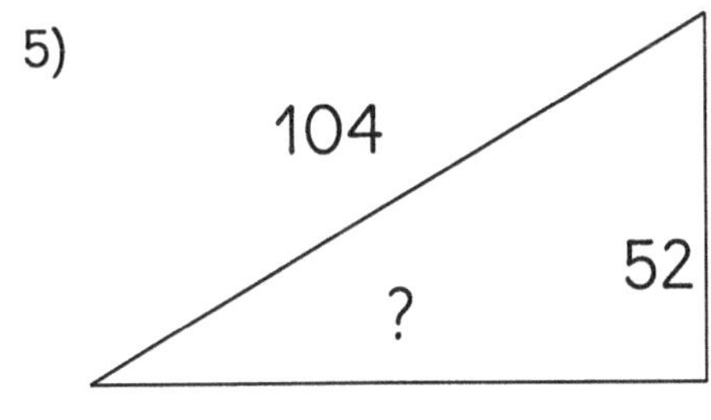

____

6)

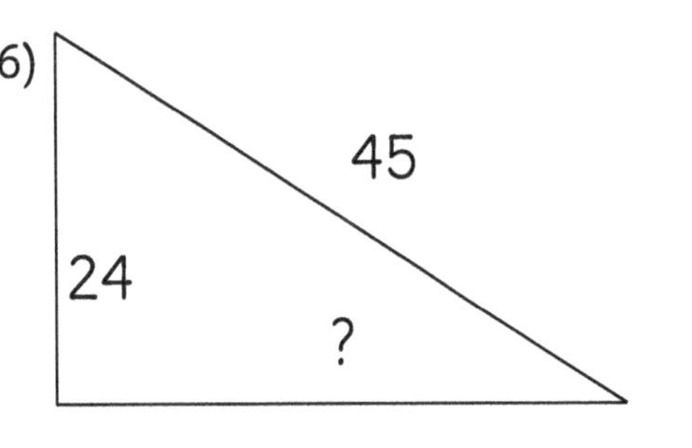

____

7)

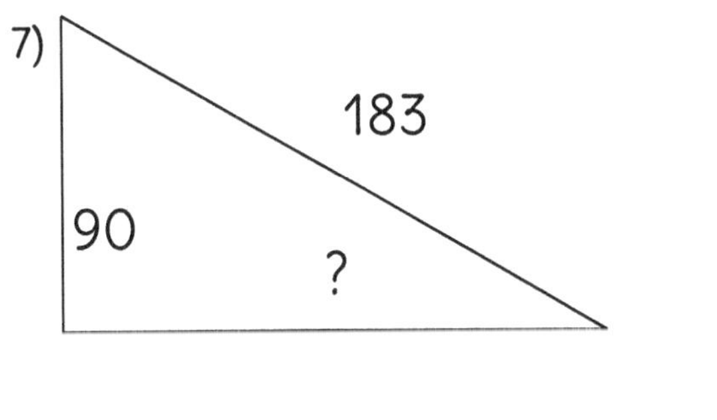

____

8)

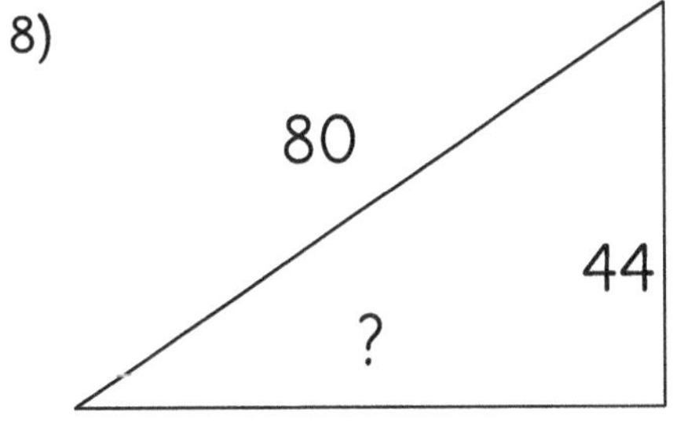

____

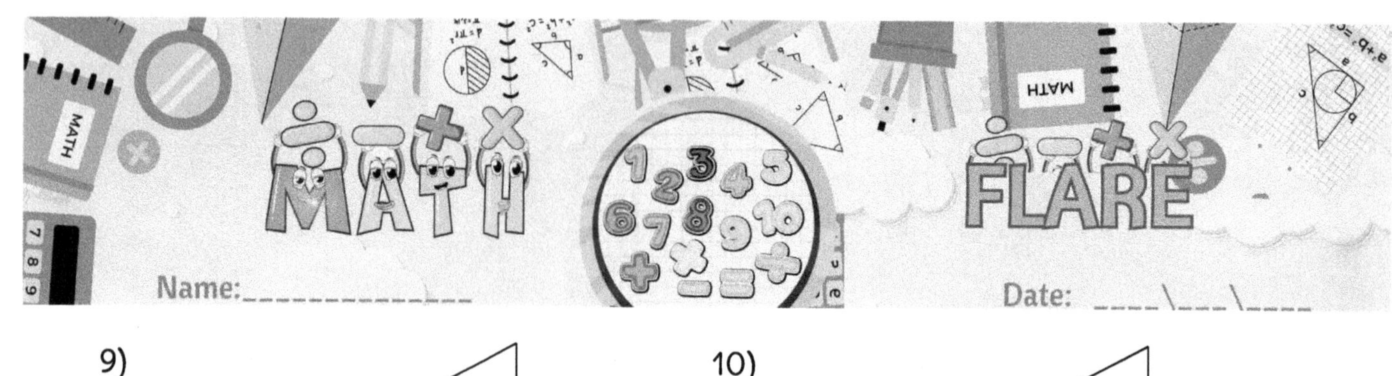

9)

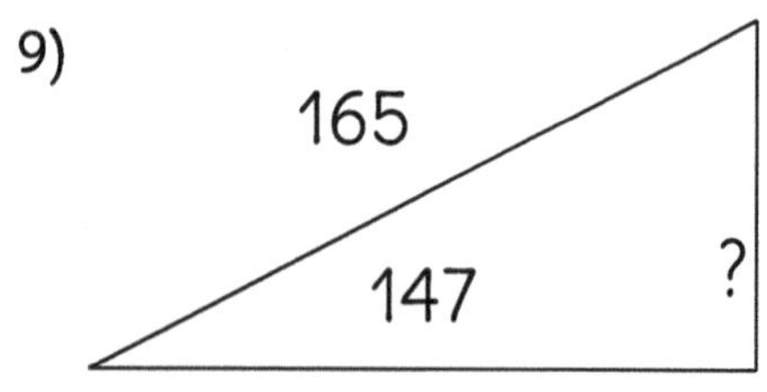

____

10)

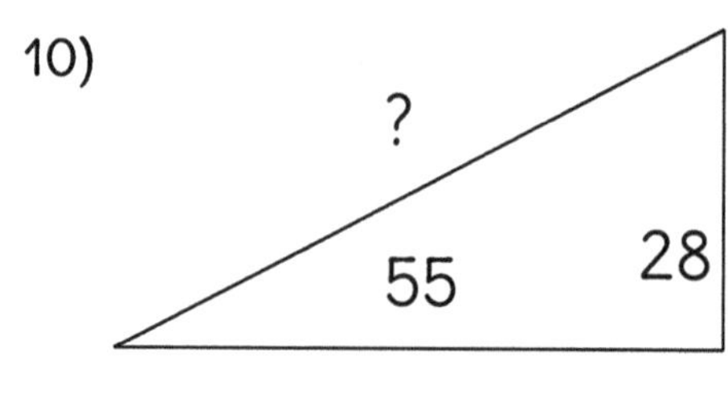

____

11)

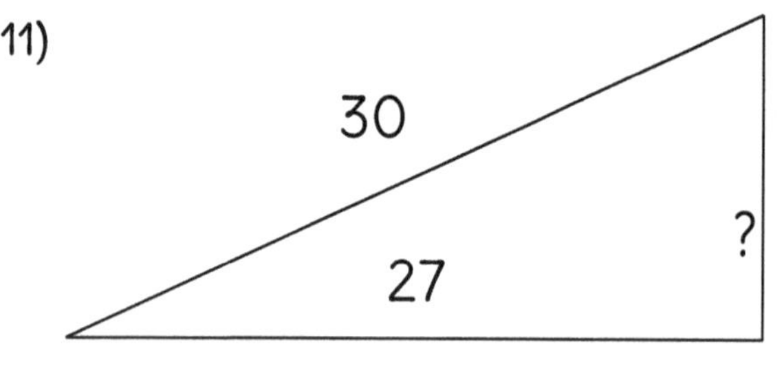

____

12)

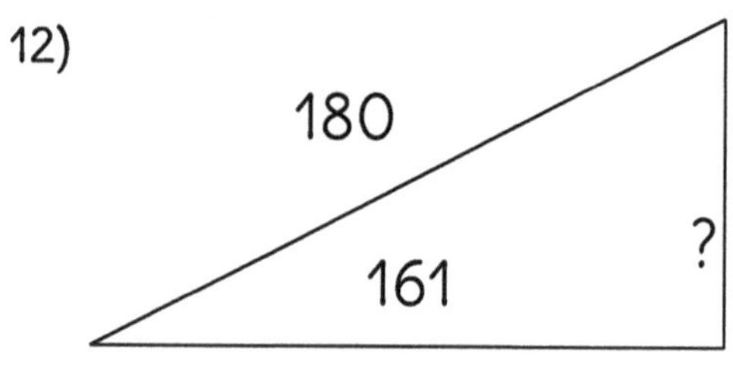

____

13)
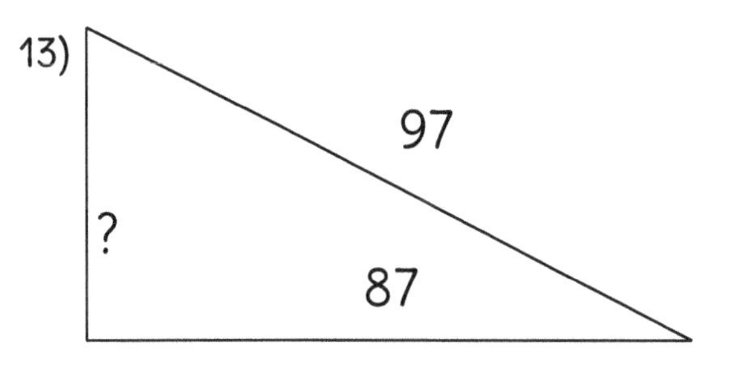

14)
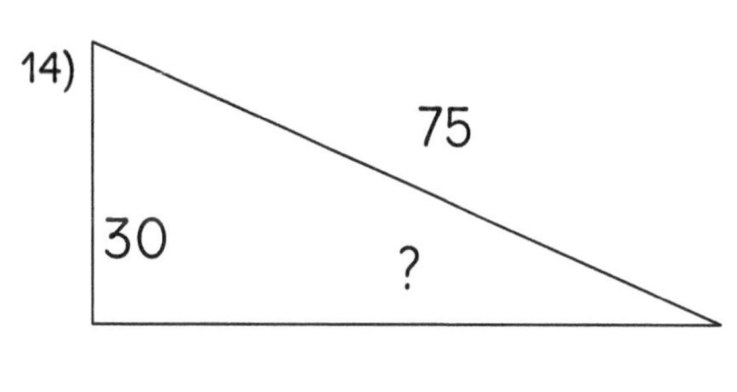

15)
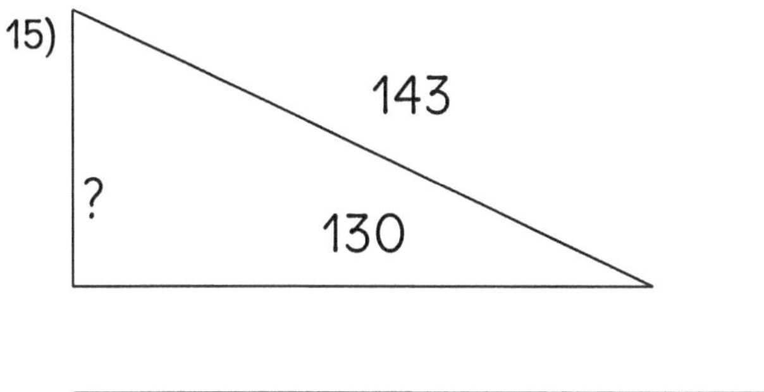

16)
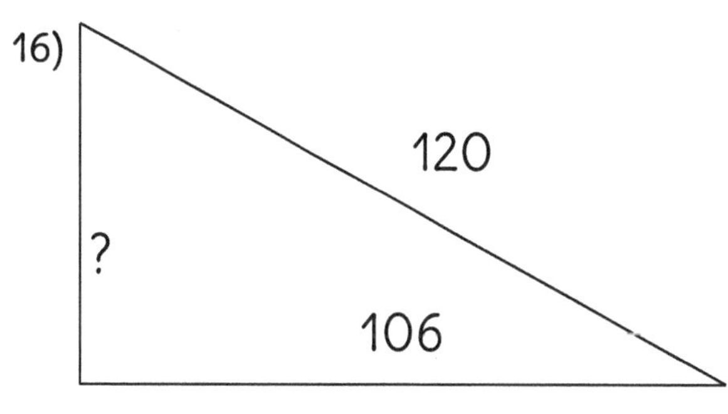

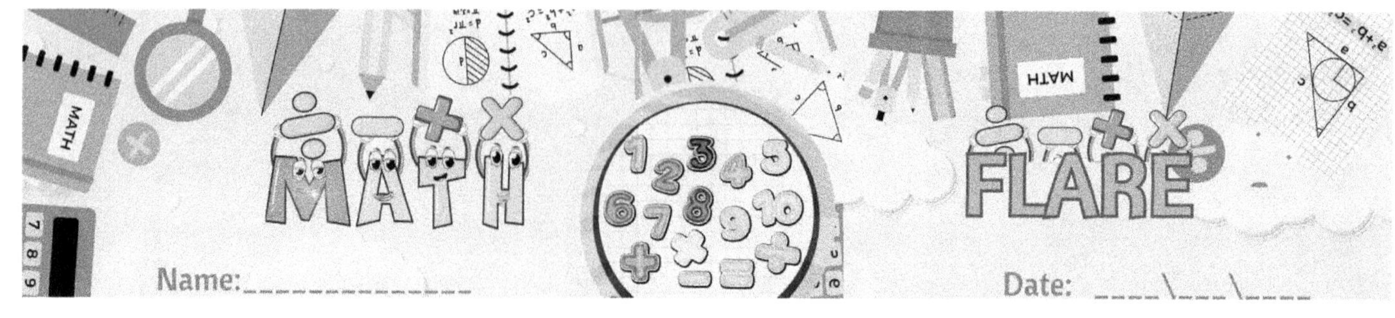

17)

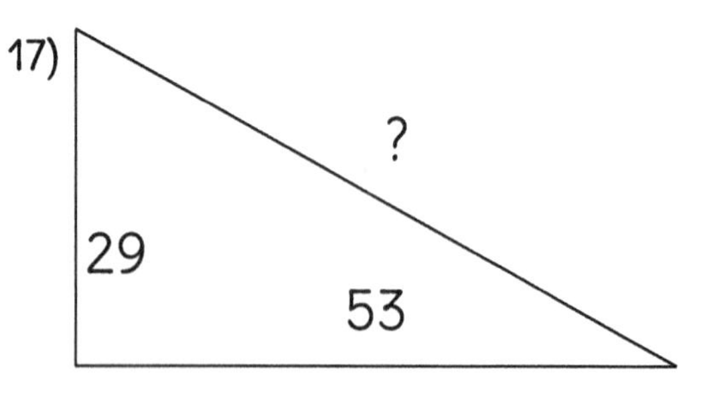

____

18)

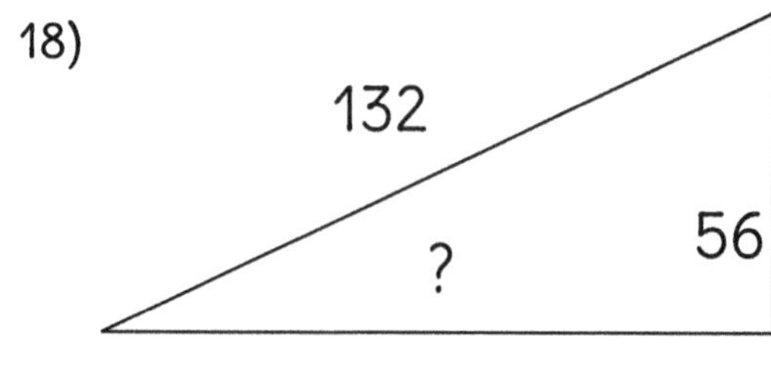

____

19)

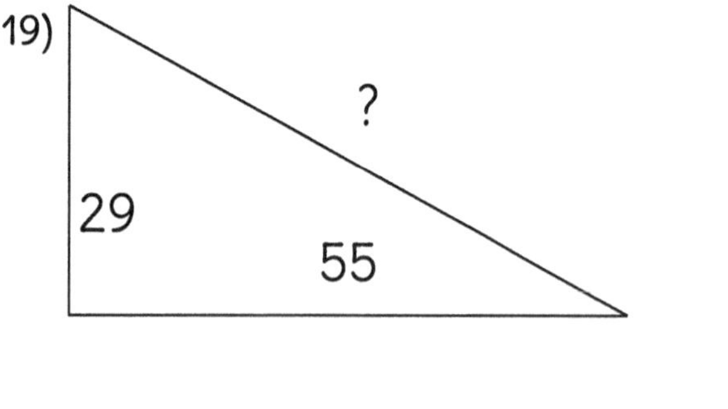

____

20)

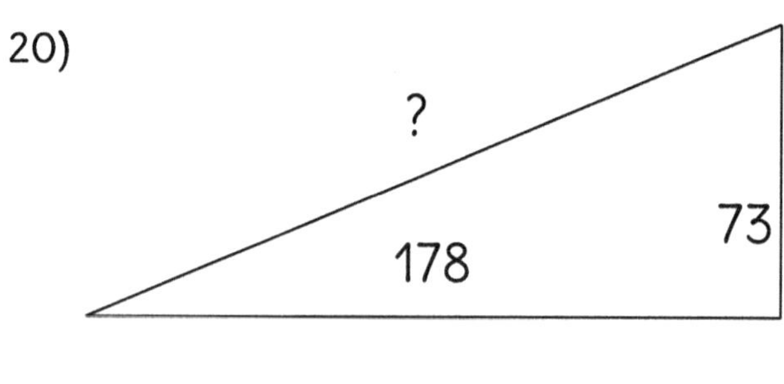

____

Volume and Surface Area

1)

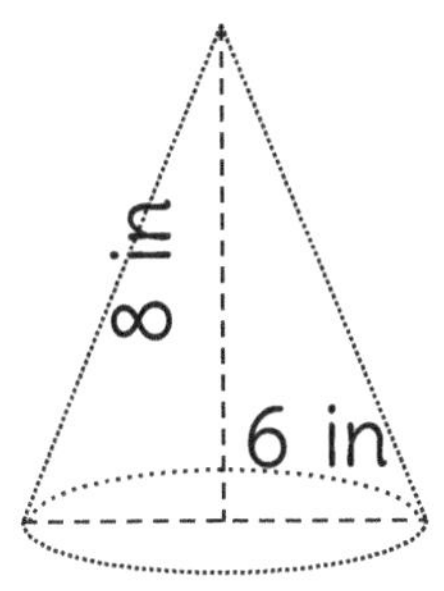

8 in

6 in

V = 75 in³

SA = 109 in²

2)

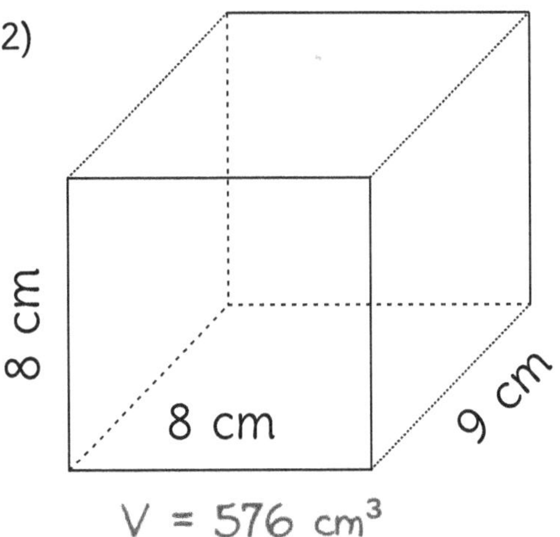

8 cm

8 cm

9 cm

V = 576 cm³

SA = 416 cm²

3)

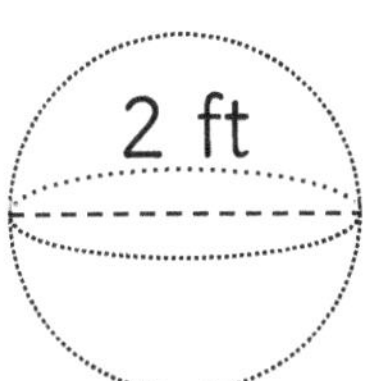

2 ft

4)

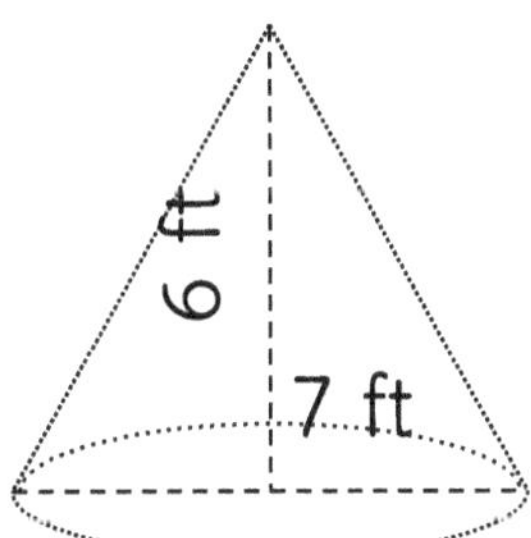

6 ft

7 ft

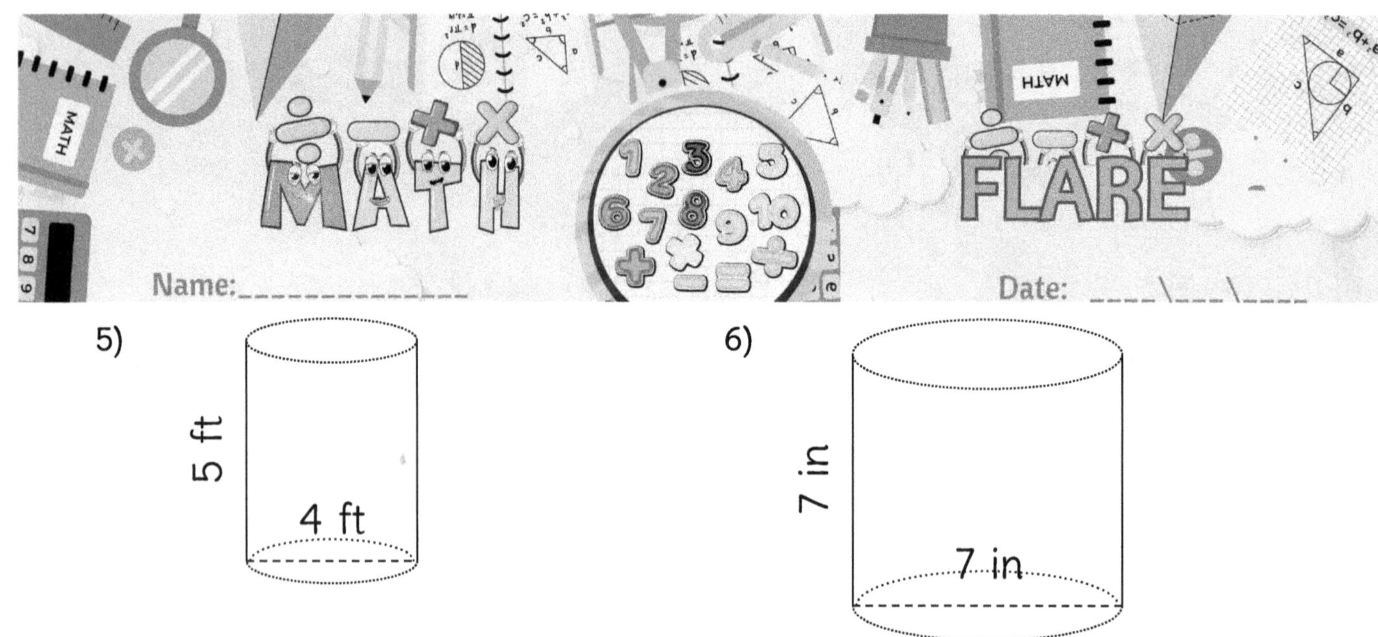

5)

5 ft

4 ft

6)

7 in

7 in

7)

6 in

5 in

8)

9 in

6 in

9 in

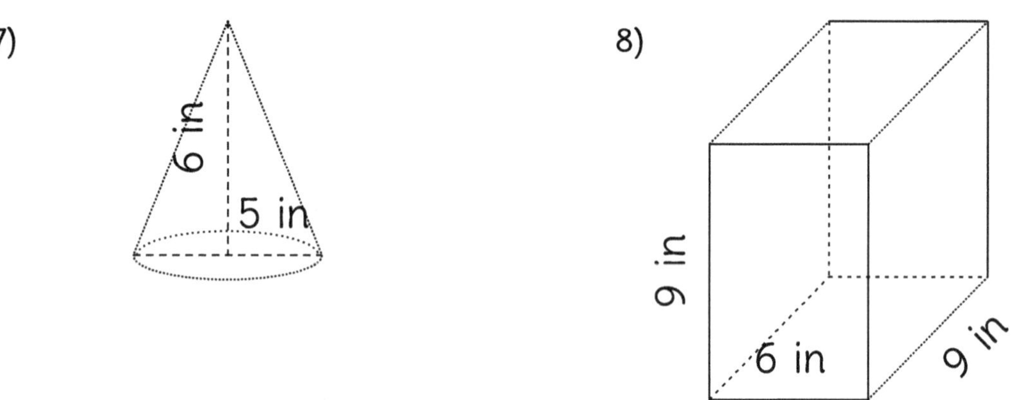

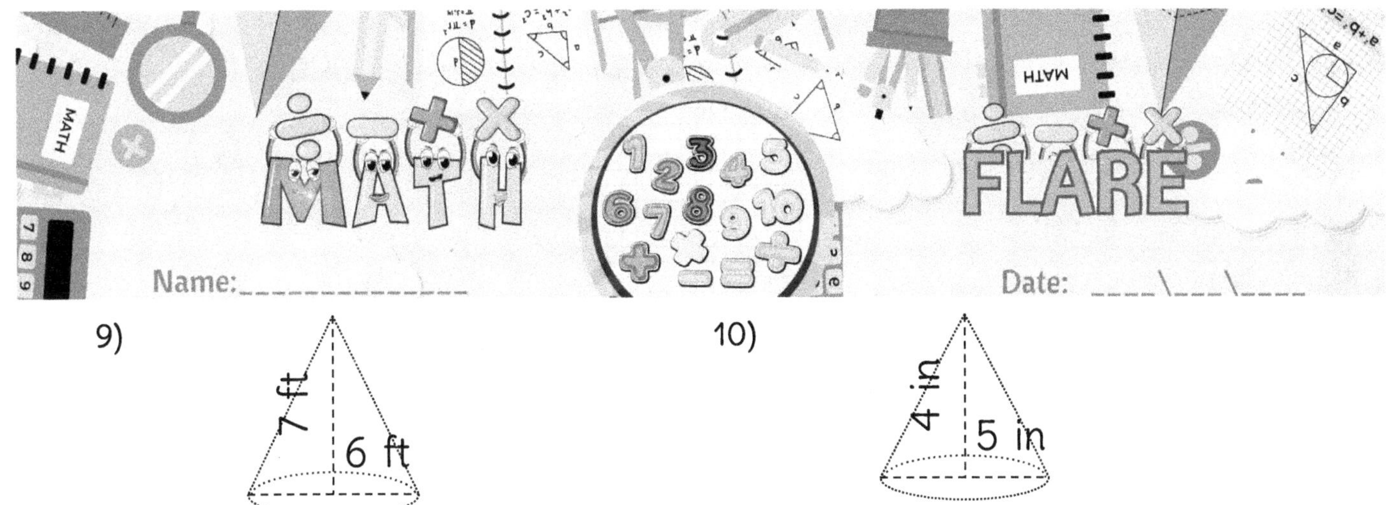

9)

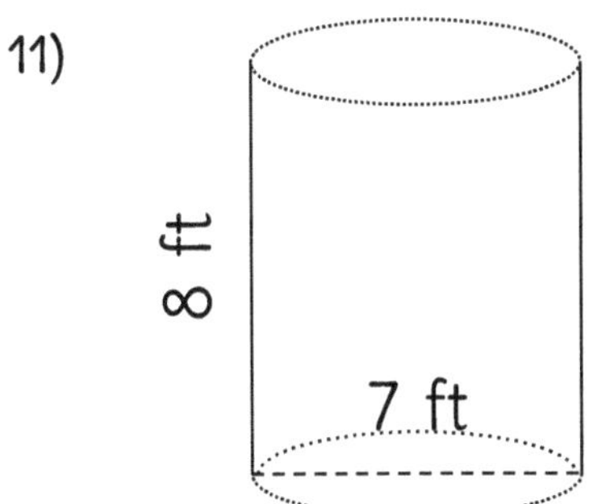

10)

11)

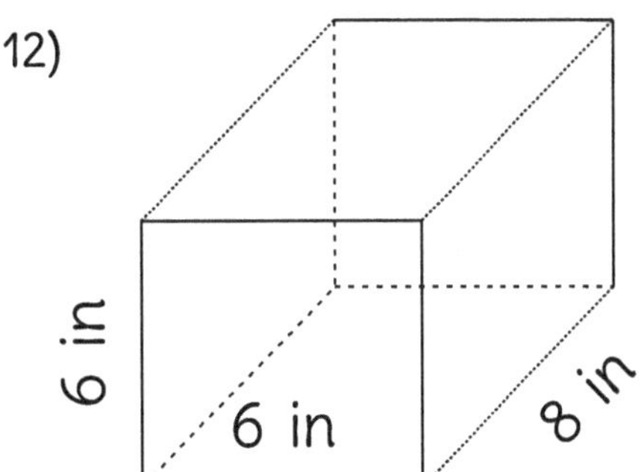

12)

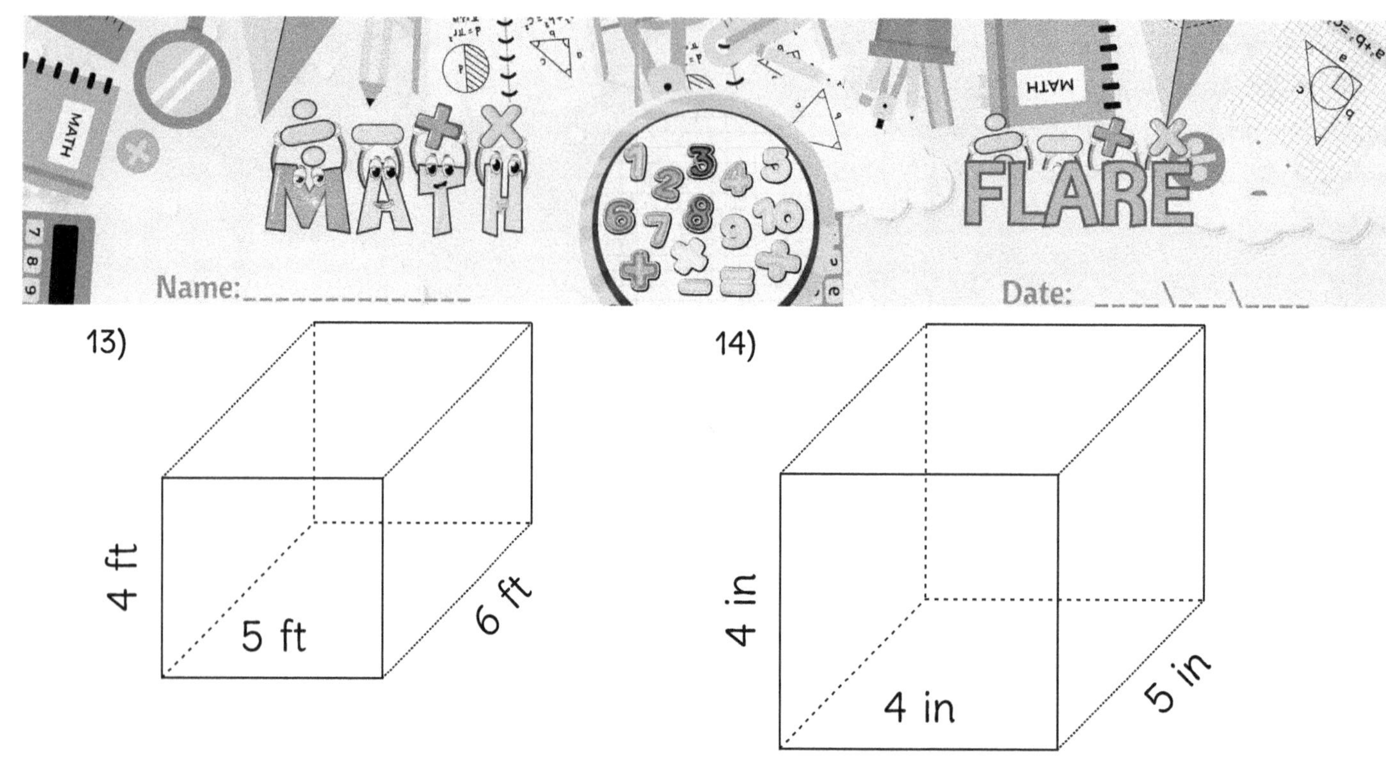

13)

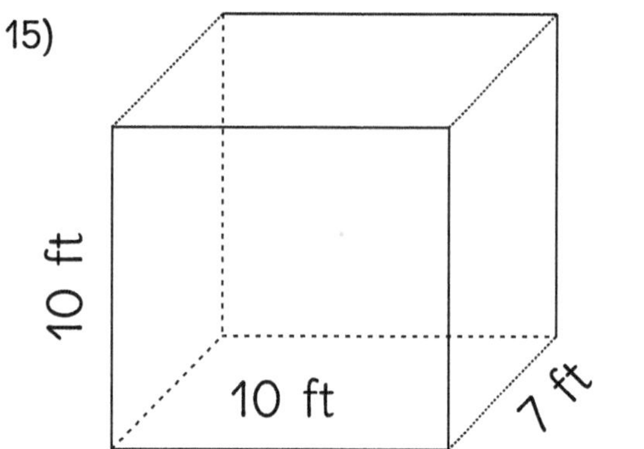

14)

15)

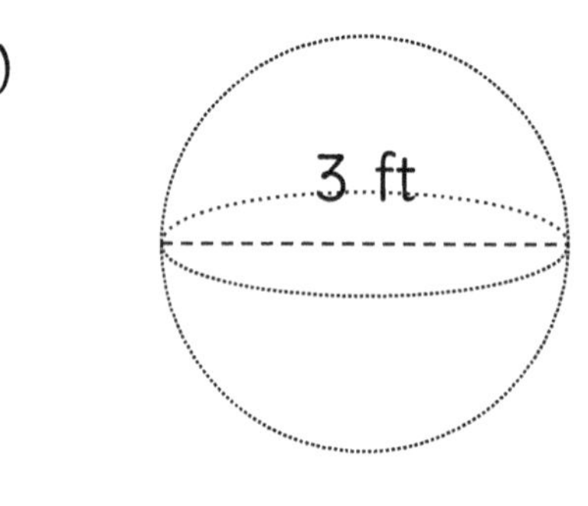

16)

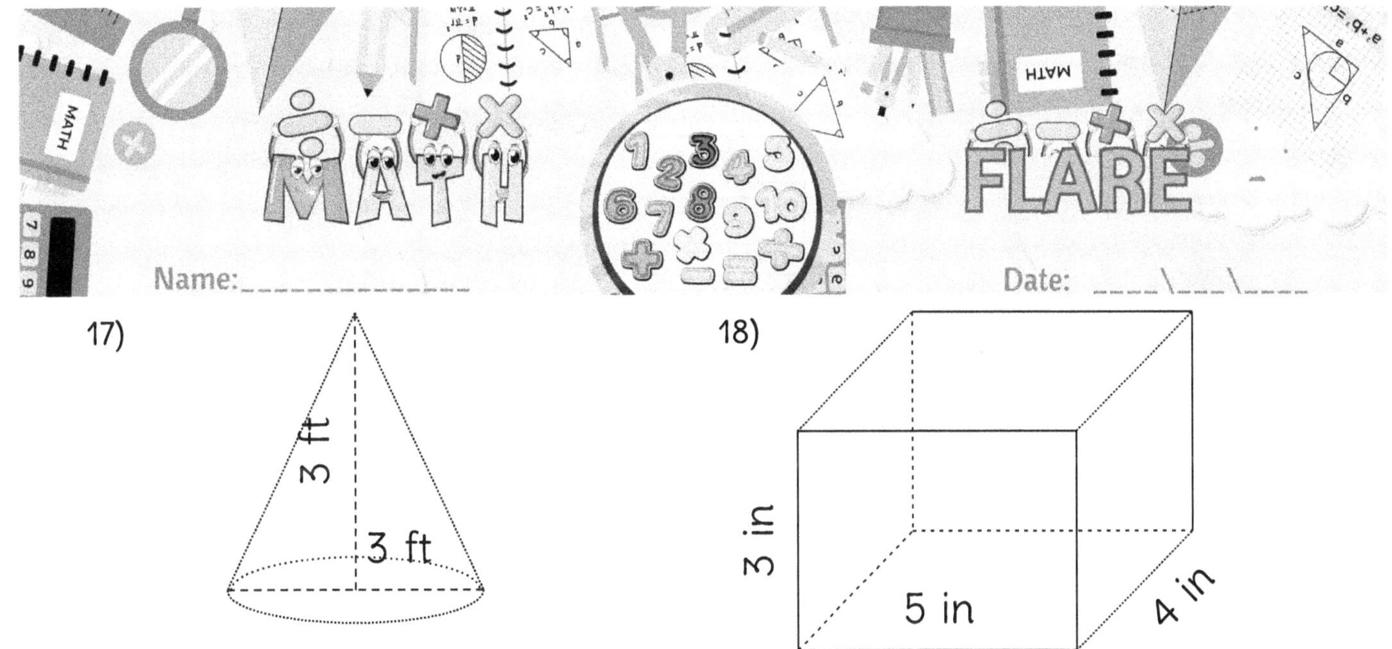

17)

18)

19)

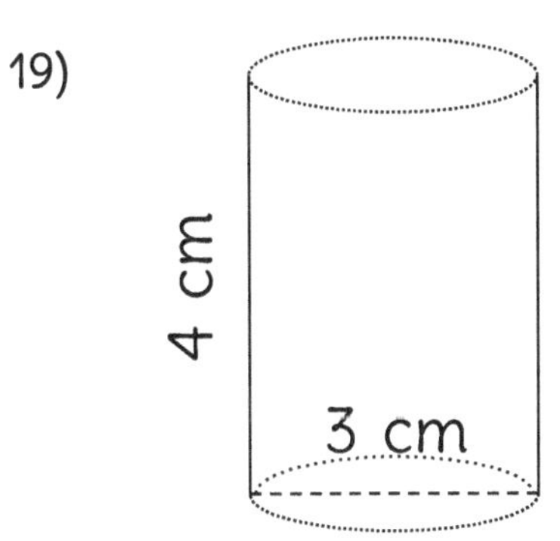

20)

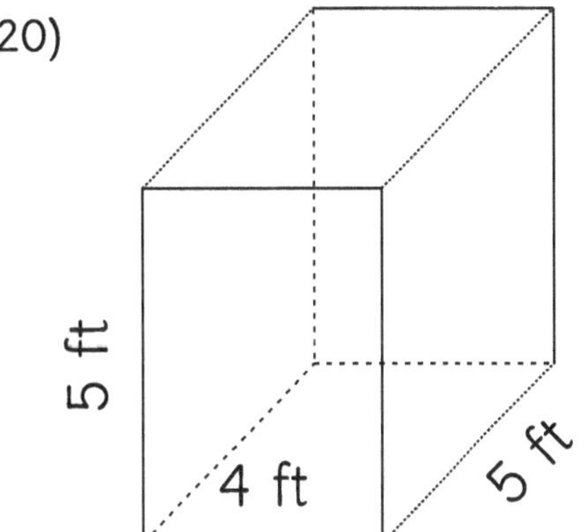

Name:________________   Date: ____________

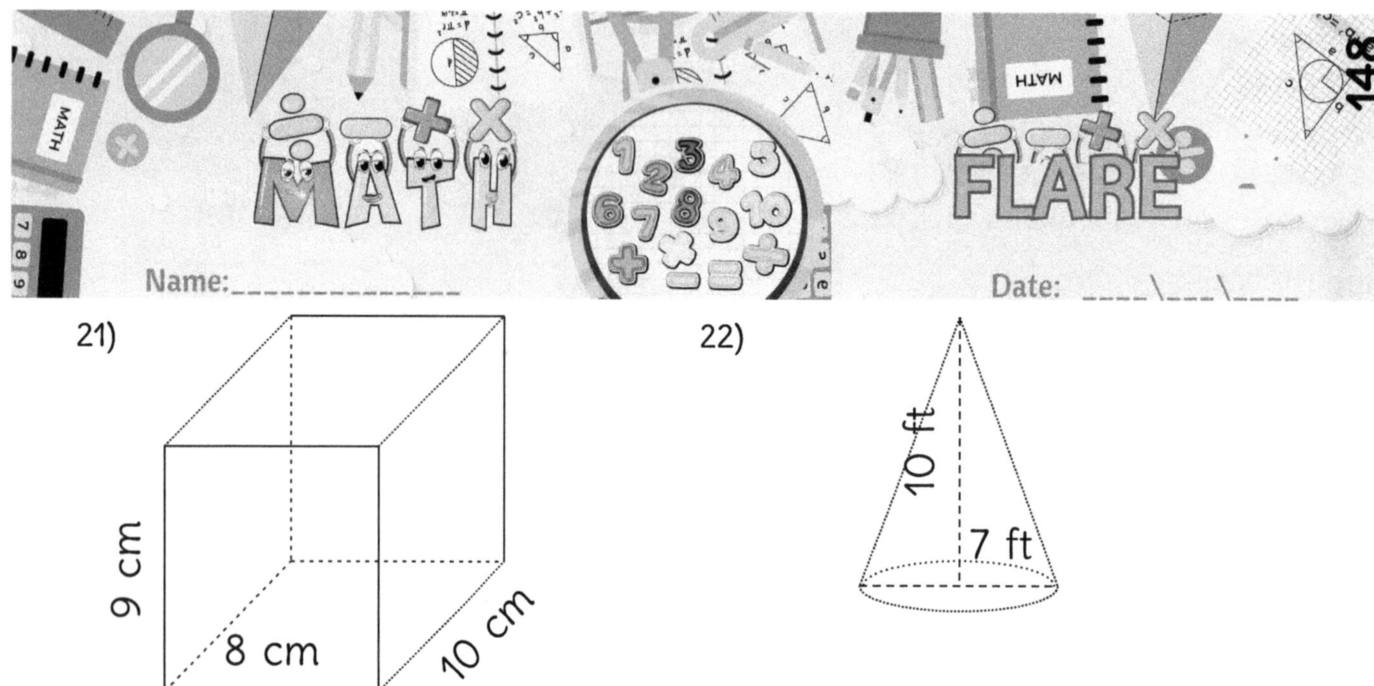

23)
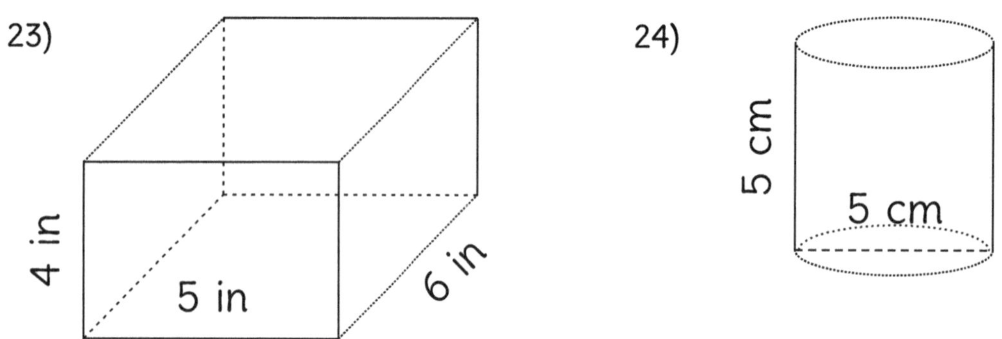

24)
5 cm
5 cm

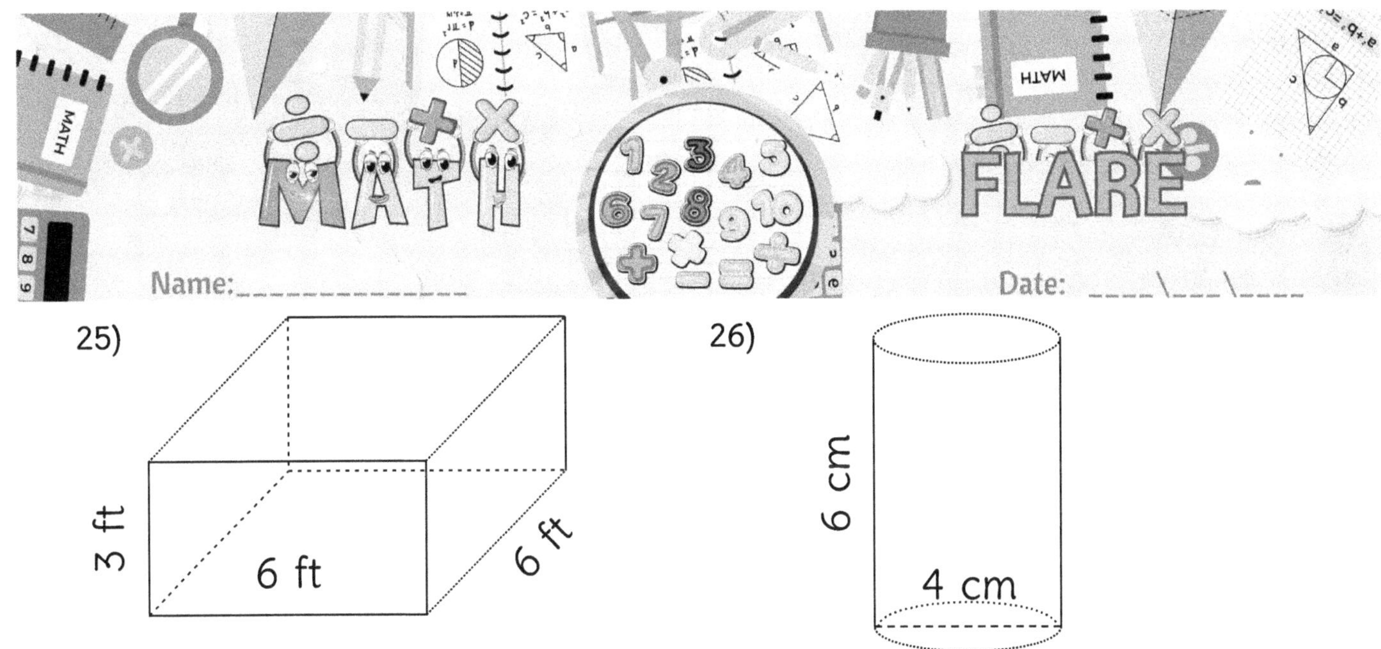

25)

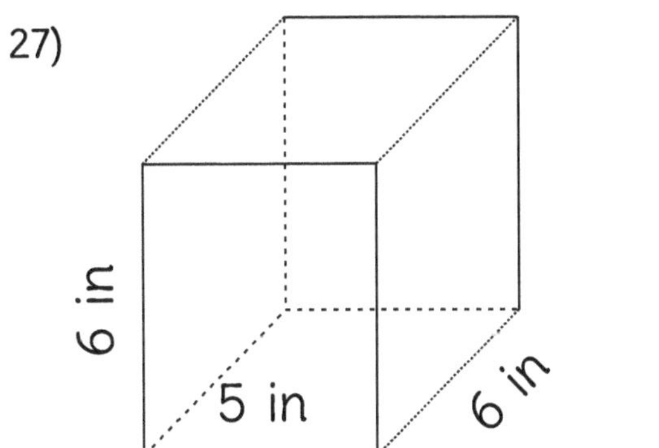

26)

27)

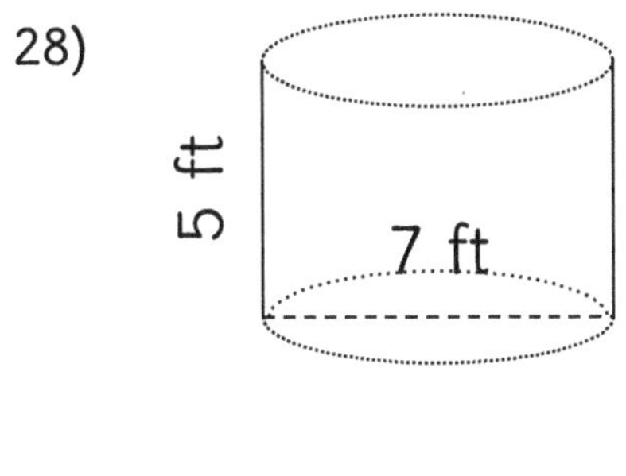

28)

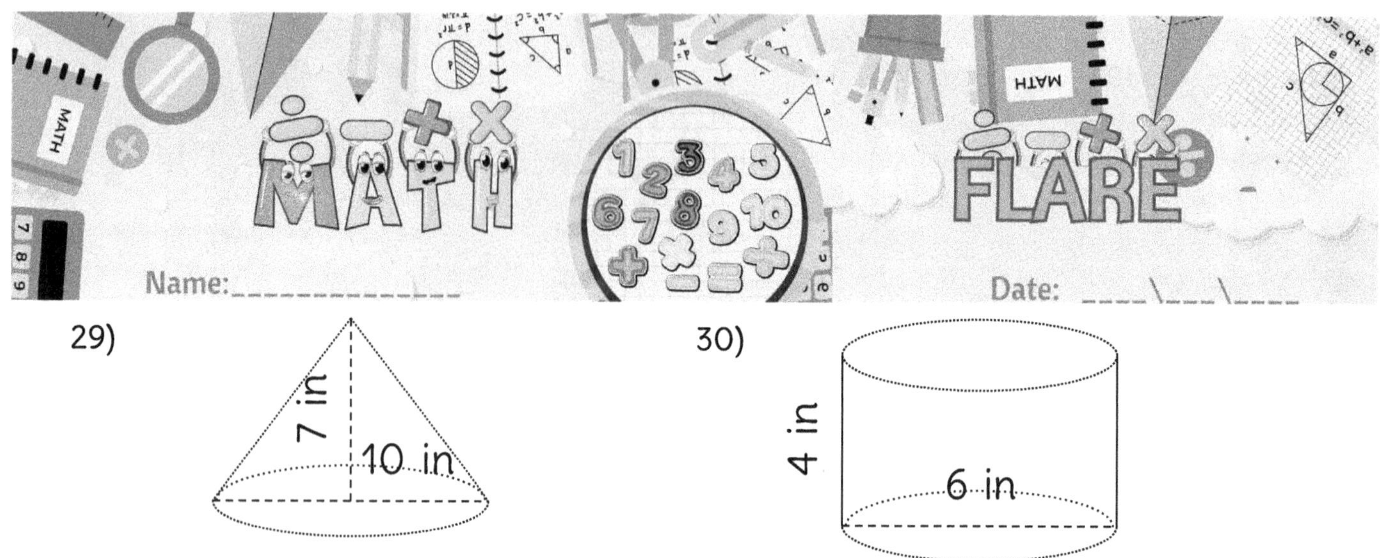

29)

30)

31)

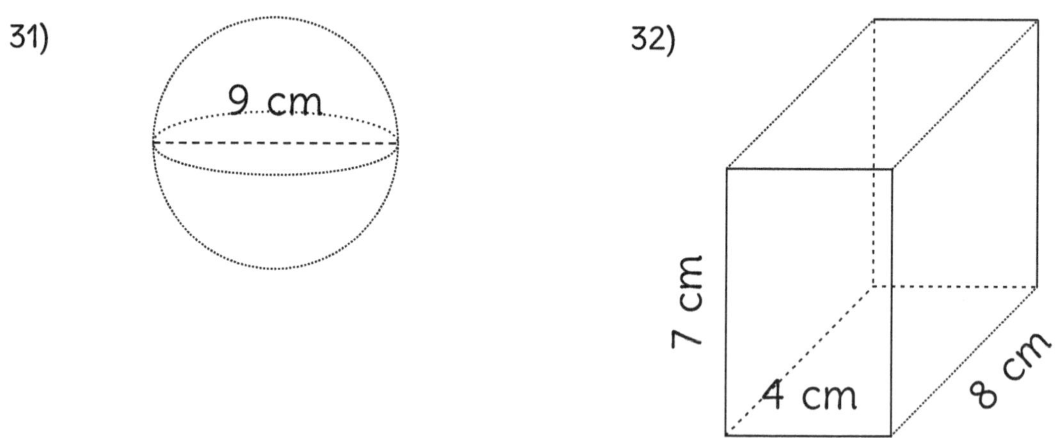

32)

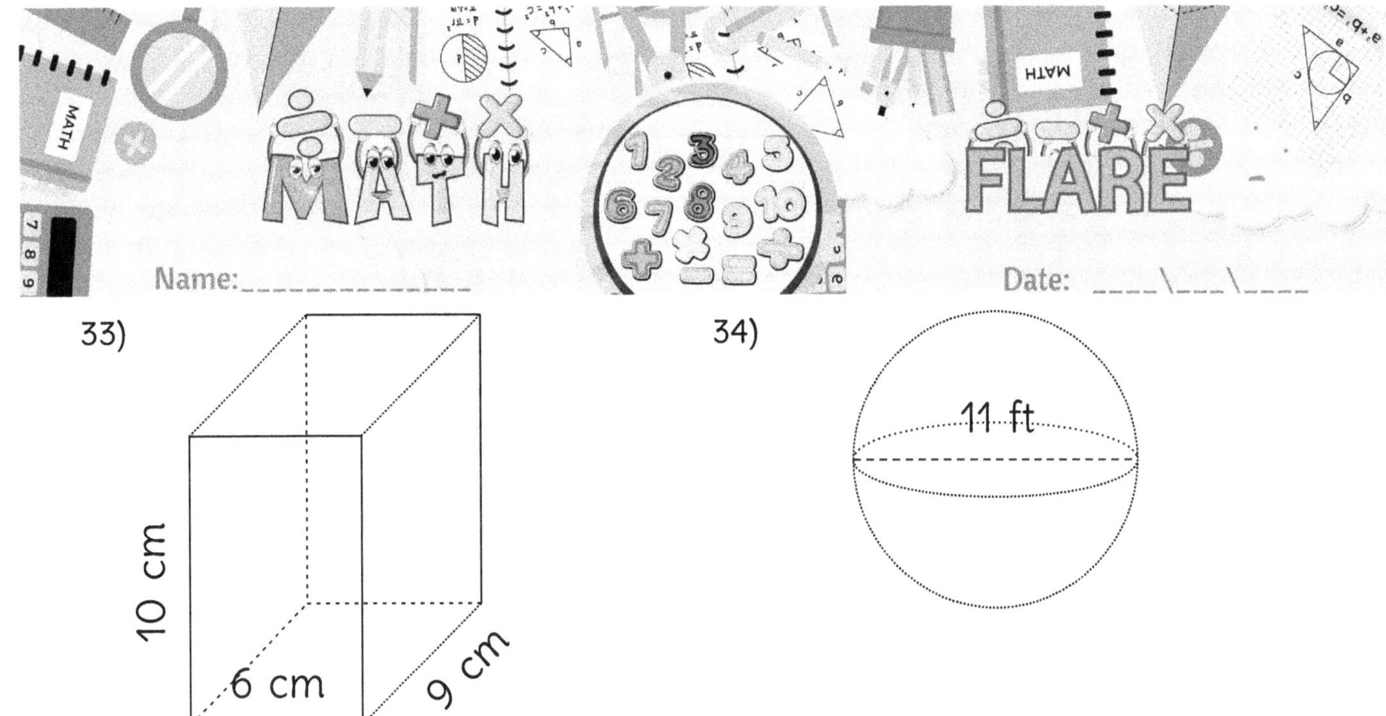

33)

34)

35)

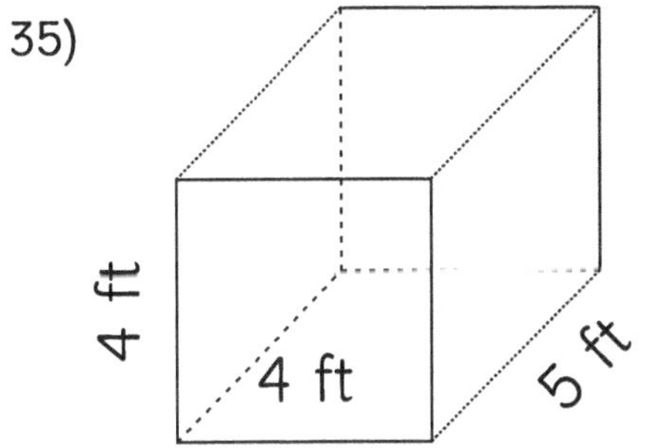

36)

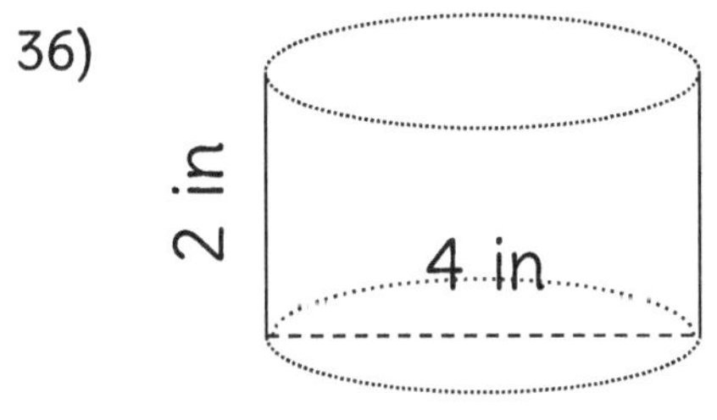

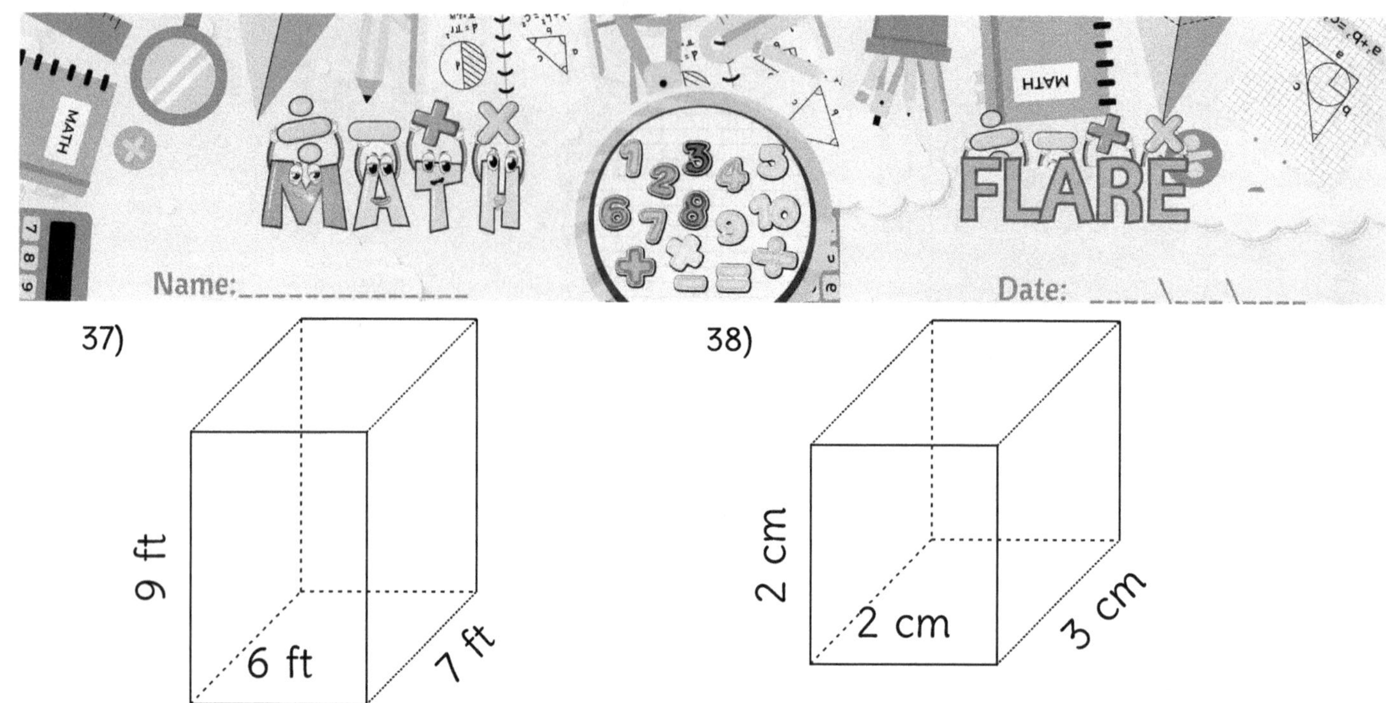

37)

9 ft
6 ft
7 ft

38)

2 cm
2 cm
3 cm

39)

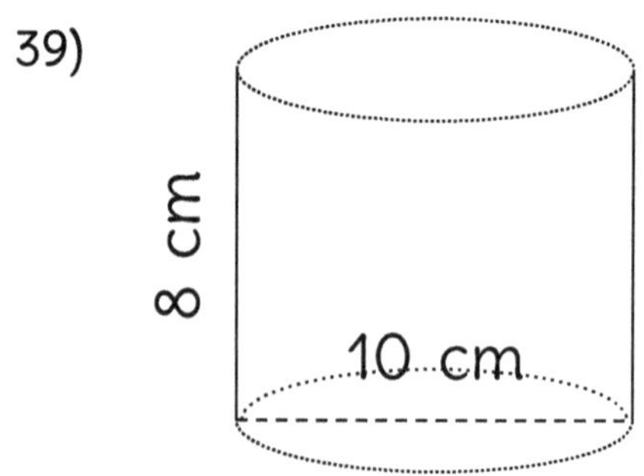

40)

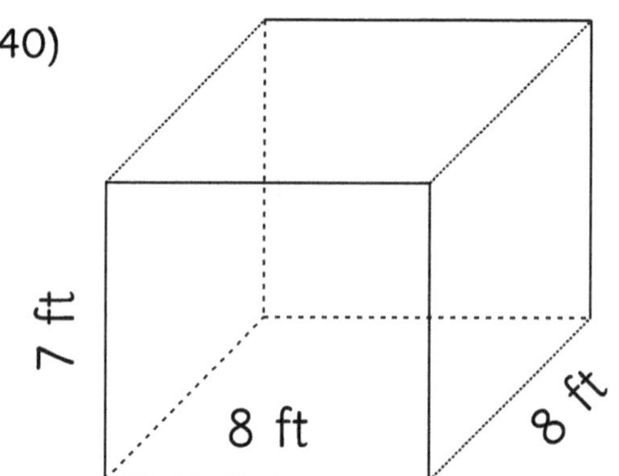

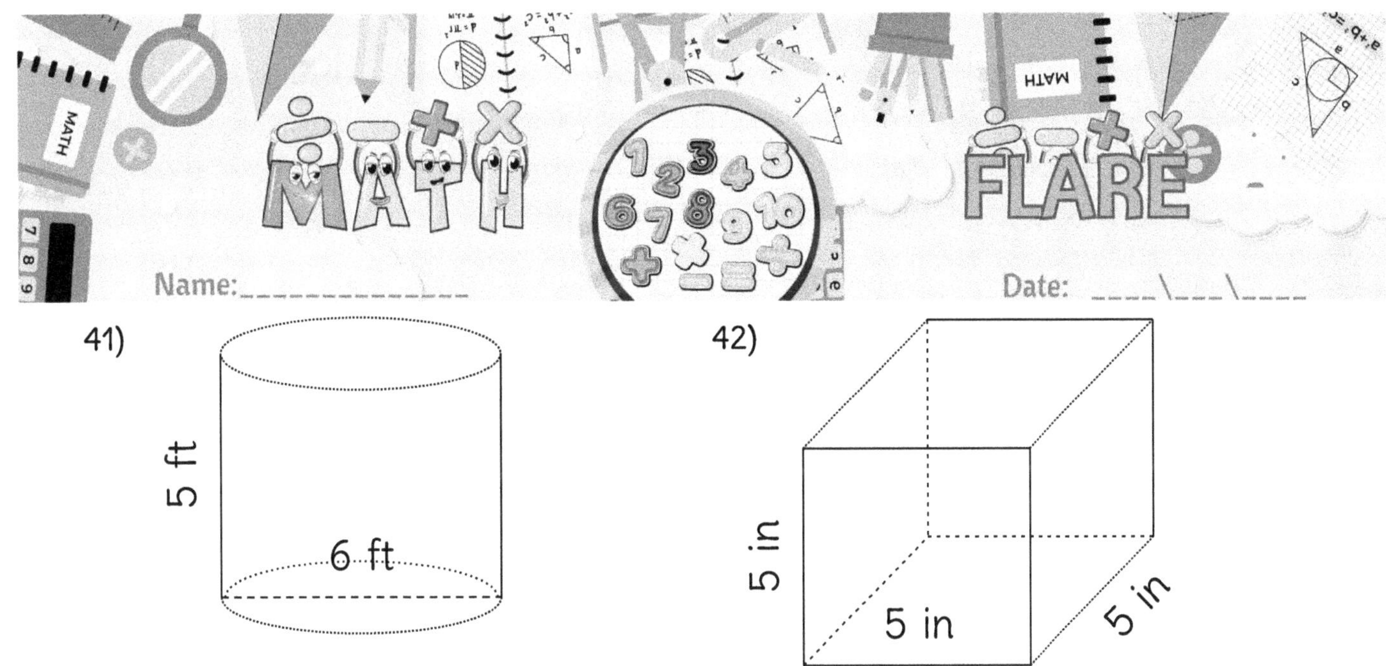

41)

5 ft

6 ft

42)

5 in

5 in

5 in

43) 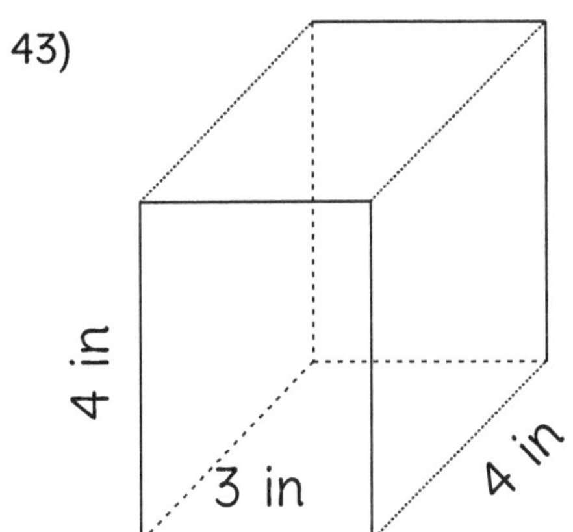

44) 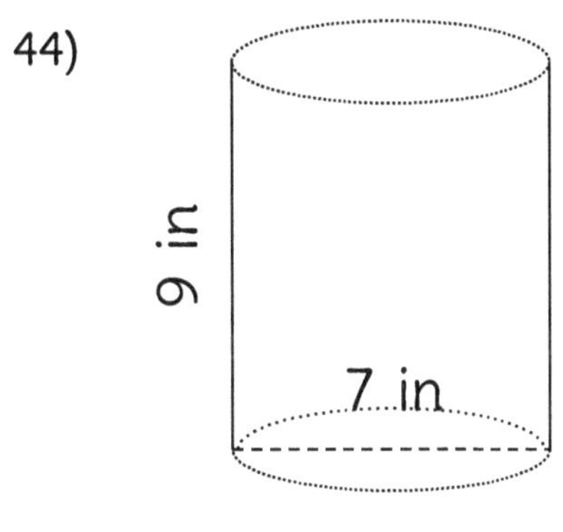

45)

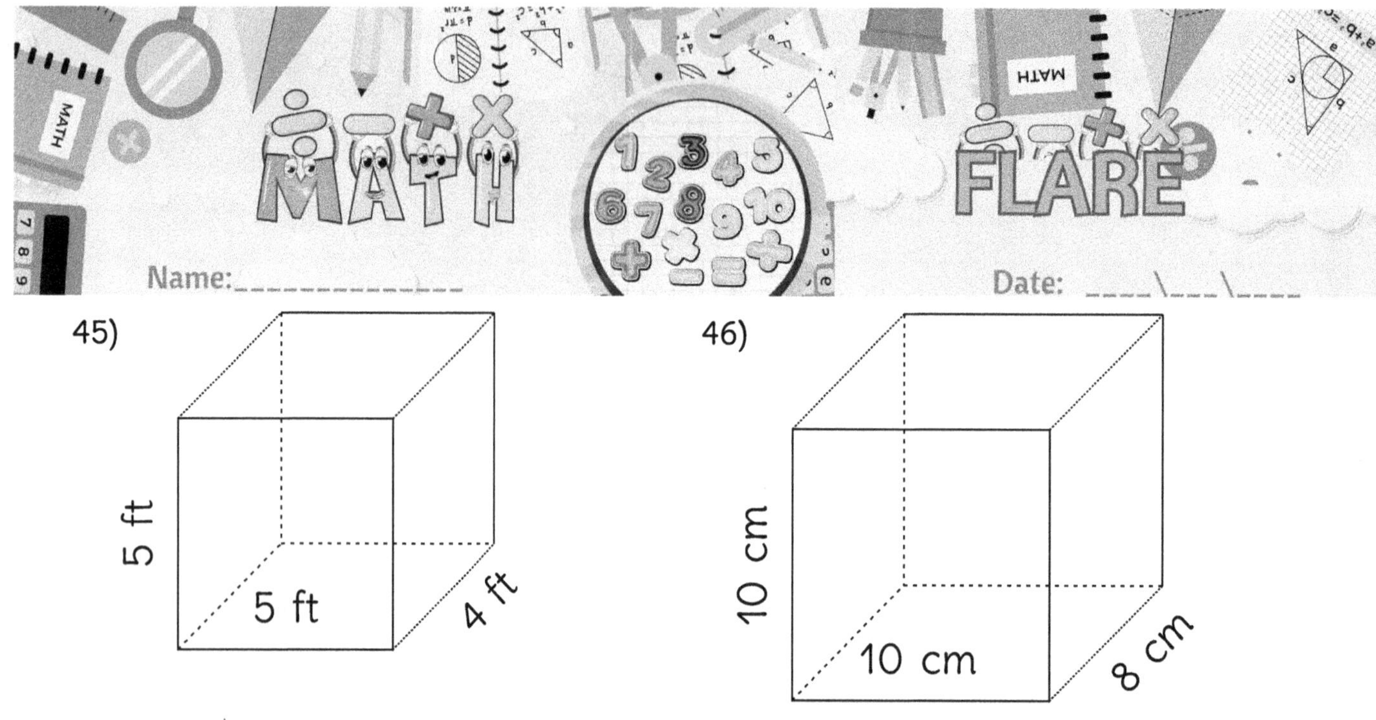

46)

47)

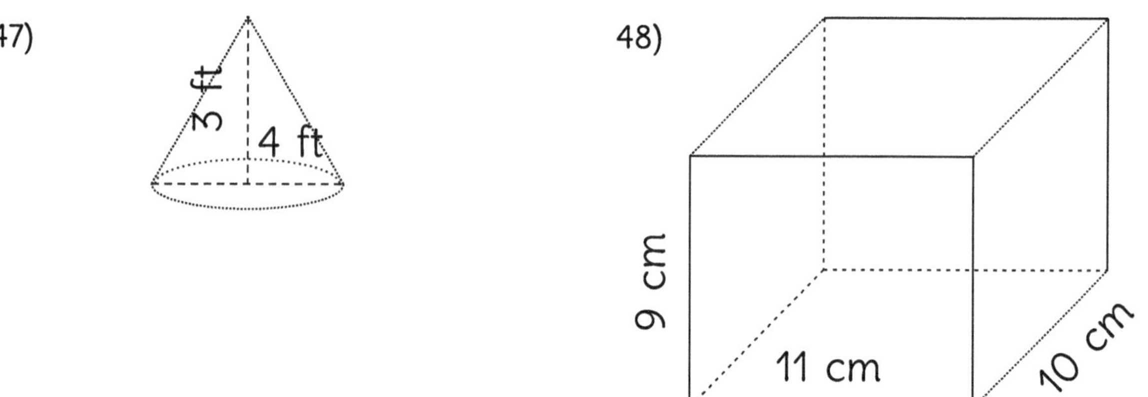

48)

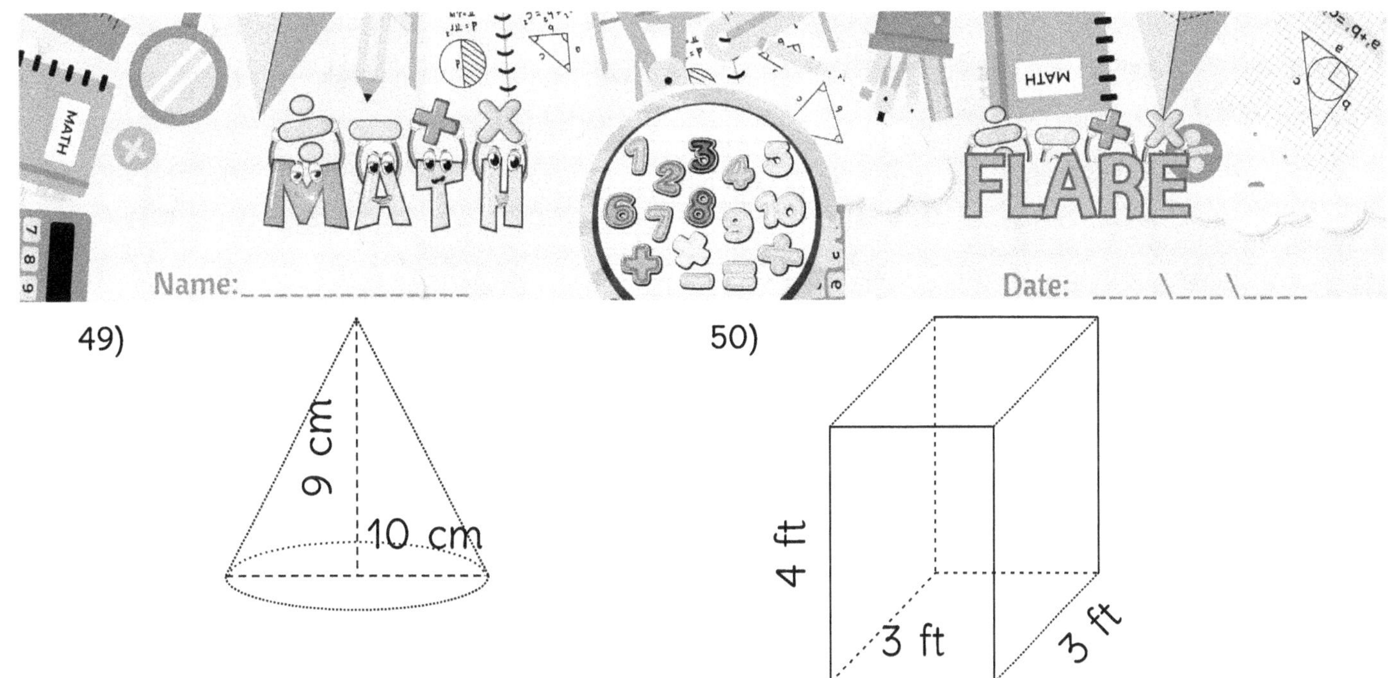

49)

50)

51)

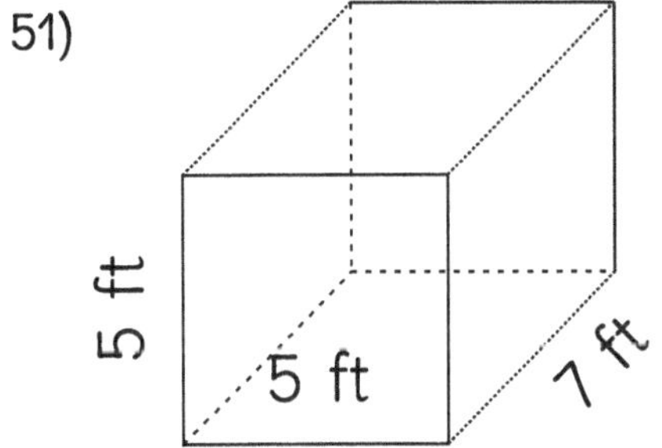

52)

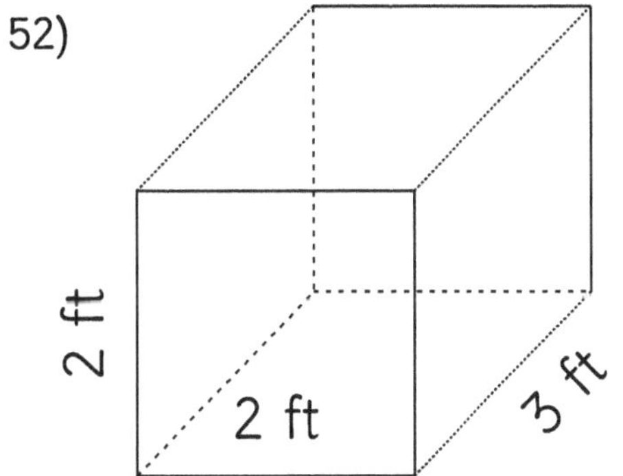

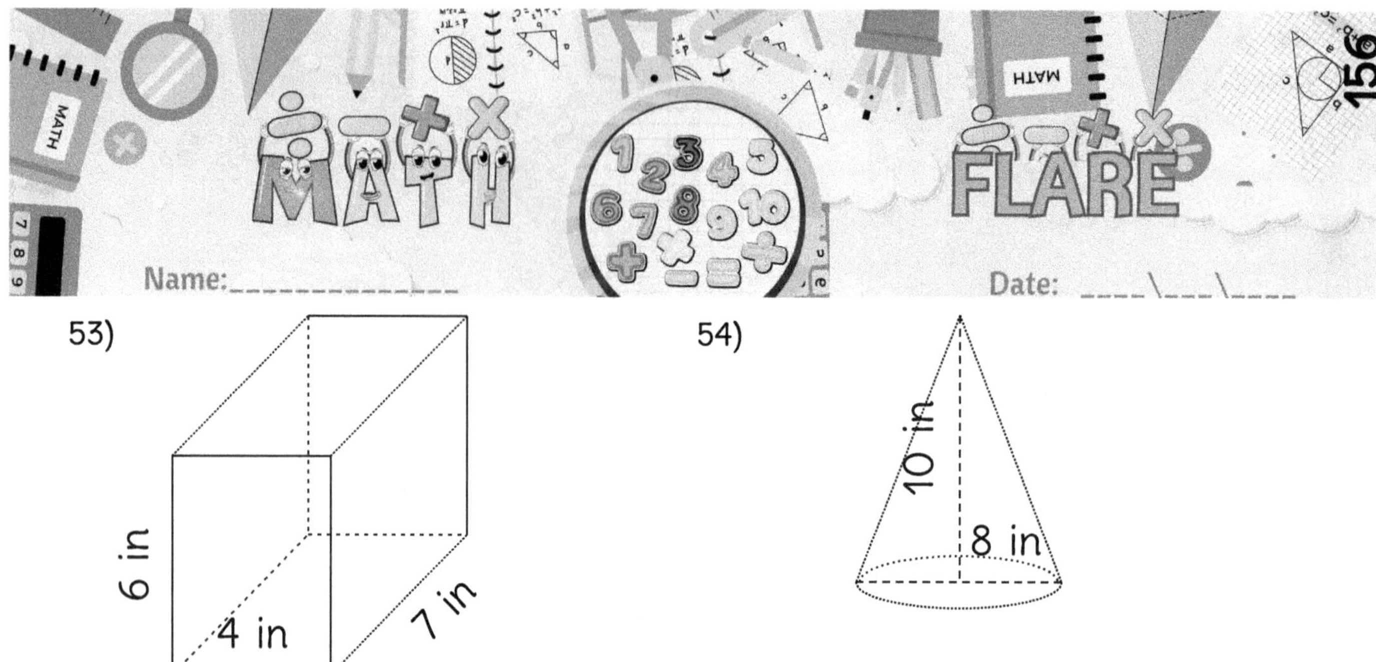

53)

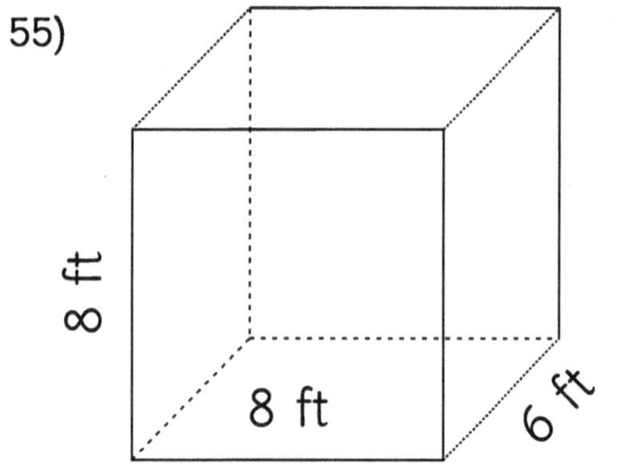

54)

55)

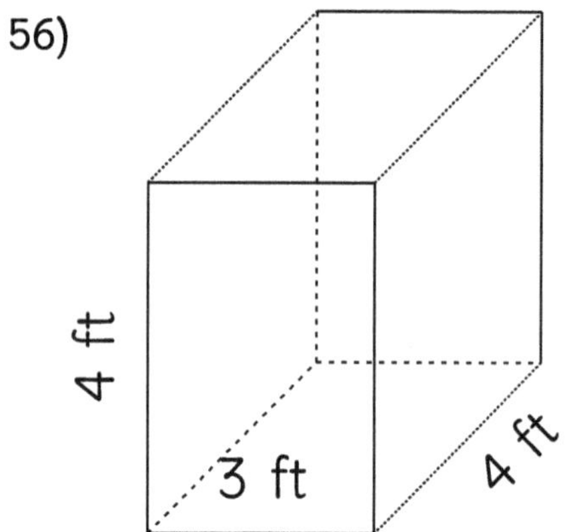

56)

MathFlare - Math Workbook 7th and 8th Grade

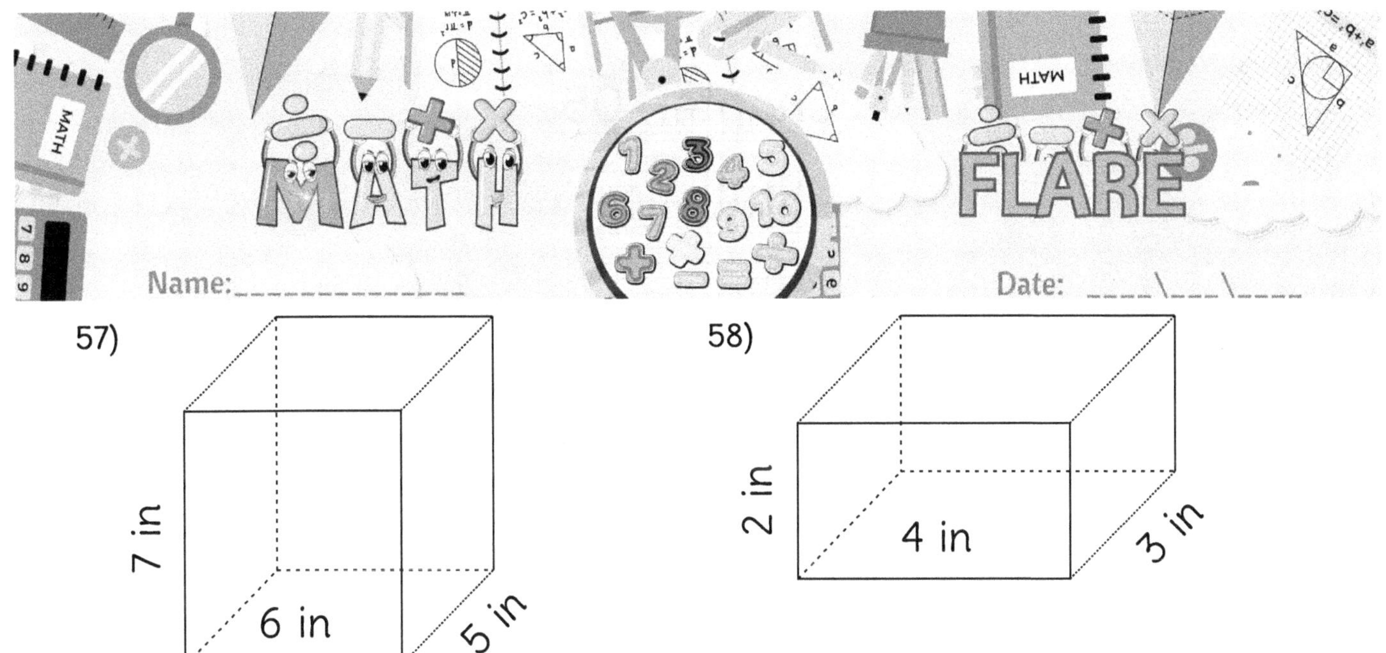

MATH
FLARE
Name:
Date:

7 in
6 in
5 in

2 in
4 in
3 in

4 ft
7 ft

2 in
2 in
2 in

57)

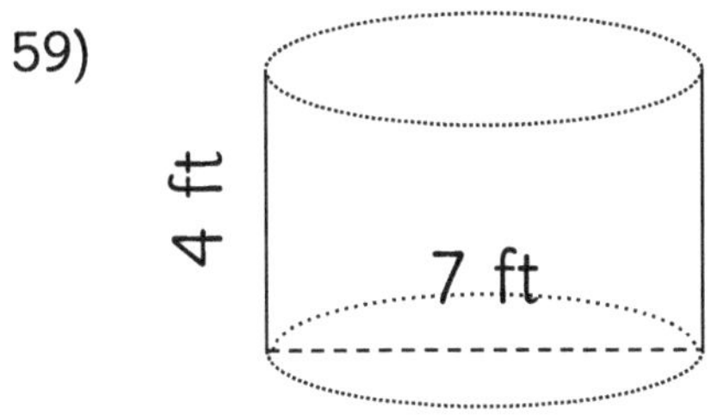

58)

59)

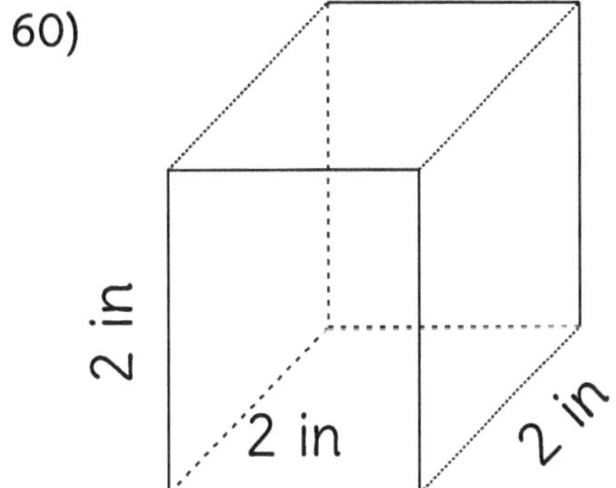

60)

Chapter. 05

Statistics

Mean

The mean, also known as the average, is a measure of central tendency.

To find the mean of a set of numbers:

- Add up all the numbers in the set.
- Divide the sum by the total count of numbers in the set.

For example: consider the set of numbers: 70, 72, 49, 69, 27, 76.

$$\text{Mean} = \frac{70 + 72 + 49 + 69 + 27 + 76}{6}$$

$$= \frac{363}{6} = 60.5$$

Median

The median is a measure of central tendency that represents the middle value of a dataset when the values are arranged in ascending or descending order.

To find the median of a set of numbers:

- Arrange the numbers in ascending or descending order.
- If the total count of numbers is odd, the median is the middle value.
- If the total count of numbers is even, the median is the average of the two middle values.

For example: consider the set of numbers: 70, 72, 49, 69, 27, 76.

$$27, 49, 69, 70, 72, 76$$

$$\text{Median} = \frac{69 + 70}{2} = \frac{139}{2} = 69.5$$

Mode

The mode in statistics refers to the value that appears most frequently in a given set of data.

Let's consider the following set of numbers:

$$\{2, 4, 4, 5, 6, 6, 6, 7, 8, 8\}$$

In this set, the number 6 appears three times, more than any other number. Therefore, the mode of this dataset is 6.

It's possible for a dataset to have more than one mode if two or more numbers appear with the same highest frequency. In such cases, the dataset is considered multimodal. If no number repeats, the dataset is considered to have no mode.

For example:

$$\{2, 4, 4, 4, 5, 6, 6, 6, 7, 8, 8\}$$

In this date set, 4 and 6 appear three times. Therefore, this dataset is multimodal.

Range

In statistics, the range refers to the difference between the largest and smallest values in a dataset. It represents the spread or variability of the data.

For example, consider the dataset $\{ 68, 13, 30, 18, 45, 76, 11\}$:

To calculate the range:

1. Arrange the data points in ascending order.

$$11, 13, 18, 30, 45, 68, 76$$

2. Subtract the smallest value from the largest value.

- The smallest value is 11.

- The largest value is 76.

$$\text{Range} = \text{Largest value} - \text{smallest value} = 76 - 11 = 65.$$

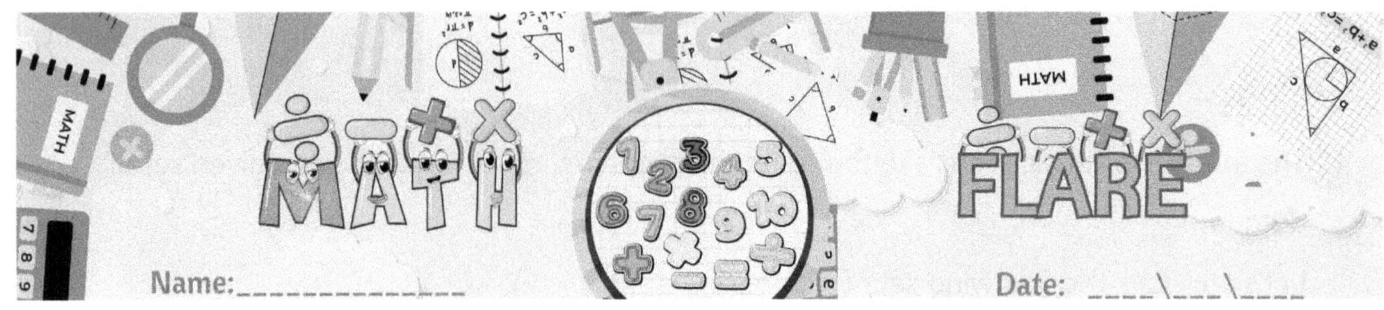

Mean, Median, Mode, and Range

Find the Mean, Median, Mode and Range of the following sets of data.

1) 32, 70, 80, 35, 79, 71, 66

Mean = 61.857   Median = 70

Mode = none   Range = 48

Range = 80 – 32

$$\text{Mean} = \frac{32, 70, 80, 35, 79, 71, 66}{7} = \frac{433}{7} = 61.857$$

Median = 32, 35, 66, 70, 71, 79, 80

70

2) 22, 30, 27, 4, 86, 2

Mean = ____   Median = ____

Mode = ____   Range = ____

3) 32, 39, 32, 4, 55, 19

Mean = ____   Median = ____

Mode = ____   Range = ____

4) 8, 83, 37, 14, 38, 49, 48

Mean = ____   Median = ____

Mode = ____   Range = ____

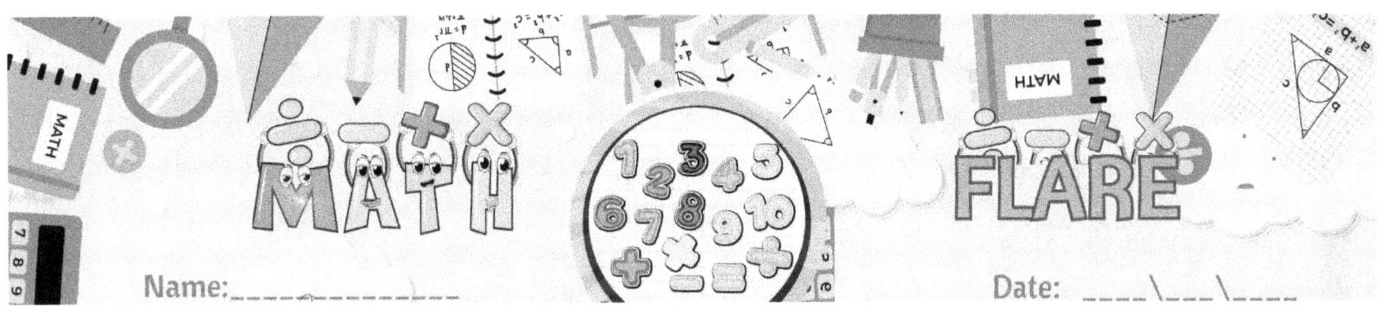

5) 99, 3, 36, 40, 97, 62, 89

   Mean = _______   Median = _____
   Mode = _______   Range = _____

6) 72, 74, 27, 99, 52, 32, 21

   Mean = _______   Median = _____
   Mode = _______   Range = _____

7) 22, 77, 83, 1, 96, 83, 91

   Mean = _______   Median = _____
   Mode = _______   Range = _____

8) 84, 15, 87, 81, 8, 90

   Mean = _______   Median = _____
   Mode = _______   Range = _____

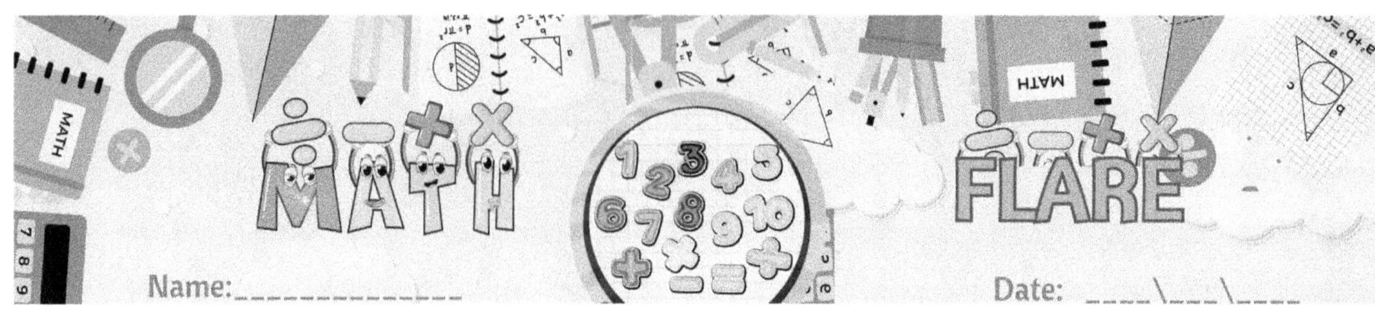

9) 83, 67, 94, 56, 42, 86

Mean = _______   Median = _____

Mode = _______   Range = _____

10) 32, 71, 63, 85, 89, 29, 41

Mean = _______   Median = _____

Mode = _______   Range = _____

11) 97, 30, 58, 13, 32, 51, 23

Mean = _______   Median = _____

Mode = _______   Range = _____

12) 97, 85, 6, 53, 13, 42, 65

Mean = _______   Median = _____

Mode = _______   Range = _____

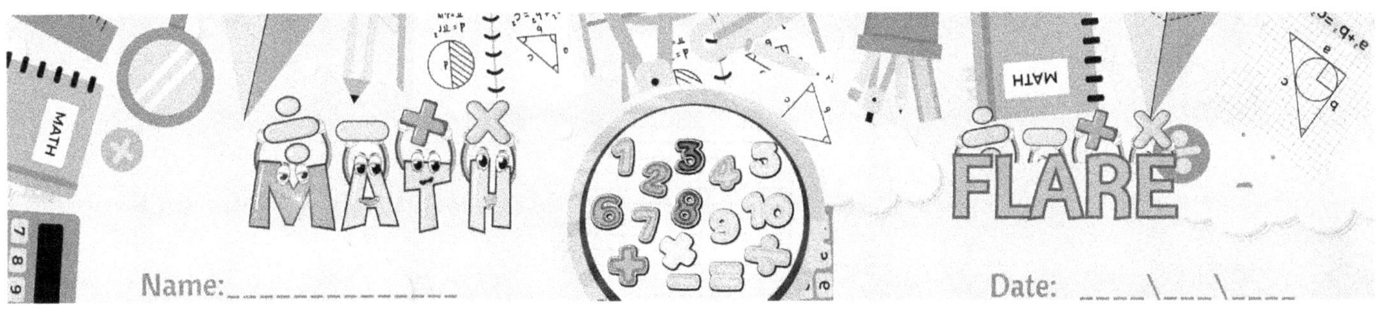

13) 57, 16, 88, 49, 59, 90, 72

Mean = _______   Median = _____

Mode = _______   Range = _____

14) 6, 6, 79, 70, 58, 66, 1

Mean = _______   Median = _____

Mode = _______   Range = _____

15) 49, 59, 91, 94, 71, 55

Mean = _______   Median = _____

Mode = _______   Range = _____

16) 85, 62, 26, 3, 55, 30, 85

Mean = _______   Median = _____

Mode = _______   Range = _____

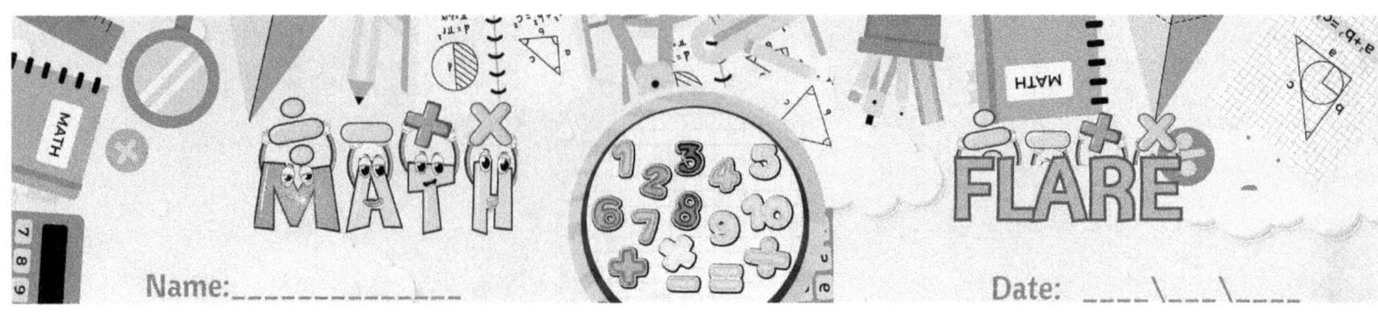

17) 92, 97, 61, 42, 44, 99, 21

Mean = _______   Median = _____

Mode = _______   Range = _____

18) 75, 56, 75, 37, 31, 39, 69

Mean = _______   Median = _____

Mode = _______   Range = _____

19) 92, 24, 78, 42, 74, 84

Mean = _______   Median = _____

Mode = _______   Range = _____

20) 22, 49, 27, 15, 59, 41

Mean = _____   Median = _____

Mode = _____   Range = _____

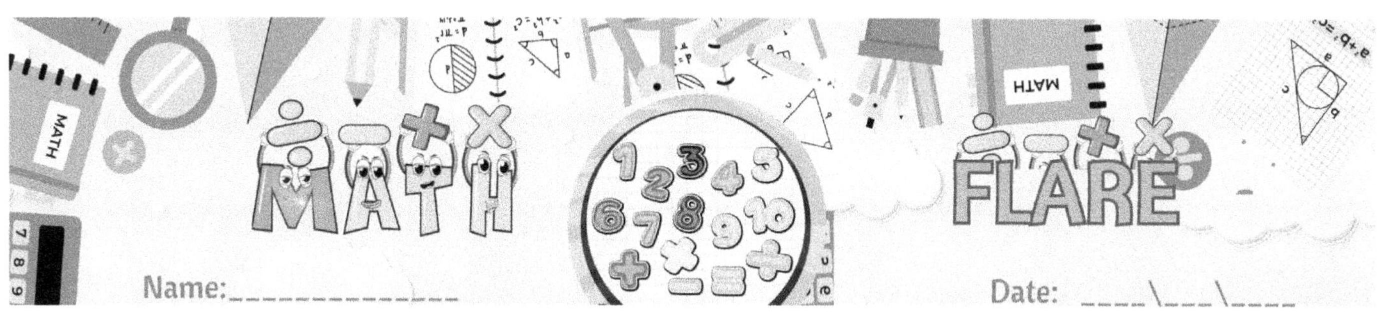

Name:______________   Date: ________________

21) 86, 79, 94, 89, 86, 94, 29

   Mean = _______   Median = _____
   Mode = _______   Range = _____

22) 6, 80, 9, 45, 38, 27

   Mean = _______   Median = _____
   Mode = _______   Range = _____

23) 58, 46, 25, 93, 84, 55

   Mean = _______   Median = _____
   Mode = _______   Range = _____

24) 64, 33, 86, 93, 38, 48, 60

   Mean = _______   Median = _____
   Mode = _______   Range = _____

ANSWERS

Page 1: Proportional Relationship

1. 17	2. 24	3. 90	4. 36	5. 4	6. 6	7. 1
8. 14	9. 60	10. 25	11. 6	12. 28	13. 57	14. 24
15. 50	16. 7	17. 16	18. 11	19. 32	20. 17	21. 4
22. 200	23. 20	24. 60	25. 24	26. 6	27. 2	28. 152
29. 8	30. 10	31. 7	32. 60	33. 18	34. 3	

Page 4: Percentage

1. 10%	2. 50%	3. 100%	4. 70%	5. 70%	6. 4%
7. 300	8. 35%	9. 18	10. 200%	11. 25%	12. 18
13. 30	14. 30	15. 240	16. 800	17. 40	18. 300
19. 72	20. 100%	21. 0.2	22. 720	23. 75%	24. 9%
25. 200	26. 20%	27. 80%	28. 5%	29. 300%	30. 20%
31. 1400	32. 300%	33. 40	34. 40%	35. 6%	36. 1%

Page 7:

1. 0.6%	2. 0.2%	3. 329	4. 7	5. 0.5%
6. 0.176	7. 927	8. 1.707	9. 0.9%	10. 0.12
11. 84	12. 2.3%	13. 5	14. 7.5%	15. 1.912
16. 323.986	17. 1.536	18. 378.72	19. 7	20. 5
21. 49.8%	22. 1.125	23. 0.126	24. 217	25. 4.526
26. 81	27. 0.7%	28. 7	29. 7.4%	30. 39.4%

31. 0.2%   32. 753   33. 18.445   34. 0.6%   35. 3

36. 0.068   37. 38.8%   38. 0.5%   39. 0.132   40. 74

41. 0.294   42. 0.9%   43. 2   44. 257   45. 162

46. 228.897

Page 11:   Word Problems: Percent

1. $171.00   2. $72.00   3. 17   4. $54.00   5. $27.00

6. 9   7. 38   8. $101.00   9. $54.00   10. 73

11. $4.00   12. 49   13. $2.00   14. 51   15. $29.00

16. 2   17. 6   18. 2   19. 1   20. 3

21. 68   22. $89.00   23. 2   24. 4   25. $74.00

26. $3.00   27. 2   28. 108   29. $53.00   30. 4

Page 18:   Ratio and Proportion Word Problems

1. 23.14   2. 14.93   3. 9.29   4. 361.4   5. 19.5

6. 11.5   7. 4.2   8. 3.56   9. 3.6   10. 6

11. 14.4   12. 544.8   13. 2.26   14. 140.8   15. 9

16. 10.71   17. 24.39   18. 36   19. 23.5   20. 272

21. 9.75   22. 33.64   23. 10.5   24. 3.55   25. 50.33

26. 5.14   27. 21.09   28. 3.71   29. 487.67   30. 1.44

Page 28: Ratio Conversions

1.

	Ratio	Fraction	Percent	Decimal
a.	12:19	12/19	63.2%	0.632
b.	1:2	1/2	50%	0.5
c.	6:10	6/10	60%	0.6
d.	1:4	1/4	25%	0.25
e.	3:14	3/14	21.4%	0.214
f.	10:18	10/18	55.6%	0.556
g.	2:5	2/5	40%	0.4
h.	11:16	11/16	68.8%	0.688
i.	3:3	3/3	100%	1
j.	4:10	4/10	40%	0.4
k.	8:11	8/11	72.7%	0.727
l.	6:16	6/16	37.5%	0.375
m.	12:18	12/18	66.7%	0.667
n.	7:19	7/19	36.8%	0.368
o.	9:12	9/12	75%	0.75

2.

	Ratio	Fraction	Percent	Decimal
a.	1:1	1/1	100%	1
b.	4:10	4/10	40%	0.4
c.	1:4	1/4	25%	0.25
d.	16:19	16/19	84.2%	0.842
e.	1:10	1/10	10%	0.1
f.	6:18	6/18	33.3%	0.333
g.	2:11	2/11	18.2%	0.182
h.	5:18	5/18	27.8%	0.278
i.	14:16	14/16	87.5%	0.875
j.	5:6	5/6	83.3%	0.833
k.	7:13	7/13	53.8%	0.538
l.	4:5	4/5	80%	0.8
m.	4:6	4/6	66.7%	0.667
n.	11:20	11/20	55%	0.55
o.	2:5	2/5	40%	0.4

3.

	Ratio	Fraction	Percent	Decimal
a.	4:4	4/4	100%	1
b.	3:14	3/14	21.4%	0.214
c.	14:20	14/20	70%	0.7
d.	9:18	9/18	50%	0.5
e.	8:16	8/16	50%	0.5
f.	13:17	13/17	76.5%	0.765
g.	9:16	9/16	56.2%	0.562
h.	1:4	1/4	25%	0.25
i.	7:14	7/14	50%	0.5
j.	1:8	1/8	12.5%	0.125
k.	1:17	1/17	5.9%	0.059
l.	6:12	6/12	50%	0.5
m.	9:12	9/12	75%	0.75
n.	7:17	7/17	41.2%	0.412
o.	1:7	1/7	14.3%	0.143

4.

	Ratio	Fraction	Percent	Decimal
a.	10:19	10/19	52.6%	0.526
b.	2:2	2/2	100%	1
c.	1:4	1/4	25%	0.25
d.	7:17	7/17	41.2%	0.412
e.	9:15	9/15	60%	0.6
f.	1:13	1/13	7.7%	0.077
g.	12:16	12/16	75%	0.75
h.	2:11	2/11	18.2%	0.182
i.	2:9	2/9	22.2%	0.222
j.	14:17	14/17	82.4%	0.824
k.	13:20	13/20	65%	0.65
l.	7:12	7/12	58.3%	0.583
m.	1:3	1/3	33.3%	0.333
n.	6:13	6/13	46.2%	0.462
o.	5:17	5/17	29.4%	0.294

5.

	Ratio	Fraction	Percent	Decimal
a.	2:9	2/9	22.2%	0.222
b.	20:20	20/20	100%	1
c.	7:20	7/20	35%	0.35
d.	12:15	12/15	80%	0.8
e.	8:10	8/10	80%	0.8
f.	11:15	11/15	73.3%	0.733
g.	12:14	12/14	85.7%	0.857
h.	3:4	3/4	75%	0.75
i.	4:20	4/20	20%	0.2
j.	1:4	1/4	25%	0.25
k.	1:10	1/10	10%	0.1
l.	4:11	4/11	36.4%	0.364
m.	3:5	3/5	60%	0.6
n.	10:18	10/18	55.6%	0.556
o.	3:6	3/6	50%	0.5

Page 33: Order of Operations (PEMDAS)

1. 160
2. 14
3. 18
4. -0.7
5. -10
6. 10
7. 9
8. 37
9. 16
10. 11
11. 117
12. 56
13. 81
14. 17
15. 22
16. 120
17. -5
18. 46
19. 49
20. 0.9
21. 23
22. -10
23. 127
24. 25
25. 9
26. 31
27. 75
28. 8
29. 12
30. 25
31. 1.7
32. 62
33. 5
34. 17
35. 405
36. 68
37. 136
38. 24
39. 388
40. 9
41. 2.6
42. -19
43. 16
44. 16
45. 10
46. 101
47. 5
48. 586

Page 38: Evaluate Expressions

1. 6	2. 7	3. 4	4. 7 or -7	5. 5 or -6
6. 2	7. 6 or -7	8. 3 or -4	9. 2 or -3	10. 2
11. 9	12. 1	13. 6	14. 3	15. 4
16. 7	17. 2 or -2	18. 6	19. 1 or -1	20. 1
21. 4	22. 9	23. 4	24. 1	25. 6
26. 5	27. 3	28. 4	29. 2	30. 1
31. 4	32. 3	33. 5	34. 2 or -2	35. 6
36. 8	37. 9	38. 8 or -5	39. 1	40. 1

Page 48: Solving Inequalities

1. $z \le -7$	2. $z \ge 2$	3. $x < -7$	4. $k < 4/5$	5. $m > 9$
6. $m < -40$	7. $k < -6$	8. $y > 0$	9. $m \ge -2$	10. $x > 4/3$
11. $x \ge 3$	12. $k \ge -48$	13. $y < -1$	14. $m < -11$	15. $z \ge 6/5$
16. $m < 7$	17. $x \le -3$	18. $k \le -10$	19. $x < -7$	20. $x \le 7$
21. $m < 19$	22. $k > -16$	23. $k \ge -12$	24. $x \ge -2$	25. $k > -5$
26. $m > -2$	27. $k > 12$	28. $k > 9$	29. $m \le 4$	30. $y \le 8$
31. $y \le 12$	32. $m > 4$	33. $m \le 27$	34. $z \ge -5$	35. $x > 3/2$
36. $m < -3$	37. $z < 35$	38. $z \ge -2/3$	39. $x < 6$	40. $x \ge -1$

Page 58: Find Numbers

1. 7	2. 10	3. 9	4. 2, 3, 4
5. 5, 6, 7, 8	6. 8	7. 4, 11, 40	8. 16

9. 7

10. 60

11. 7, 28

12. 8

13. 11

14. 11, 8

15. 10

16. 4

17. 4, 6

18. 8, 18

19. 6, 7, 8, 9

20. 6

21. 9, 11

22. 4, 16

23. 8, 1

24. 6, 8, 10

25. 2

26. 10

27. 5, 15

28. 15

29. 1

30. 8

31. 13

32. 35

33. 9, 4

34. 0, 0

35. 7

36. 6

37. 7, 8, 9

38. 4

39. 3

40. 8

41. 8

42. 4, 3

43. 6

44. 6

45. 2, 1

46. 6, 8

47. 13

48. 4

49. 3, 4, 5

50. 8, 9, 10, 11

51. 2

52. 7, 9

53. 12

54. 8, 10, 12

55. 6

56. 6, 8, 10

57. 1, 3

58. 2, 9, 16

59. 3, 5

60. 3

Page 73: Solving Equations: (One Step)

1. $x = 20$

2. $x = 17$

3. $k = 10$

4. $y = 20$

5. $k = 9$

6. $y = 288$

7. $k = 10$

8. $m = 9$

9. $z = 56$

10. $k = 9$

11. $m = 18$

12. $y = 8$

13. $m = 100$

14. $m = 10$

15. $m = 9$

16. $k = 7$

17. $m = 4$

18. $k = 15$

19. $x = 10$

20. $m = 3$

21. $y = 7$

22. $x = 200$

23. $y = 15$

24. $k = 16$

25. $z = 16$

26. $x = 11$

27. $z = 17$

28. $k = 10$

29. $k = 11$

30. $y = 13$

31. $k = 16$

32. $z = 5$

33. $y = 17$

34. $k = 19$

35. $m = 11$

36. x = 11   37. z = 17   38. y = 7   39. k = 11   40. m = 17

41. k = 1   42. x = 18   43. z = 16   44. z = 4   45. m = 11

46. m = 4   47. z = 12   48. m = 5   49. k = 16   50. z = 12

51. x = 208   52. k = 14   53. k = 104   54. y = 5   55. k = 16

56. z = 16   57. y = 8   58. z = 5   59. y = 306   60. y = 6

61. z = 3   62. k = 9   63. m = 12   64. m = 1   65. k = 12

66. x = 15   67. z = 18   68. m = 20   69. z = 2   70. z = 6

71. k = 1   72. x = 2   73. z = 20   74. m = 20   75. m = 10

76. k = 2   77. y = 5   78. y = 12   79. z = 5   80. y = 6

81. x = 1   82. x = 5   83. z = 14   84. k = 9   85. m = 153

86. z = 10   87. y = 13   88. k = 13

Page 82: Equations (Two Steps)

1. k = 1   2. x = 6   3. x = 3   4. x = 1   5. k = 5   6. z = 8

7. m = 4   8. x = 1   9. z = 3   10. y = 5   11. z = 8   12. m = 9

13. x = 7   14. y = 5   15. y = 8   16. z = 8   17. z = 2   18. k = 5

19. k = 5   20. x = 5   21. z = 4   22. x = 4   23. y = 8   24. m = 6

25. k = 6   26. k = 2   27. y = 1   28. y = 9   29. x = 8   30. x = 7

31. x = 3   32. m = 1   33. m = 2   34. z = 3   35. y = 1   36. z = 2

37. m = 2   38. y = 4   39. k = 3   40. z = 9   41. m = 7   42. x = 8

43. z = 4   44. m = 6   45. y = 7   46. z = 5   47. y = 8   48. m = 7

49. x = 8   50. m = 6   51. k = 6   52. x = 1   53. y = 9   54. m = 9

55. m = 3   56. y = 7   57. z = 5   58. k = 2   59. x = 3   60. z = 6

61. k = 4   62. y = 2   63. z = 4   64. m = 2   65. m = 1   66. x = 9

67. k = 6   68. y = 7   69. z = 5   70. z = 9   71. x = 6   72. m = 3

73. z = 1   74. k = 9   75. k = 4   76. x = 7   77. y = 9   78. x = 3

79. y = 7

Page 98: Cartesian Coordinates

1.

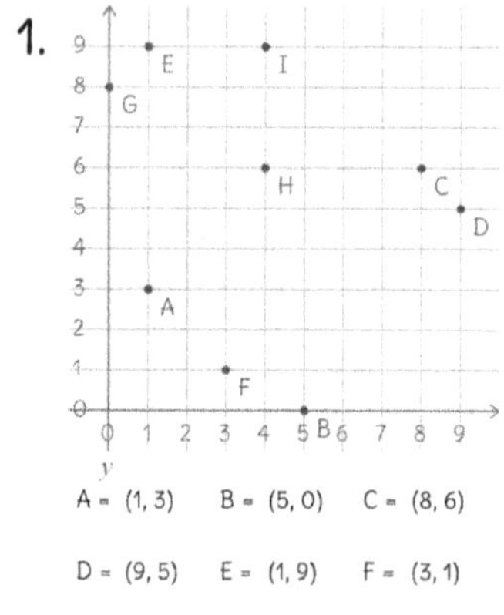

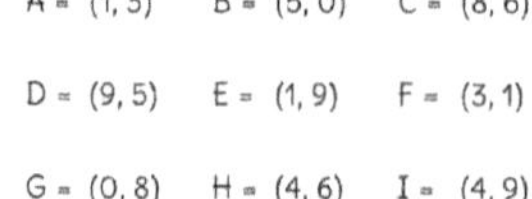

A = (1, 3)   B = (5, 0)   C = (8, 6)

D = (9, 5)   E = (1, 9)   F = (3, 1)

G = (0, 8)   H = (4, 6)   I = (4, 9)

2.

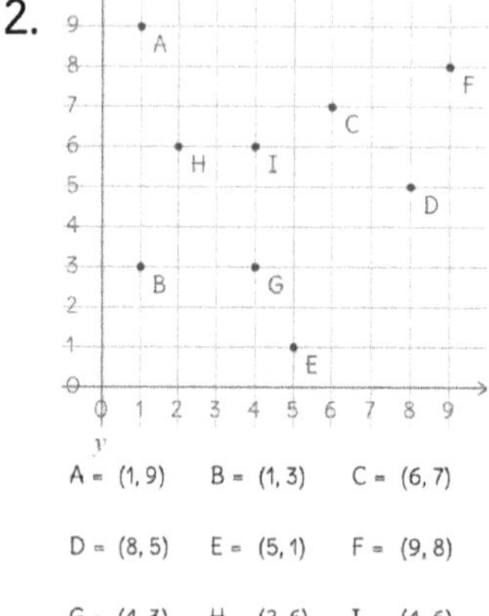

A = (1, 9)   B = (1, 3)   C = (6, 7)

D = (8, 5)   E = (5, 1)   F = (9, 8)

G = (4, 3)   H = (2, 6)   I = (4, 6)

3.

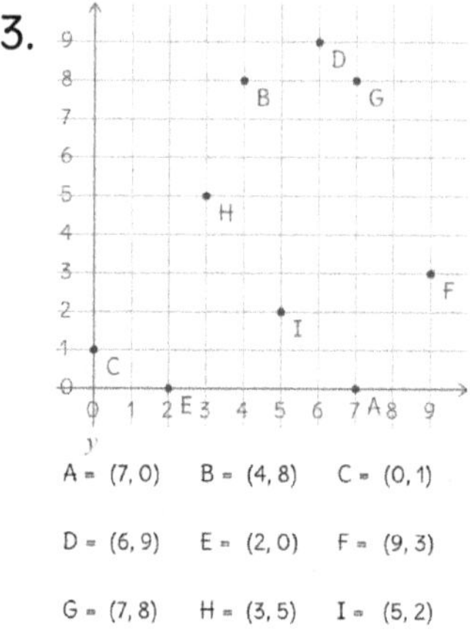

A = (7, 0)   B = (4, 8)   C = (0, 1)

D = (6, 9)   E = (2, 0)   F = (9, 3)

G = (7, 8)   H = (3, 5)   I = (5, 2)

4.

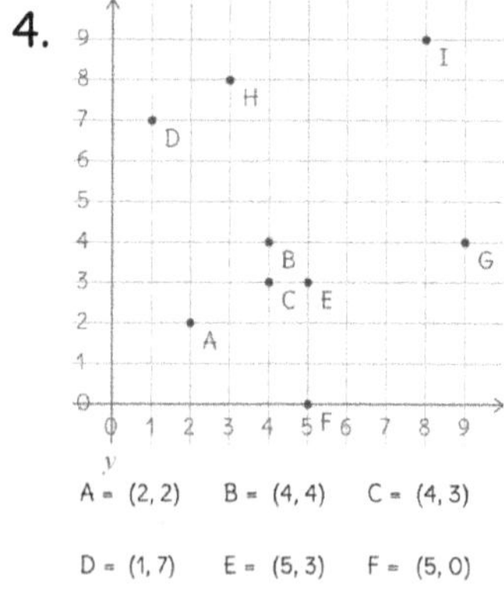

A = (2, 2)   B = (4, 4)   C = (4, 3)

D = (1, 7)   E = (5, 3)   F = (5, 0)

G = (9, 4)   H = (3, 8)   I = (8, 9)

5.

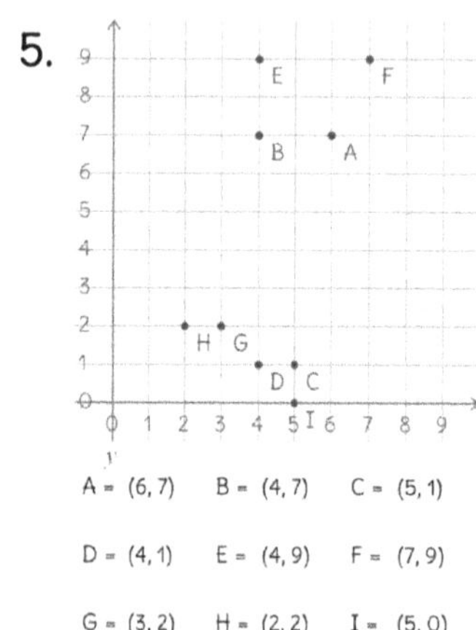

A = (6, 7)   B = (4, 7)   C = (5, 1)

D = (4, 1)   E = (4, 9)   F = (7, 9)

G = (3, 2)   H = (2, 2)   I = (5, 0)

Page 103:   Cartesian Coordinates

1.

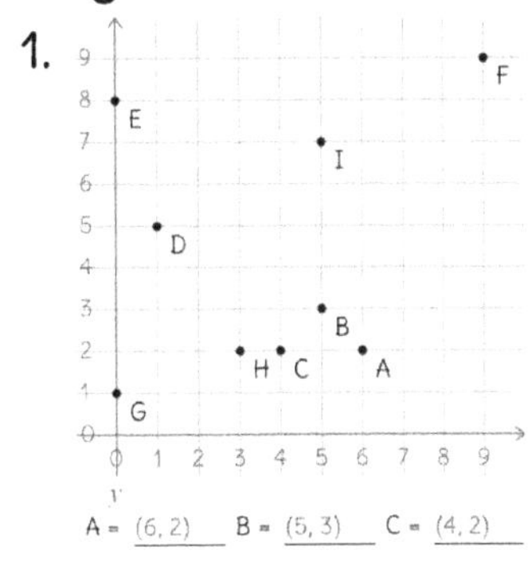

A = (6, 2)   B = (5, 3)   C = (4, 2)

D = (1, 5)   E = (0, 8)   F = (9, 9)

G = (0, 1)   H = (3, 2)   I = (5, 7)

2.

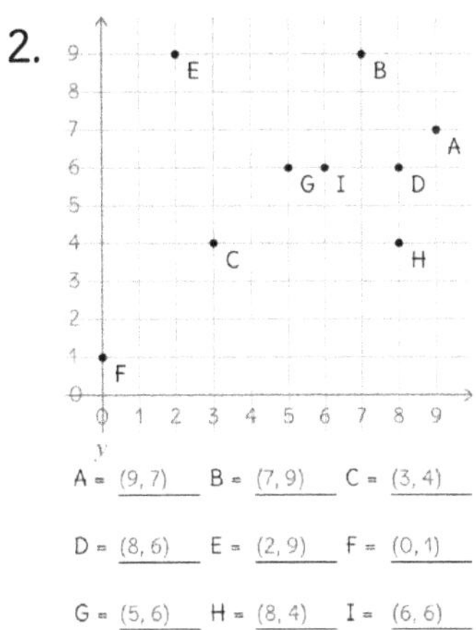

A = (9, 7)   B = (7, 9)   C = (3, 4)

D = (8, 6)   E = (2, 9)   F = (0, 1)

G = (5, 6)   H = (8, 4)   I = (6, 6)

3.

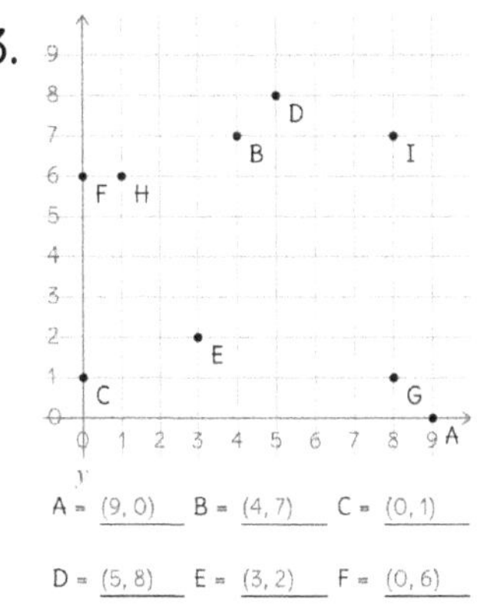

A = (9, 0)   B = (4, 7)   C = (0, 1)

D = (5, 8)   E = (3, 2)   F = (0, 6)

G = (8, 1)   H = (1, 6)   I = (8, 7)

4.

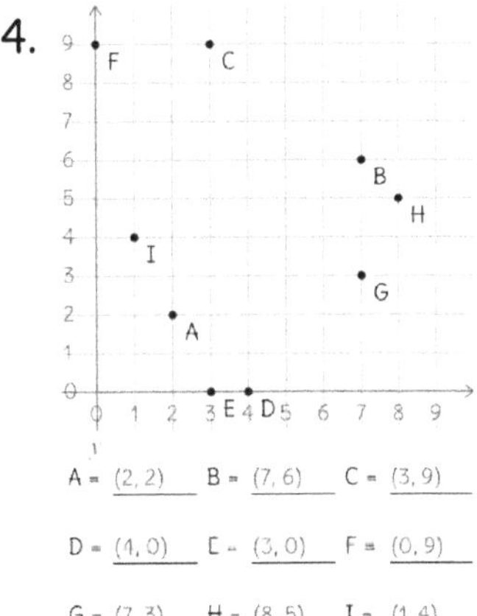

A = (2, 2)   B = (7, 6)   C = (3, 9)

D = (1, 0)   E = (3, 0)   F = (0, 9)

G = (7, 3)   H = (8, 5)   I = (1, 4)

5.

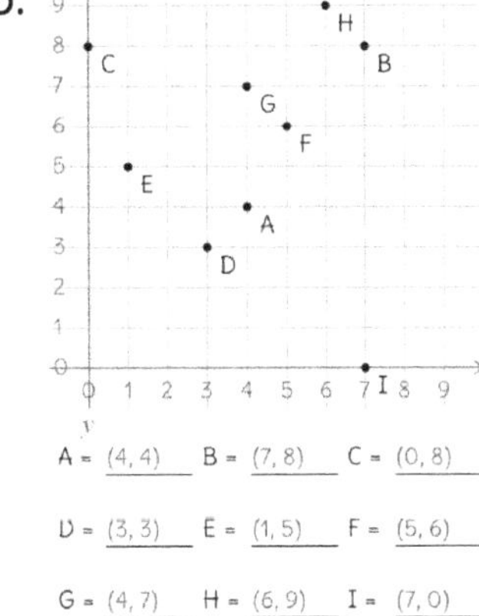

A = (4, 4)   B = (7, 8)   C = (0, 8)

D = (3, 3)   E = (1, 5)   F = (5, 6)

G = (4, 7)   H = (6, 9)   I = (7, 0)

Page 108:   Cartesian Coordinates With Four Quadrants

1.

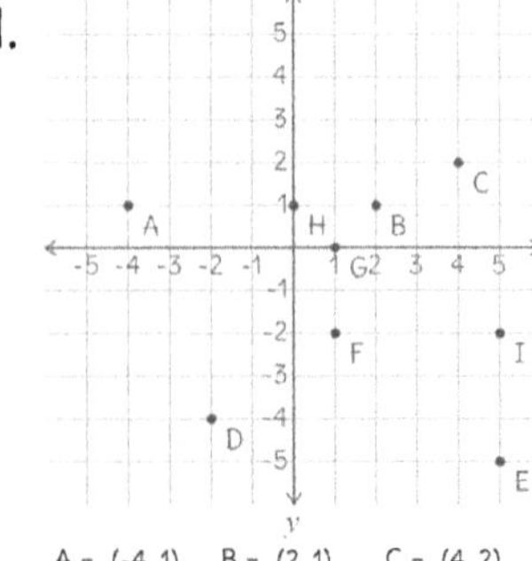

A = (-4, 1)   B = (2, 1)   C = (4, 2)

D = (-2, -4)   E = (5, -5)   F = (1, -2)

G = (1, 0)   H = (0, 1)   I = (5, -2)

2.

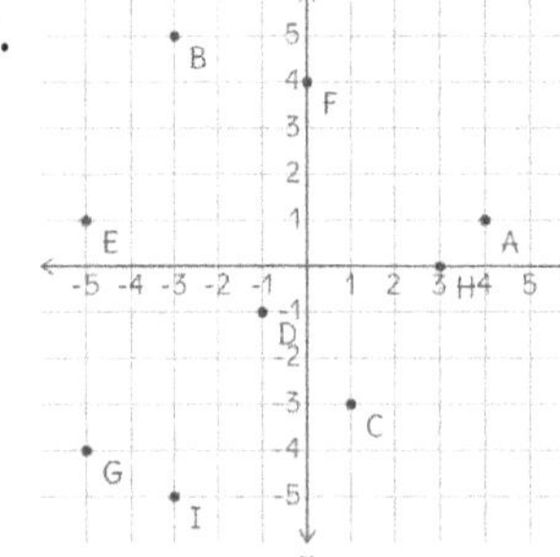

A = (4, 1)   B = (-3, 5)   C = (1, -3)

D = (-1, -1)   E = (-5, 1)   F = (0, 4)

G = (-5, -4)   H = (3, 0)   I = (-3, -5)

3.

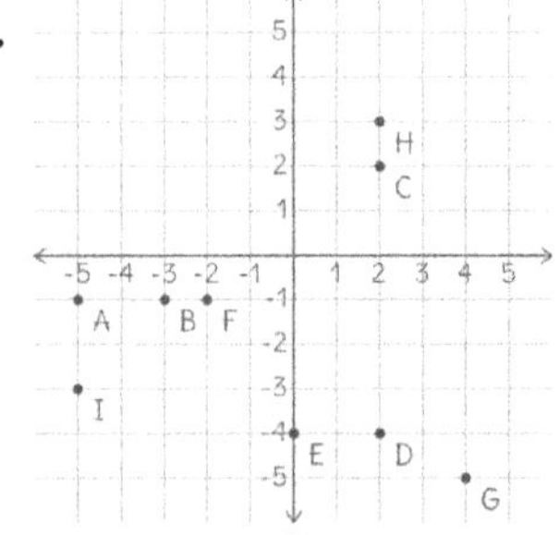

A = (-5, -1)   B = (-3, -1) C = (2, 2)

D = (2, -4)   E = (0, -4)   F = (-2, -1)

G = (4, -5)   H = (2, 3)   I = (-5, -3)

4.

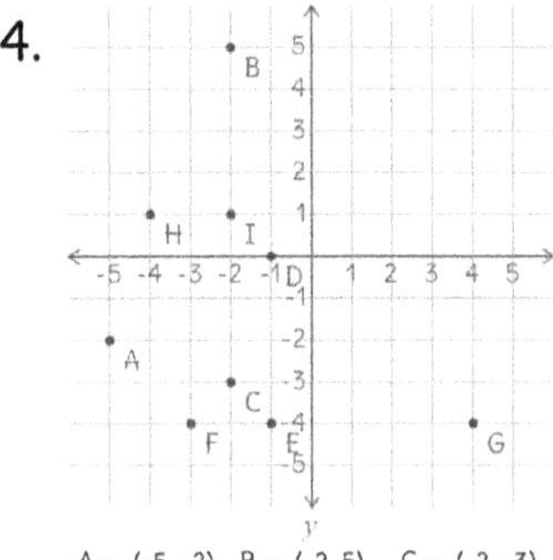

A = (-5, -2)   B = (-2, 5)   C = (-2, -3)

D = (-1, 0)   E = (-1, -4) F = (-3, -4)

G = (4, -4)   H = (-4, 1)   I = (-2, 1)

5.

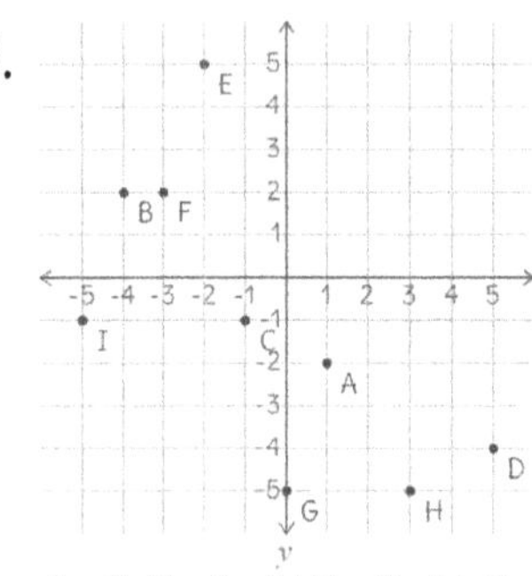

A = (1, -2)   B = (-4, 2)   C = (-1, -1)

D = (5, -4)   E = (-2, 5)   F = (-3, 2)

G = (0, -5)   H = (3, -5)   I = (-5, -1)

Page 113: Cartesian Coordinates With Four Quadrants

1.

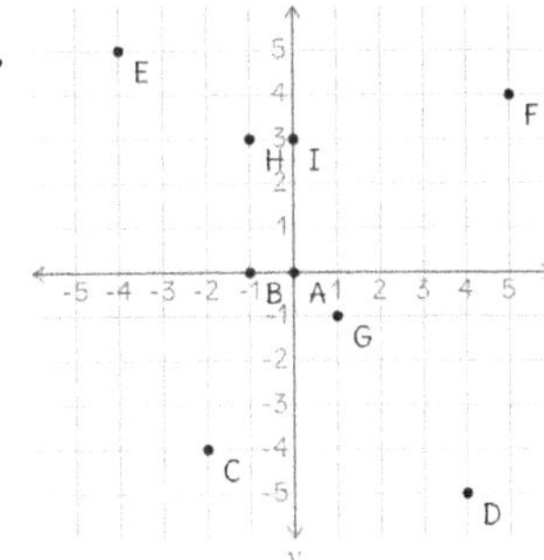

A = (0, 0)   B = (-1, 0)   C = (-2, -4)

D = (4, -5)   E = (-4, 5)   F = (5, 4)

G = (1, -1)   H = (-1, 3)   I = (0, 3)

2.

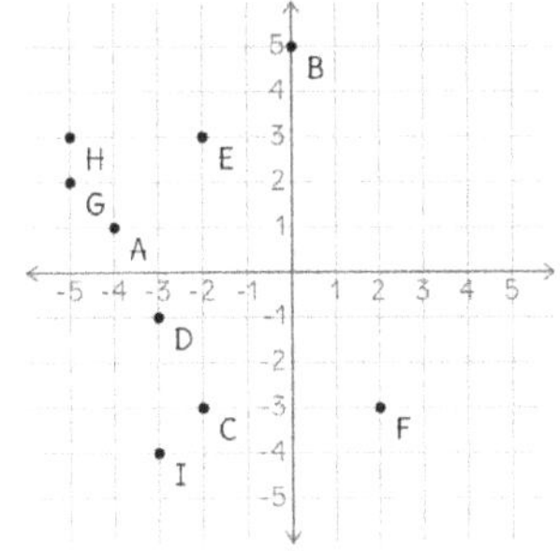

A = (-4, 1)   B = (0, 5)   C = (-2, -3)

D = (-3, -1)   E = (-2, 3)   F = (2, -3)

G = (-5, 2)   H = (-5, 3)   I = (-3, -4)

3.

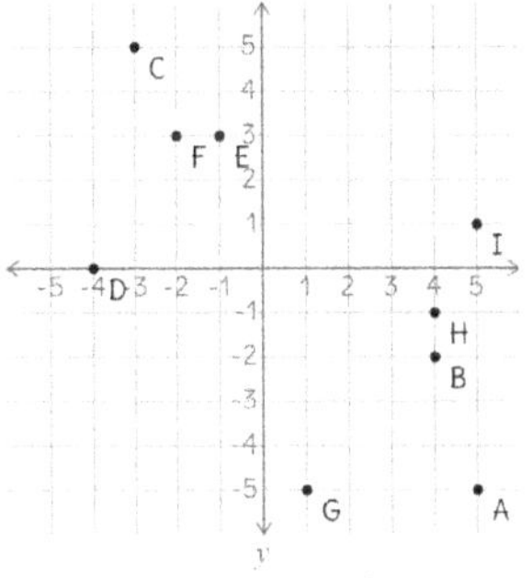

A = (5, -5)   B = (4, -2)   C = (-3, 5)

D = (-4, 0)   E = (-1, 3)   F = (-2, 3)

G = (1, -5)   H = (4, -1)   I = (5, 1)

4.

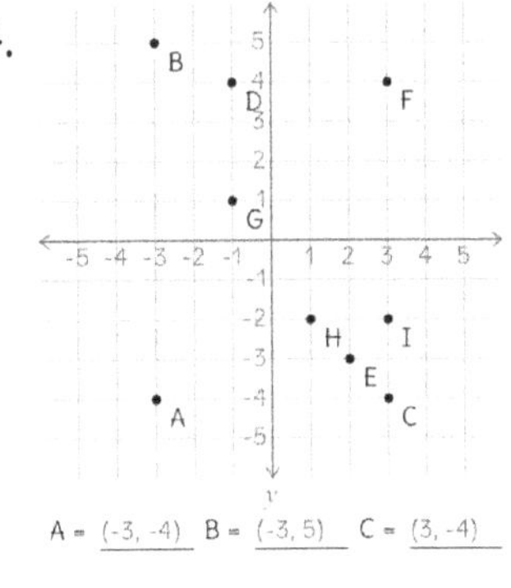

A = (-3, -4)   B = (-3, 5)   C = (3, -4)

D = (-1, 4)   E = (2, -3)   F = (3, 4)

G = (-1, 1)   H = (1, -2)   I = (3, -2)

5.

A = (-5, 2)   B = (-5, 0)   C = (0, 4)

D = (2, -3)   E = (5, 2)   F = (3, 0)

G = (1, -4)   H = (4, -5)   I = (-3, 3)

Page 118: Area and Perimeter

1. P=33 A=38.71

2. P=46 A=90

3. P=33 A=39.9

4. P=42 A=78

5. P=26 A=35

6. P=42 A=86

7. P=58 A=110

8. P=28 A=49

9. P=66 A=230

10. P=44 A=85

11. P=46 A=88

12. P=42 A=70.38

13. P=54 A=132

14. P=18 A=20

15. P=42 A=78

16. P=39 A=66

17. P=32 A=37.44

18. P=50 A=124

19. P=31 A=45.18   20. P=34 A=60   21. P=32 A=32.72

22. P=38 A=80   23. P=26 A=25   24. P=56 A=110

25. P=37 A=59.67   26. P=70 A=182   27. P=32 A=49

28. P=32 A=45   29. P=33 A=52.39   30. P=28 A=40

31. P=36 A=70   32. P=46 A=88   33. P=54 A=121

34. P=22 A=22   35. P=19 A=16.35   36. P=31 A=36

37. P=50 A=98   38. P=28 A=36.68   39. P=40 A=54

40. P=33 A=52.42   41. P=52 A=112.5   42. P=21 A=21.22

43. P=40 A=82   44. P=44 A=101   45. P=50 A=121

46. P=26 A=28   47. P=54 A=112   48. P=16 A=15

49. P=60 A=165   50. P=40 A=70   51. P=22 A=22.26

52. P=46 A=96   53. P=23 A=21   54. P=36 A=55

55. P=36 A=65   56. P=32 A=48   57. P=36 A=62.34

58. P=50 A=90   59. P=40 A=65   60. P=51 A=110.5

61. P=34 A=49.5   62. P=64 A=145   63. P=36 A=69

64. P=40 A=100   65. P=42 A=86   66. P=52 A=140

67. P=46 A=111   68. P=36 A=72   69. P=26 A=27

70. P=68 A=222   71. P=28 A=36.68   72. P=54 A=180

73. P=34 A=70   74. P=50 A=154   75. P=28 A=36

76. P=42 A=77   77. P=41 A=72   78. P=36 A=54

79. P=22 A=20   80. P=38 A=58.5

Page 138:   Pythagorean Theorem

1. S=89.554   2. S=35.777   3. S=27.495   4. S=177.395

5. S=90.067   6. S=38.066   7. S=159.339   8. S=66.813

9. S=74.940   10. S=61.717   11. S=13.077   12. S=80.492

13. S=42.895   14. S=68.739   15. S=59.573   16. S=56.249

17. S=60.415   18. S=119.532   19. S=62.177   20. S=192.388

Page 143:   Volume and Surface Area

1. V=75 in³ in³ SA=109 in² in²

2. V=576 cm³ cm³ SA=416 cm² cm²

3. V=4 ft³ ft³ SA=13 ft² ft²

4. V=77 ft³ ft³ SA=115 ft² ft²

5. V=62.83 ft³ ft³ SA=88 ft² ft²

6. V=269.39 in³ in³ SA=231 in² in²

7. V=39 in³ in³ SA=71 in² in²

8. V=486 in³ in³ SA=378 in² in²

9. V=66 ft³ ft³ SA=100 ft² ft²

10. V=26 in³ in³ SA=57 in² in²

11. V=307.88 ft³ ft³ SA=253 ft² ft²

12. V=288 in³ in³ SA=264 in² in²

13. V=120 ft³ ft³ SA=148 ft² ft²

14. V=80 in³ in³ SA=112 in² in²

15. V=700 ft³ ft³ SA=480 ft² ft²

16. V=14 ft³ ft³ SA=28 ft² ft²

17. V=7 ft³ ft³ SA=23 ft² ft²

18. V=60 in³ in³ SA=94 in² in²

19. V=28.27 cm³ cm³ SA=52 cm² cm²

20. V=100 ft³ ft³ SA=130 ft² ft²

21. V=720 cm³ cm³ SA=484 cm² cm²

22. V=128 ft³ ft³ SA=155 ft² ft²

23. V=120 in³ in³ SA=148 in² in²

24. V=98.17 cm³ cm³ SA=118 cm² cm²

25. V=108 ft³ ft³ SA=144 ft² ft²

26. V=75.40 cm³ cm³ SA=101 cm² cm²

27. V=180 in³ in³ SA=192 in² in²

28. V=192.42 ft³ ft³ SA=187 ft² ft²

29. V=183 in³ in³ SA=214 in² in²

30. V=113.10 in³ in³ SA=132 in² in²

31. V=382 cm³ cm³ SA=254 cm² cm²

32. V=224 cm³ cm³ SA=232 cm² cm²

33. V=540 cm³ cm³ SA=408 cm² cm²

34. V=697 ft³ ft³ SA=380 ft² ft²

35. V=80 ft³ ft³ SA=112 ft² ft²

36. V=25.13 in³ in³ SA=50 in² in²

37. V=378 ft³ ft³ SA=318 ft² ft²

38. V=12 cm³ cm³ SA=32 cm² cm²

39. V=628.32 cm³ cm³ SA=408 cm² cm²

40. V=448 ft³ ft³ SA=352 ft² ft²

41. V=141.37 ft³ ft³ SA=151 ft² ft²

42. V=125 in³ in³ SA=150 in² in²

43. V=48 in³ in³ SA=80 in² in²

44. V=346.36 in³ in³ SA=275 in² in²

45. V=100 ft³ ft³ SA=130 ft² ft²

46. V=800 cm³ cm³ SA=520 cm² cm²

47. V=13 ft³ ft³ SA=35 ft² ft²

48. V=990 cm³ cm³ SA=598 cm² cm²

49. V=236 cm³ cm³ SA=240 cm² cm²

50. V=36 ft³ ft³ SA=66 ft² ft²

51. V=175 ft³ ft³ SA=190 ft² ft²

52. V=12 ft³ ft³ SA=32 ft² ft²

53. V=168 in³ in³ SA=188 in² in²

54. V=168 in³ in³ SA=186 in² in²

55. V=384 ft³ ft³ SA=320 ft² ft²

56. V=48 ft³ ft³ SA=80 ft² ft²

57. V=210 in³ in³ SA=214 in² in²

58. V=24 in³ in³ SA=52 in² in²

59. V=153.94 ft³ ft³ SA=165 ft² ft²

60. V=8 in³ in³ SA=24 in² in²

Page 158: Mean, Median, Mode, and Range

1. Mean = 61.857, Median = 70, Mode = none, Range = 48

2. Mean = 28.5, Median = 24.5, Mode = none, Range = 84

3. Mean = 30.167, Median = 32, Mode = 32, Range = 51

4. Mean = 39.571, Median = 38, Mode = none, Range = 75

5. Mean = 60.857, Median = 62, Mode = none, Range = 96

6. Mean = 53.857, Median = 52, Mode = none, Range = 78

7. Mean = 64.714, Median = 83, Mode = 83, Range = 95

8. Mean = 60.833, Median = 82.5, Mode = none, Range = 82

9. Mean = 71.333, Median = 75, Mode = none, Range = 52

10. Mean = 58.571, Median = 63, Mode = none, Range = 60

11. Mean = 43.429, Median = 32, Mode = none, Range = 84

12. Mean = 51.571, Median = 53, Mode = none, Range = 91

13. Mean = 61.571, Median = 59, Mode = none, Range = 74

14. Mean = 40.857, Median = 58, Mode = 6, Range = 78

15. Mean = 69.833, Median = 65, Mode = none, Range = 45

16. Mean = 49.429, Median = 55, Mode = 85, Range = 82

17. Mean = 65.143, Median = 61, Mode = none, Range = 78

18. Mean = 54.571, Median = 56, Mode = 75, Range = 44

19. Mean = 65.667, Median = 76, Mode = none, Range = 68

20. Mean = 35.5, Median = 34, Mode = none, Range = 44

21. Mean = 79.571, Median = 86, Mode = 86, 94, Range = 65

22. Mean = 34.167, Median = 32.5, Mode = none, Range = 74

23. Mean = 60.167, Median = 56.5, Mode = none, Range = 68

24. Mean = 60.286, Median = 60, Mode = none, Range = 60